OXFORD c.1375

| 0 | yards | 220 |
| 0 | metres | 200 |

Augustinian Friary

llege

St. Cross

Holywell mill

13

ITCH

Crowell

Exeter College

Queen's College

St. Peter-in-the-East

3

St. Mary the Virgin

HIGH STREET

6

East Gate

Hospital of St. John

7

Oriel College

St. Frideswide's Grange

East Bridge

Canterbury College

Merton College

R. Cherwell

9

St. Frideswide's Priory

GRANDPONT

Trill mill

R. Cherwell

16

Shire Lake stream

New Gate

The Life and Times
of John Trevisa,
Medieval Scholar

The Life and Times of John Trevisa, Medieval Scholar

by

DAVID C. FOWLER

UNIVERSITY OF WASHINGTON PRESS

Seattle and London

For Mary Gene Stith Fowler

Library of Congress Cataloging-in-Publication Data

Fowler, David C., 1921–
    The life and times of John Trevisa, medieval scholar / by David C. Fowler.
    p. cm.
    Includes bibliographical references and index.
    ISBN 0-295-97427-3 (cloth : acid-free paper)
    1. Trevisa, John, d. 1402. 2. Authors, English—Middle English, 1100–1500—Biography. 3. Latin language—Translating into English (Middle)—History. 4. Catholic Church—England—Berkeley—Clergy—Biography. 5. England—Intellectual life—1066-1485. 6. Translators—England—Biography. 7. Scholars—England—Biography. I. Title.
PR2148.T7Z65   1995
428′.0271′092—dc20
[B]
                                                    95-7886
                                                     CIP

Endsheet map of Oxford c. 1375 reproduced by permission of the General Editor, C. R. Elrington, from *Victoria County History: Oxfordshire,* Volume IV. Map drawn by K. J. Wass from a draft by Janet M. Cooper.

The paper used in this publication meets the minimum requirements of American National Standard for Information Sciences—Permanence of Paper for Printed Library Materials, ANSI Z39.48-1984.

Contents

Preface

This is a book that required thirty-five years to research and write, and this means that many of the people who helped me along the way are no longer here to receive my thanks. If it seems, in this preface, that I address them as if they are still alive, that is because to me they are. I am surrounded by a cloud of witnesses, I thank them one and all for their help, and hope that they will forgive me for taking so long to finish this work.

My predecessor, A. J. Perry, brought out his edition of Trevisa's minor works in 1925. Of course I never met him, yet I feel close to him for two reasons. One is that we were both students, though decades apart, in the University of Chicago, he a student of J. M. Manly and T. A. Knott, and I of a near-contemporary of theirs, J. R. Hulbert. The other reason is that I did locate and visit his widow, Mrs. Perry, who spent her retirement years north of the border in Victoria, British Columbia. Thanks to her generosity, I now have her husband's own copy of his book on Trevisa on my desk, inscribed with his clear but minuscule hand: "Aaron Jenkins Perry, Univ. of Man[itoba], 1932." Every student must be greatly indebted to this pioneer in the study of Trevisa's life and works.

As I began my own work on Trevisa, there may have been moments when it seemed that I was alone in my interest, but this was never true. I soon learned that there were others at work in this vineyard, as the Bibliography in this volume attests. But I am particularly indebted to Michael Seymour for seeing through to completion the monumental edition of Trevisa's translation of Bartholomaeus Anglicus, *On the Properties of Things* (1975–92); to A. S. G. Edwards for his work on numerous manuscripts of Trevisa's works and the chapter on Trevisa in his guide to Middle English prose (1984); and to Ronald Waldron for beginning a much needed new edition of the *Polychronicon* translation. In my own country I am encouraged to see that the interest in Trevisa is growing, as witnessed by the number of Americans who worked with Michael Seymour on *Properties*, whose interest in Trevisa continues. In particular I want to thank Ralph Hanna of the University of California at Irvine for a valuable critique of this book. While there may still be matters we disagree on, I believe this study is much better than it would have been without his generous suggestions for its improvement. Finally I welcome the interest of Charles F. Briggs of the University of North Carolina at Chapel Hill in Trevisa's translation of Aegidius Romanus, *De Proprietatibus Rerum*, and hope that together we may see this as yet unpublished text through to publication.

In numerous trips to England over the years I was supported with sabbaticals by my own institution, the University of Washington, and with fellowships by the Guggenheim Foundation in 1962–63 and 1975–76. I thank the officials of these institutions, public and private, for giving me the means to carry out my research in Cornwall, Oxford, Berkeley, and London.

Cornwall is filled with people who love their land, and take kindly to anyone who shows a serious interest in it. My wife, our two daughters, and I were fortunate to find a home there with Mr. and Mrs. E. G. R. Hooper of Camborne, who were both intensely involved in the revival of the Cornish language and culture. Our circle of acquaintances grew thereafter to include R. Morton Nance, Charles Thomas, L. R. Moir, and Canon J. H. Adams, then vicar of Landulph, whose wife Marion now lives in St. Agnes. Through the good offices of the National Trust I was able to visit the Earl of Mount Edgcumbe at Mount Edgcumbe, and Captain J. T. Coryton at Pentillie Castle in pursuit of documents still in private hands. The Earl and the Captain were both gracious, in their different fashions, in dealing with my fanatical devotion to research on Trevisa, the former often responding to my pronouncements with "To be sure!" and the latter usually replying with a personal counterstatement of his own, followed by "Don't you agree?" The more accessible public records of Cornwall were in the care of distinguished officials to whom I am also much indebted: H. L. Douch, then curator of the County Museum, Royal Institution of Cornwall, and Peter L. Hull of the County Record Office, both located in Truro.

For most of the many visits to England, Oxford was our home, and the Bodleian Library my research headquarters. I thank all the members of the staff who helped me over the years in so many ways that words fail me. Even those whose scholarship and high station should have excused them from answering the questions of a novice were always willing to help: from R. W. Hunt in my early days there, to David Vaisey in recent years. Above all I must thank Neil Ker, who as paleographer steered me through the intricacies of manuscript study, both in his seminar on the subject and on several occasions in Duke Humphrey, when he found me struggling with a difficult scribal hand. Among many who were of service to me in the college libraries, I must mention the Queen's College archivist, John M. Kaye, whose analysis of the issues involved in Trevisa's expulsion is included in this volume at the end of the fifth chapter. The Oxford faculty in the medieval field is one of the greatest, and I have never ceased to be amazed at their willingness to help others beyond the call of duty: Professor Norman Davis (Merton), Sir Idris Foster (Jesus), J. I. M. Stewart (Christ Church), J. A. W. Bennett (then of Magdalen), Beryl Smalley (St. Hilda's), Pamela Gradon (St. Hugh's), and Anne Hudson (Lady Margaret Hall). These scholars not only helped me with matters related to their own interests, but also often directed me to colleagues elsewhere in the country. A most fortunate example of the latter was Anne Hudson's suggestion that I consult Alison McHardy of Aberdeen University, leading to the discovery of the clerical subsidy roll which in turn contributed to the hypothesis concerning Trevisa's installation as vicar of Berkeley.

There were some surprises. During our sabbatical of 1969–70, we stayed in the upstairs apartment of a home in north Oxford, while on the ground floor lived our landlord, Sir Owen O'Malley and his wife (whose pen name is Ann Bridge). Sir Owen was a career diplomat and man of qualities. We were told that as the time of our arrival approached, he would look in at the office of the nearby lodge where we had reservations and call out in the hearing of all, "Where are my Americans?" Lady O'Malley was a dedicated gardener as well as an engaging conversationalist. They were wonderful neighbors. And it was Sir Owen who steered me to Lord Ernle's book on English farming (which he had read years ago as a student in Oxford), which contained an important reference to the farming practices of Thomas III, Lord Berkeley, based on manorial records in Berkeley Castle. Another surprise came a few years later, when I learned of the interest of Derek Hall, president of Corpus Christi College, in court records of the hundred of Penwith in the fourteenth century, leading directly to the discovery of documents on a case involving a member of the Trevisa family in 1333. This filled a crucial gap in the evidence leading to identification of the family home as Trevisa in St. Enoder. Let me mention one more

Oxford memory: in my first visit there in 1959 I met Father Thomas P. Dunning of University College, Dublin. We had a common interest, of course, in *Piers the Plowman*, but he also became my mentor in Oxford, a lifelong friend, and our host during a visit to Dublin.

Berkeley is a small town in Gloucestershire, but we soon came to know members of that community, both as friends and informants. Canon J. H. W. Fisher and Canon J. E. Gethyn-Jones, both (in that order) vicars of Berkeley during most of our visits, had done valuable work on the history of Berkeley parish church and were helpful to me in my efforts to gain admittance to the muniment room of Berkeley Castle. I am indebted also to the countess, Mary Berkeley, and the trustees of the estate, for eventual permission to consult the records there with the kind assistance of Brian Smith, Records Officer of Gloucester. This is perhaps the appropriate place to thank officials in other localities for similar favors: Dr. B. S. Benedikz of the University Library, Birmingham, in his capacity as consultant librarian to the dean and chapter of Worcester Cathedral, who searched meticulously (though in vain) for mention of Trevisa in the *Liber Albus*; Dr. R. F. Hunnisett of the Public Record Office, London, for favors too numerous to specify here; and Mr. Paul Yeats-Edwards, Librarian of the Winchester College Fellows' Library, who was very helpful when I came there to examine the recently discovered Winchester manuscript (33) of Trevisa's translation of the *Gospel of Nicodemus*.

Returning at last to the western hemisphere, I salute Roy M. Haines of Dalhousie University in Halifax, Nova Scotia, for his thoughtful elucidation of a decree by Bishop Wakefield, the result of an effort to compel Trevisa to appoint a chaplain for the village of Stone in Berkeley parish. This is a personal debt, over and above what I owe him from reading his published work.

In my own University of Washington I want to thank Paul Pascal for his patience with my requests for help with medieval Latin, Lionel Friedman for similar guidance in deciphering Old French, and Mícéal Vaughan for all of the above as well as other advice and counsel over the last half of the project. Sherry Laing has proved over the years both knowledgeable in the field (medieval studies) and a perfectionist when it comes to making sense out of my handwriting: I am very much in her debt for typing more than one version of this book. Graduate students have helped me in many ways over the years, not only those whose dissertations are listed in the Bibliography, but also some whose work is still in the formative stages.

My wife has been involved in this project from its inception, and has maintained a movable family feast under trying conditions all of these years. This book is appropriately completed in the year of our fiftieth wedding anniversary (1943–93), and is dedicated to her with these words which Chaucer used to describe his beloved Duchess Blanche: "she was alway so trewe."

Abbreviations

Add.	Additional
AV	Authorized Version of the Bible (1611)
BL	British Library
BRUO	*Biographical Register of the University of Oxford* (A. B. Emden)
CCR	Calendar of Close Rolls
CPR	Calendar of Patent Rolls
CPR/L	Calendar of Papal Registers (Papal Letters)
DA	Dissertation Abstracts (to 1969)
DAI	Dissertation Abstracts International (1969–)
DMA	*Dictionary of the Middle Ages*, 13 vols. (1982–89)
EETS	Early English Text Society (OS=Original Series)
ELN	*English Language Notes*
fol(s)	folio(s)
HUO	*History of the University of Oxford* (1984–)
IPM	*Inquisitions Post Mortem*
JWCI	*Journal of the Warburg and Courtauld Institutes*
KAS/RB	Kent Archaeological Society, Records Branch
MAE	*Medium AEvum*
MED	*Middle English Dictionary* (Ann Arbor, Michigan)
MLN	*Modern Language Notes*
MLQ	*Modern Language Quarterly*
MP	*Modern Philology*
N&Q	*Notes and Queries*
NM	*Neuphilologische Mitteilungen*
Poly.	*Polychronicon*
PQ	*Philological Quarterly*
PRIA	*Proceedings of the Royal Irish Academy*
PRO	Public Record Office, London
RES	*Review of English Studies*
RS	Rolls Series
RSV	*Registrum Sede Vacante*
VCH	*Victoria County History*

WB(EV)	Wyclif Bible (Early Version)
WHS	Worcestershire Historical Society
YES	*Yearbook of English Studies*

The Life and Times
of John Trevisa,
Medieval Scholar

Introduction

John Trevisa was born in Cornwall, studied at Oxford University, and, having come to the attention of the Berkeley family, was instituted vicar of Berkeley, a position he held until his death in 1402. Even these few facts are not easy to come by, and I must confess to a complete ignorance of this man until some ten years after completing my graduate work in English. At that time I was writing a book on *Piers the Plowman*, a fourteenth-century alliterative poem existing in three versions, the earliest of which (the "A" text) I had edited as a dissertation and later published (1952), in posthumous collaboration with Thomas A. Knott. Since the circumstances of my discovery of Trevisa are importantly related to some of the theories presented in this volume, it seems only proper to explain briefly how he came to my attention.

The book I was working on was *Piers the Plowman: Literary Relations of the A and B Texts* (1961), and one of the problems I faced in writing it was identifying, in a chapter entitled "Principles of Order in the B-Continuation," the literary sources or influences that determined the shape of the latter half of the "B" text, or second version of *Piers the Plowman* (B passus XI–XX). One of those influences, I concluded, was the fourteenth-century Latin chronicle by Ranulph Higden known as the *Polychronicon*. Almost immediately this brought Trevisa to my attention, since his English translation was included in the Rolls Series edition of the Latin *Polychronicon* published in nine volumes in 1865–86.

One of the distinctive features of Trevisa's translation of the *Polychronicon* (to be discussed in Chapter 4) is his inclusion of notes, usually prefixed by his name, commenting on the text he is translating. These notes are often quite opinionated, and I noticed right away that the views of Trevisa seemed in close harmony with those of the author of the B text of *Piers the Plowman* (who is separate in my mind from the author of the A text). In one instance Higden, author of the Latin text and himself a monk, relates that when Roger, earl of Shrewsbury, was on his deathbed, he was made a monk in the Benedictine abbey of Shrewsbury (which he himself had founded), in hopes this would

3

bring him some assurance of salvation (*ad succurrendum* [*animae suae*]). To this Trevisa (a secular priest) appends the following note (*Poly.* vii, 355): "A wise man would ween that Earl Roger had as much meed of that he was a monk, as Malkyn of her maidenhood, that no man would have, and not a deal more." Could Trevisa have known *Piers the Plowman*? In the earliest version of the poem the author is addressing wealthy men, and warns them against relying on external religiosity as a means of achieving salvation (A I 157–58):

> Ye haue no more merit in mass ne in houres
> Than Malkyn of hire maydenhod that no man desireth.

The traditional allusion to Malkyn as a country girl of loose morals is not at issue here, since this Malkyn has her virginity intact (whether or not it is to her own credit), a point stressed epigrammatically in both of these quotations and nowhere else to my knowledge.

In addition to the *Polychronicon*, another source of influence in the shaping of the B-continuation of *Piers the Plowman*, it seemed to me, was the medieval drama. Yet after I had read through the four major biblical cycles in Middle English, with one eye on the B version, passus XI–XX, I was disappointed in that, apart from certain general parallels (and one important connection with the Chester *Doomsday*), there was nothing very specific to authenticate my conviction that the poet was influenced by the drama. Then I remembered a fact acquired in graduate school. There was a fifth cycle of medieval drama in England, little known because it was in a different language: the Cornish *Ordinalia*.

Not really expecting to find much, but for the sake of completeness, I began plowing through the ten thousand lines of Cornish biblical drama, with the aid of a translation by Edwin Norris (1859). What I found, in brief, were two important passages that were remarkably similar to corresponding passages in the B-continuation of *Piers*, thus supporting my belief that the drama had indeed influenced the poet. But the Cornish drama? How many people outside Cornwall could have understood it? I can still remember the moment when these two separate discoveries, one in Trevisa's *Polychronicon* and the other in the Cornish *Ordinalia*, came together in my mind with the recollection of an old rhyme:

> By tre, pol, and pen
> Ye shall know the Cornish men.

That is, Trevelyan, Polwhele, Penrose—and, of course, I thought *Trevisa*!

My eventual conclusion from all this was that Trevisa, although too young to have been the author of the A text of *Piers* (ca. 1362), may possibly have been responsible for the revision and continuation of that text in the two forms known as the B and C texts. On the strength of this belief I added a chapter to *Literary Relations* entitled "About the Author" in which I frankly set forth the Trevisa hypothesis. But subsequently my main efforts were directed toward learning more about the man himself and his corner of the world: medieval Cornwall. Before going to Britain for the first time, I taught a seminar in the Cornish language, barely keeping ahead of the students in the small grammar by Caradar (A. S. D. Smith) that we were using. Two of the students in this seminar eventually visited Cornwall and did significant work in Cornish literature.

In the spring of 1959, I went to Cornwall and enjoyed the hospitality of Mr. E. G. R. Hooper, who was named Grand Bard of Cornwall later that same year (after the death of R. Morton Nance), and there I learned for the first time of the movement to revive the Cornish language, which had died out some century and a half previously. Quite apart from the documentary research that I did there, the experience of meeting people like Mr. and Mrs. Hooper enabled me to get a sense of the Cornish culture within Britain, still seeking to maintain itself even after all the centuries that had passed since the time of Trevisa. My indebtedness to many friends in Cornwall gained over the years can never be fully expressed.

In addition to the Cornish phase of my studies I wanted to follow Trevisa's path, first to Oxford and eventually to Berkeley (including some time in London at the British Museum and Public Record Office). In Oxford I learned much that was new by consulting the long rolls of Queen's College, as well as having the experience of seeing Oxford itself and working there for the first time. Much of what I learned there is incorporated in Chapter 5 of this book, and for this I am deeply indebted to the late Neil Ker, then Reader in Paleography, whose learning was matched by his generosity in helping novices like me find their way in the study of medieval manuscripts. Excellent as was my graduate training at Chicago, nothing I learned then could have prepared me for the complex task that I faced in the Bodleian Library in 1959.

Going to Berkeley was perhaps to some extent a sentimental journey: I simply wanted to see the castle and the church where Trevisa had been vicar in the final years of his life. Yet the possibility of new discoveries also beckoned, since the muniment room of the castle contained much of importance, and had not been available to researchers for many years. Even A. J. Perry, whose edition of Trevisa's minor works (1925) contains the fullest and best account of the translator's life, was unable to have access to the castle.

My efforts over several years to gain entry to the Berkeley muniment room (ultimately successful) will not be detailed here. Needless to say, I am very much indebted to Major John Berkeley and to the trustees of the estate for making it possible for me to work there. What is still vivid in my mind from that first visit to Berkeley in 1959 is the church, which is very little changed from what was likely to have been its appearance when Trevisa was vicar. I arrived there on a beautiful spring afternoon, completely anonymous, intent only on visiting the church for my own satisfaction. The setting is beautiful: it is very near the castle but hidden by a wall and almost surrounded by a grove of trees. The birds were singing and sunlight illuminated the glass of the west window as I entered. In the south aisle was the tomb of Thomas III, Lord Berkeley, who (as we shall see) may have originally been responsible for giving Trevisa the opportunity to study at Oxford.

While I was sitting in one of the pews, thinking fourteenth-century thoughts, and completely alone in that large church, in walked a black-robed figure, a man who turned out to be the vicar of Berkeley. When I was later recounting this experience to a colleague in Seattle, he responded anxiously: "Do you mean the *present* vicar of Berkeley?" And indeed it was Canon J. H. W. Fisher, vicar from 1945 to 1967. I am much indebted to him, as well as to Canon J. E. Gethyn-Jones, vicar from 1967 to 1976, whose interest in Trevisa has found expression in an ingenious fictional recreation of his life (*Trevisa of Berkeley*, 1978). On the occasion of my first visit there, Canon Fisher rolled back the carpet and showed me the stone which local tradition says marked the burial place of John Trevisa. He also generously placed at my disposal everything he had been able to discover from local sources, especially concerning the restoration of Berkeley church by Sir Gilbert Scott in 1866.

Although I have since been occupied with other kinds of research in subsequent visits to England, with generous support from the Guggenheim Foundation, in 1962–63, 1969–70, 1975–76, and the summer of 1979, my interest in Trevisa has persisted, and my memory of the original visit of 1959 remains a strong factor in motivating this present effort to undertake a biography of John Trevisa, an effort made possible by a leave of absence from the University of Washington for the academic year 1982–83. The life of a somewhat obscure fourteenth-century scholar and translator can scarcely be called "biography" in the modern sense, because the facts are few, and about all one can do is try to fit these facts into a hypothetical account within a historical setting (a procedure that I find myself referring to as "drawing lines to connect the dots"). In the case of Trevisa we have a little more evidence of personal views than might be expected, in his notes to the *Polychronicon*; without these we might well despair of ever getting inside his mind.

Even the facts about Trevisa have been strangely elusive, however, perhaps in part because there has been no standard biography, and even the valuable introduction to his life published by Perry in 1925 is not widely known. Probably most readers would rely on the *Dictionary of National Biography*, where there are two columns devoted to him which contain more than a half-dozen misleading statements: both dates are wrong; he was not born at Crocadon; he was not a canon of Westbury-on-Severn; the verses from the Apocalypse written on the walls of a chapel is not in Berkeley church; he is not the translator of the Methodius tract or Vegetius's *De Re Militari* (the latter was indeed completed in 1408, but that was six years after Trevisa's death); there is no internal evidence (beyond the allegation of John Shirley) that the *Gospel of Nicodemus* was translated at the request of Lord Berkeley; and finally Ussher (1690, p. 123) does not attribute a genealogy of King David of Scotland to Trevisa (a mistake originating with Tanner and published in 1748). On the other hand, it should be said in defense of C. L. Kingsford, who wrote the *DNB* article before 1909, that when he does his own verifying of sources, he is very accurate indeed. Thus he correctly states that Trevisa was at Exeter College from 1362 to 1369, even though the authoritative *Registrum Collegii Exoniensis*, edited by C. W. Boase (1894), indicates that Trevisa remained in Exeter College only until the winter of 1365.

The comedy of errors surrounding efforts to determine the dates of Trevisa's birth and death may serve to illustrate the problems facing a would-be biographer. Even Chaucer's birth date is not known, so it is not surprising that we have no record of the year of Trevisa's birth. And it is to the credit of the earliest writers who refer to him that they do not try to guess the date, but merely affirm that he was born in Cornwall. But beginning with Thomas Fuller in the seventeenth century, efforts were made to fix upon a date, with the result that Trevisa is said to have been born at times ranging from 1322 "or before" to 1342. This wide divergence, however, can be explained.

The very early dates for Trevisa's birth are guesses based on William Caxton's curious change in the date of completion of the translation of Higden's *Polychronicon*. Trevisa had written the following conclusion (modernized):

> God be thanked of all his deeds. This translation is ended in a Thursday, the eighteenth day of April, the year of our Lord 1387, the tenth year of King Richard the second after the conquest of England, the year of my lord's age, sir Thomas lord of Berkeley, that made me make this translation, five and thirty.

For whatever reason, Caxton in 1482 printed this same passage with the completion date changed to 1357. It was not a mere misprint, for he then proceeded to change the regnal date to "the 31st year of King Edward the Third," which is correct for the earlier date he had inserted. Afterwards when John Smyth of Nibley was writing his *Lives of the Berkeleys* (about 1622, though the work was not published until much later), he accepted Caxton's date, but noticed that the age of Thomas lord Berkeley did not accord with the date 1357. Thomas III, who died in 1361, was sixty-five in 1357, and so Smyth records the completion of the *Polychronicon* as in "the year of my lord's age . . . the 65th," adding in the margin, "misprinted 35 for 65." Smyth apparently did not notice that 1387 *was* the 35th year of Thomas IV, and furthermore he failed to realize (something that Ussher did notice later) that the eighteenth of April fell on a Thursday in 1387 whereas in 1357 it did not. But such was the power of Caxton's influence that almost every subsequent effort to fix the date of Trevisa's birth was affected by the supposition that the translation of the *Polychronicon* was completed in 1357.

This can be seen easily in the speculations of Thomas Fuller, writing in the middle of the seventeenth century:

> . . . [Trevisa] died full of honour, quiet, and age, little less than ninety years old. For,
>
> 1. He ended his translation of *Policronicon*, (as appeareth by the conclusion thereof) the 29th of *Edward* the third, when he cannot be presumed less than 30 years of age.

2. He added to the end thereof, *fifty* (some say more) years of his own historical observations.

It is this sort of conjecture that gave rise to the assortment of early dates that we find in most later notices. Thus Boase and Courtney (1874–82) have 1326, and this is repeated by Kingsford in the *Dictionary of National Biography*, who gives Trevisa's dates as 1326–1412.

A death date is usually easier to find: we know that Chaucer died in 1400. But even here Trevisa did not escape the curse of inaccuracy. The first person to cite the date of his death was John Smyth of Nibley (in his *Lives of the Berkeleys*, ca. 1622, 2:22), who gives it as 1412, citing the Worcester episcopal register. This date is repeated toward the end of the seventeenth century by Henry Wharton (who consulted Smyth), and thereafter by Tanner, Towneley, Babington, Rogers, Boase and Courtney, Cooke, Jeayes, C. W. Boase, and Kingsford in the *Dictionary of National Biography*. It was not until the present century that Wilkins (1915) and Perry (1925) discovered the correct date (1402) in the Worcester Episcopal Register of Bishop Clifford. The earliest birth date cited is 1322 (Cooke, Wilkins), and this seems to be based partly on Fuller's speculations ("little less than ninety years old") and partly on the erroneous death date, since 1322 subtracted from 1412 yields ninety years. Wilkins adds "or before," since he knew that 1412 was wrong, but failed to realize that Fuller's calculations were based on the erroneous date for completion of the *Polychronicon* translation.

Ironically, the best guess for the date of Trevisa's birth (1342) first appears in Fabricius (1735) as an apparent misreading of an entry on Trevisa in Bale's *Catalogus* (1557), which erroneously states that Trevisa's continuation of the *Polychronicon* extended from 1342 to 1397. Fabricius seems to have read the first figure as Trevisa's birth date. This is then picked up by Rogers (1870), who states flatly that Trevisa was "born in the year 1342." To my knowledge the only person to arrive at the date 1342 by the same route I have (based on the date of his arrival in Oxford: 1362) is C. W. Boase in his edition of the Registry of Exeter College (1894), where he gives the date of Trevisa's birth as "about 1342." But old traditions die hard. Even the *New Cambridge Bibliography of English Literature*, 1:467 (1974), cautiously gives the birth date as ca. 1330.

One might suppose that this discussion of dates is much ado about nothing, but in the case of Trevisa, at least, this is not so, because important inferences have been made by the use of these dates. Thus the attribution to Trevisa of the pedigree of the Berkeley family, for example, which records the birth dates of children ending with the birth of John on 21 January 1351, is based on the assumption that he was already an educated adult attached to Lord Berkeley in the 1350s. John Smyth had first proposed this in his *Lives* (1:7), whence it was picked up by Shrapnell in 1808 (Perry 1925, p. cxxviii), and in turn by Jeayes, who, in his published catalogue of the muniments in Berkeley Castle (1892), carries it a step further and says that Select Roll 102 (the document in question) "was the original production, if not in the very handwriting of John Trevisa." Both Wilkins and Perry list this roll among Trevisa's works without doubt. A translation of Vegetius's *De Re Militari* is dated 1408, and was attributed to Trevisa until this century, when the true date of his death was discovered. I should add that some uncertainty remains: when did Trevisa become chaplain to Lord Berkeley? when vicar of Berkeley?

The first three chapters (on Cornwall, Oxford, and Berkeley) will deal directly with Trevisa's life, beginning in each case with what is known or can be inferred. The chapter on translations will discuss Trevisa's known works, and a final chapter and an appendix will present hypotheses in which I have associated Trevisa with translation of the Early Version of the Wyclif Bible (in the 1370s), and with authorship of the revisions of *Piers the Plowman* (B version, 1378–83; C version, ca. 1388 or later). Students of medieval literature will already be aware that these matters are highly theoretical, but it is well at this point to remind the reader that the final chapter and appendix do not represent a generally accepted point of view. Naturally it is my hope that subsequent research by others, with more specialized knowledge than I have, will disprove or—preferably— confirm the truth of these two hypotheses concerning Trevisa, who has suffered enough (as we have seen) from the slings and arrows of misinformation.

1

CORNWALL

Even though there is no direct evidence concerning Trevisa's life before his arrival in Oxford in 1362, commentators have not been slow to supply the needed information. The earliest writers say only that he was born in Cornwall: thus John Bale in 1557 ("genere ac patria Cornubiensis"), Holinshed in 1577 ("a Cornish man borne"), and Richard Carew in 1602, who speaks of "Crocadon, the mansion of Mr. Trevisa, a gentleman deriving himself from the ancient and well-deserving chronicler of that name." Crocadon is in eastern Cornwall, and the occupant referred to is Peter Trevisa, who died in 1598. I have not been able to find any evidence to connect the Trevisa family with Crocadon before the sixteenth century, and it is clear that Carew says no more than that Peter Trevisa is a *descendant* of John. Nevertheless, in his *Church History of Britain* (1655), Thomas Fuller says that John Trevisa was "born at Crocadon in Cornwall." Yet in his *History of the Worthies of England* (1662), he says: "John Trevisa was born at Caradock in this county" (i.e., Cornwall). Fuller either had second thoughts or this could simply be a slip, since I know of no place in Cornwall with that name. This aberration is echoed in Tanner (1748) and Towneley (1821), but most later commentators agree that John Trevisa was "born in 1326 at Crocadon in St. Mellion, near Saltash, Cornwall," as the *Dictionary of National Biography* specifies. Since it is quite evident that the traditional assertion of Trevisa's birthplace is founded on Fuller's misinterpretation of Carew, we may now consider what evidence remains to support Trevisa's Cornish origin, and whether it is possible to locate him geographically within the county.

That Trevisa comes from Cornwall is supported by his name, the record of his ordination, and some remarks in his notes to the *Polychronicon*. The name *Trevisa* means "lower town," the element *trev-* being from the Indo-European root **treb* found in Latin *trabs, trabis* (English *thorpe, thrupp*); *-isa, ysa* is a formation from the root represented by Latin *pes, pedis* (English *foot*), with characteristic loss of initial *p* in Celtic languages; see Pokorny (1959, pp. 790, 1090). It is interesting that the arms of the Trevisa family, as reported by Carew, are Gules, a Garbe

Or (a wheat-sheaf in gold against a red background). Mr. Hooper once pointed out to me that many family emblems are based on puns, and offered the ingenious suggestion that the Trevisa sheaf may be intended as a pun in Cornish on -*ysa*, alluding to the Cornish word *ys*, "corn," "grain."

Trevisa's initial attachment to Exeter College, Oxford, strongly suggests that he comes from Cornwall, since the county was then a part of the diocese of Exeter (Devon and Cornwall), and Exeter College had been founded by Bishop Walter Stapeldon in 1312 specifically for students from that area. The likelihood of the connection is increased by the stipulation in the record of Trevisa's ordination (about which more later) that he was released from Exeter diocese by letters dimissory. Such letters were required when a candidate was being ordained outside his own diocese; and, as we shall see, Trevisa was in fact ordained in 1370 by Simon Sudbury, then bishop of London.

Apart from the name *Trevisa*, we have in two additions to the *Polychronicon* some indirect evidence that our translator comes specifically from Cornwall. Early in the *Polychronicon*, Higden lists the shires of England, omitting Cornwall, and citing as his source Alfred of Beverley (II, 91):

> *Trevisa.* It is wonder why Alfred summeth the shires of England somedeal as a man that dreameth; for Alfred telleth the sum of shires in this manner: "There be in England six and thirty shires without Cornwall and without the islands." Why sayeth he not in this manner? " . . . In England be seven and thirty shires, and so is Cornwall accounted with the other shires"; and that is skilful. For Cornwall is a shire of England . . . , and is departed in hundreds, and is ruled by the law of England, and holdeth shire days, as other shires do. If Alfred sayeth nay to that, he wot not what he maffleth.

This attitude, of course, contrasts sharply with that of modern British (and Scottish) groups that emphasize devolution and the preservation of regional differences. Trevisa had been introduced to an exciting new world when he departed from his home county, and he clearly was anxious that Cornwall become a part of that world.

In a later note, Trevisa referred to the parable of the wheat and tares (Matt. 13:25) as "the example of wheat and *evre* that some men clepeth darnel" (VII, 525). What the King James Bible of 1611 calls "tares" was translated in the Wyclif Bible (Early Version) as "darnel" or "cocle" (the latter used also by Chaucer). Trevisa's word *evre* appears to be of Cornish origin, and in fact survives in the modern Cornish dialect (of English) variously spelled *eaver, heaver(s), hayver(s)*, with cognates in Welsh (*efrau*) and Breton (*ivre*). Whatever its ultimate origin (Joseph Wright in his *English Dialect Dictionary* says Old French *evraie*/Modern French *ivraie*), it does seem to have been a genuine Cornish word known to Trevisa, a fragile reminder that his native language may have been Cornish rather than English.

In the fourteenth century the Cornish language was already strongly under the influence of English, especially in matters of vocabulary (like modern Welsh), an influence accelerated by the fact that Cornwall, unlike Wales, had no mountains to serve as a barrier to the Anglo-Saxon tide. But the decline of the language itself (though more investigation of this topic is needed) seems to have been very slow before the Reformation of the sixteenth century. Perhaps only in eastern Cornwall would English have established itself in the time of Trevisa. No doubt it was for this reason that R. Morton Nance, thinking (as we all did) of Trevisa as having been born at Crocadon in the east, raised the question (in conversation) whether Trevisa would have been able to speak Cornish. Obviously the specific place of Trevisa's birth in the county is important to the determination of his native language, and so it is to this problem that we now turn.

In the period we are concerned with, a person's name often provided a genuine clue to his place of birth, and such indeed would appear to be the case with *Trevisa*. There are, however, perhaps four localities in Cornwall identified by something like a form of that name. There is a *Trevyssa* in the parish of Towednack, *Trevessa* in St. Erth, *Trevease* in Constantine, and *Trevessa* in St. Enoder. Of these four, the least likely is *Trevease* in Constantine, which, in the fourteenth century, was spelled phonetically as *Trefeas* or *Trefyas*, showing that it is a different word altogether. But on phonological grounds, at least, the other three Trevessas are equally plausible.

Variations in spelling may or may not be significant. The alternation of *i* and *y* or *v* and *w* can often be ignored, but the replacement of *-isa* by *-essa* or *-issa* could be important. Oliver Padel (1985, pp. 237–38) suggests, for example, that the second element of Trevessa (St. Erth) may be derived from *ussa* "outermost," perhaps because of the early variant spelling *Trefussa* in the Assize (Plea) Rolls (dated 1284). The same reasoning could be applied to *Trevessa* in St. Enoder, since Gover cites *Trefussamur* and *Trefussabyan* from the *Calendar of Patent Rolls*

(1430), meaning *Great* and *Little Trefussa* in St. Enoder. The case of *Trevyssa* in Towednack differs in that the spelling is consistent in the two medieval sources cited by Gover: Feudal Aids in 1428 (Trevyssa), and the Lay Subsidy Rolls in 1523 (Trevissa). I ignore the questionable variant *Trevidgia* cited from an eighteenth-century map of Cornwall, though Gover for some reason treats this as the principal form of the place name. Nevertheless, I am inclined to set aside these orthographic variants, at least as they relate to St. Enoder, since, as we shall see, the spelling of both the place name and the family name in the documents mentioned below consistently supports the traditional form: *Trevisa* or *Trevysa*.

The eighteenth-century Cornish historian William Hals was the first to conjecture that the family name might be derived from *Trevisa* in St. Enoder. But support for this is hard to find, and Hals, as Charles Thomas remarks (1974), "cannot rank as a reliable historian." There is evidence, however, some previously unnoted, of the existence of a Trevisa family in Cornwall in the fourteenth century, and this evidence consistently associates the family with *Trevisa* in St. Enoder. In the *Register* of John de Grandisson, bishop of Exeter, under the date 27 October 1328, Johannes de Treuysa is named (with several others) to a sequestration of the revenues of the late Master Richard Flamank, rector of the church of Roche. A further order in connection with this sequestration was issued on 12 November of the same year, and again John de Trevysa is mentioned. The date is much too early, of course, for us to suppose that this Trevysa could be our author (born ca. 1342); but the entries do suggest that a Trevisa family was residing at this time in central Cornwall. For if this John de Trevysa lived at *Trevisa* in St. Enoder, his home was less than ten miles southwest of the parish church of Roche, to which he was ordered for the sequestration. The late rector Richard Flamank, mentioned in the bishop's order, bears the name of a venerable Cornish family, one branch of which had a residence in Goonrounson in St. Enoder, little more than a mile due east of *Trevisa*.

More decisive evidence appears in the Cornwall County Court Rolls in the Public Record Office (SC 2/161/74), for which reference I am greatly indebted to the late Derek Hall, former president of Corpus Christi College, Oxford (Hall 1978). John de Trevisa is mentioned in a number of court cases in the hundreds of Powder and Pyder. Most of the cases in which he is involved are listed under Pyder, the hundred in which *Trevisa* is situated, but one case (of particular interest here) is entered under Powder, since it appears that Trevisa's cows strayed across the line into the town of Mitchell (m. 2):

Johnnes de Trevisa by attorney complains of Guy of St. Aubyn and William Aly appearing by attorney in a plea of the seizing of cattle. And thereof he complains that they unjustly seized six cows of the same John in the vill of Mitchell (*Medesole*) in a place which is called Goenmargh and impounded them at Arrallas (*Argalles*) etc. to his damage of one hundred shillings. And Guy avows the seizure for himself and for William for this, that he found them in the vill of Arrallas doing damage and not in the vill and place aforesaid, and prays that it may be investigated.

This entry is dated 5 July 1333 (7 Edward III), just five years after the sequestration (discussed above) ordered by Bishop Grandisson. It seems reasonable that this is the same John de Trevisa mentioned earlier, and it is even clearer that he is associated with *Trevisa* in St. Enoder, which is very near the town of Mitchell, where Trevisa alleges his cattle were seized.

Another person of some prominence in Cornwall in the fourteenth century was Ralph Trevisa, who was a member of parliament for Lost-withiel (1351), Liskeard (1357), Bodmin (1360), Lostwithiel again (1360, 1362), Helston (1368), Truro (1369), and Launceston (1370–71). It is not possible to deduce Ralph Trevisa's home from his political career. But a list of rentals for the Berkeley manor of Tygembreth (Degembris) in Cornwall, which I found among the muniments in Berkeley Castle (Box 14.12), strongly suggests that this Ralph, like John before him, lived in St. Enoder. The list is written on parchment in a hand of the early fifteenth century, and appears to be a copy of an earlier list dating from the latter half of the fourteenth century, in the lifetime of our John (Fowler 1971).

My interest in the list was aroused when I observed that it represented a manor in central Cornwall, precisely the locale (as we have seen) for the activities of John de Trevisa in 1328 and 1333. The name of the manor, Tygembreth, was not familiar, but then I noticed that one of the places named was *Trevisa*: "The heirs of Ralph Trevisa hold one Cornish acre of land in *Trevysa* and two acres of land in *Penscawen*, and render per annum six shillings three pence, and suit of the common court and multure." A total of thirty entries like this one go to make up the manor of Tygembreth, owned by the Berkeley family in the fourteenth and early fifteenth centuries. Furthermore, there can be no doubt that the *Trevisa* in question is the one in St. Enoder parish, the only place of that name in Cornwall with a *Penscawen* immediately adjoining; and all of the thirty places named in the roll form a tight cluster in the center of the county to the north and northwest of the town of Mitchell.

Other traceable names in this same rental clearly refer to contemporaries of the Ralph Trevisa cited under *Trevysa and Penscawan*. Thus Robert Tresawell died in 1388, as is evident from an inquisition taken in the eleventh year of Richard II. Robert Trevanyon appears to have been the son of Sir John Trevanyon, M.P. for Lostwithiel in the time of Edward III (died 1377). Ralph Kayell's daughter was married in 1377. Finally, Thomas Peverell married Margaret Courtney about 1350. These four examples accord well with the dates established for Ralph Trevisa's political career (1351–71).

The conclusions to be drawn from this recently discovered evidence are modest enough, but there are several points to be made of considerable significance for the life of John Trevisa. First, identification of his birthplace with *Trevisa* in St. Enoder is strengthened, while it seems possible that the various documents put us in touch with at least three generations of the family: John (1328–33), Ralph (1351–71), and John Trevisa himself (1342–1402). It likewise follows (recognizing the limits of our knowledge of the decline of the Cornish language) that if John was born in central Cornwall about 1342, his native language is likely to have been Cornish rather than English; or at the very least it is likely that he would have been able to speak and understand Cornish from an early age. Nor should we overlook the fact that a Berkeley was lord of the manor to which *Trevisa* belonged: we may even conjecture that it was this ownership of the Trevisa homestead that brought young John to the attention of the Berkeley family.

Thomas III was Lord Berkeley from 1326 until his death in 1361, and is the man who would certainly have been Trevisa's original benefactor if indeed the Berkeley connection prompted his departure for Oxford. But with all of his lands and other responsibilities, would Lord Berkeley ever have bothered to visit a manor so remote as Tygembreth in Cornwall? Lord Ernle, author of *English Farming Past and Present* (revised, 1961), was one of the very few scholars early in this century who made use of the manorial records of Berkeley Castle, and he singles out Thomas III as a medieval prototype of "farmer George," and an illustration of the maxim

that "the master's foot fats the soil" (pp. 31ff.). Hence it is not entirely
fanciful to suppose that this lord actually visited his Cornish properties,
there encountered Trevisa at an early age, and, as his benefactor, made
it possible for him to study at Oxford and eventually to go to Berkeley
and become chaplain to his grandson Thomas IV.

Where might Trevisa have received his initial training? By far the
most important center of education in Cornwall from the thirteenth
to the fifteenth centuries was the Collegiate Church of St. Thomas
of Canterbury, otherwise known as the Collegiate Church of Glasney
in Penryn. It was founded in 1265 by Walter Bronescombe, bishop of
Exeter. Concerning the importance of Glasney, Thurston C. Peter in
his history of the school (1903) has this to say (p. xiii):

> It was the foundation here of the Collegiate Church of Glasney, in 1265, that
> gave Penryn its chief importance, and made it a place known all over England,
> and, indeed, Europe. The following pages will show how men came hither
> from all parts, and how those who were connected with the college travelled
> to and from Rome and elsewhere on the Continent. For three hundred years
> Glasney was a favourite establishment of the bishops of Exeter, and many men
> of high standing in the Church held prebends therein. It was a centre from
> which important orders were frequently promulgated, and excommunications
> pronounced, and indeed was the centre of Church life in West Cornwall.

The Collegiate Church of Glasney was allotted a faculty of thirteen secular canons, one of whom served as provost. Of particular interest for the
present discussion is the manner in which these canons were supported.
In general the bishops arranged for each canon to receive the living of
one of the local parish churches, with the privilege of appointing a vicar
to serve for him in the parish. This meant that during most of its history,
Glasney College benefited from the income of some thirteen or more
appropriated livings. As might be expected, a majority of the churches
were in the vicinity of Penryn: St. Kea, St. Feock, Mylor, St. Gluvias,
Budoc, Manaccan, and St. Sithney. Somewhat farther removed were
St. Allen, Lanmorek (Mevagissey), and St. Goran. But the most remote
parishes appropriated to Glasney were, to the west, Zennor and St. Just
(in Penwith), and, to the northeast, St. Colan and St. Enoder.

The ties between St. Enoder parish and the Collegiate Church of
Glasney strengthen the possibility that Trevisa went to school in Penryn.
The living of St. Enoder was appropriated to Glasney virtually through-
out the history of the college, from 1270 to the sixteenth century, and

it seems to have been an especially desirable assignment. In 1271 the house formerly occupied by Walter, provost of Glasney, was allotted to the vicar of St. Enoder, and the *Valor Ecclesiasticus* of Henry VIII reveals that St. Enoder provided the largest single income of all the sixteen appropriated tithes there listed.

In light of this system of appropriations, it is not difficult to see why the canons and prebendaries of Glasney would take a particular interest in the parishes over which they legally presided, and from which they derived their income. The influence of the College in these areas must have been very strong. One of the most famous activities at Glasney was the production of the Cornish *Ordinalia*, to which reference has been made above (in the Introduction). These biblical dramas in the Cornish language contain amusing allusions to local places, most of them clustered around Penryn, suggesting that the text in its present form reflects a production staged at Glasney in the fourteenth century. It can scarcely be coincidence, I think, that one of the two surviving remains of the Cornish *plen an gwary* or "playing place" is to be found in St. Just in Penwith, a parish appropriated to Glasney in 1355. Archae-ological evidence, such as that uncovered by Charles Thomas (1964) at Lanivet near Bodmin, suggests that modification of these ancient Cornish rounds for use as outdoor stages had been undertaken by the mid-fourteenth century. And Bishop Grandisson, on 10 December 1360, issued a prohibition addressed to (among others) the provost and chapter of Glasney, forbidding the acting of plays during the holidays under pain of excommunication. If Trevisa did indeed go to school at Glasney, there is good reason to believe that he may have witnessed a performance of the Cornish *Ordinalia*, which, in its present form, as I have tried to show elsewhere (1961a), belongs to the third quarter of the fourteenth century.

Perhaps the best of all educational opportunities open to a Cornish boy in the fourteenth century was appointment as a "clerk of the first form" in Glasney College. Here he would be able not only to study, to serve as a chorister, and to assist at Mass, but also to learn from men who had traveled widely, and even a few who had studied at the University of Oxford. Some of the young clerks of Glasney could look forward merely to the attainment of minor orders; others could hope eventually to achieve ordination as priests; but there were also the fortunate few for whom Glasney was a stepping stone on the way to Exeter College in Oxford (then known as Stapeldon hall after its founder). Such was the good fortune, as we know, of John Trevisa, whether he went there from Glasney or from some other Cornish school. No doubt it is likely that students who, like Trevisa, were sent to Oxford were those of exceptional ability. At the same time, however, most students needed the support of a patron, preferably a wealthy and powerful lord, who could intercede for them, and perhaps also give them some kind of financial assistance "wherwith to scoleye."

The Berkeley historian John Smyth (1883–85) documents the fact that the Berkeleys had important holdings in Cornwall over a long period. But their interests were not limited to the lands they held there. For a brief time, in 1327, James Berkeley, son of Thomas II (1281–1321), was bishop of Exeter. Peter Berkeley, son of Maurice III, was a canon of the Collegiate Church of Glasney, 1331–34. Sir Maurice de Berkeley, also a son of Maurice III, interceded with the king in 1329 on behalf of certain canons and prebendaries of Glasney, that they should retain their benefices for life, and the king granted his request. Thomas III, though there is no record of his having interceded at Glasney, had considerable business in Cornwall, as we have seen, and he was also not without interest in the welfare of promising young students. In 1327 he gave "to William Stinchcomb an hopeful Scholler, five pounds a year for his better maintenance untill hee shall be promoted to a benefice of twenty pounds a yeare." Likewise Thomas III's younger brother, Eudo de Berkeley, was engaged in study at Oxford. Being a member of a wealthy family, Eudo celebrated the completion of his studies in fine style, as reported by Smyth (1:270):

> At whose inception there, (soe is the word,) the twentieth of Edward the second, the parson of Slimbridge, (which I conceive to bee his Vncle James,) presented him with a boare, which in the feedinge had eaten one Quarter and two Bushells of beanes.

Thus we see that the Berkeleys possessed lands in Cornwall, including the *Trevisa* homestead, that one member of the family was for a time canon of Glasney Collegiate Church, and that another member interceded there on behalf of certain canons in the college. If we add to this the significance of James Berkeley's brief tenure as bishop of Exeter (until his death on 24 June 1327), the concern of the lords of the Berkeleys for "hopeful scholars," and their interest in Oxford University, it is not difficult to imagine how a young man from a remote parish in Cornwall might hope, with the aid of such a family, to rise eventually to a position of importance in fourteenth-century England.

The man who succeeded James Berkeley was John de Grandisson, bishop of Exeter from 1327 until his death in 1369, at which time John Trevisa was about twenty-seven and studying at Oxford. We do not have evidence of any direct connection between these two men, but it is very likely that, as Canon Gethyn-Jones (1978) suggests, Trevisa came under the influence of this great bishop. Grandisson was born of a distinguished family in Ashperton (Ashton), Hereford, in 1292. He studied at Paris from 1313 to 1317 under the Cistercian Jacques Fournier, the man who eventually became Pope Benedict XII (1334–42), and later served as Fournier's chaplain in Avignon, where he was when James Berkeley died. Grandisson also seems to have studied at Oxford, before or after his sojourn in Paris, but the exact time of his stay there is uncertain.

When Grandisson arrived in Exeter in the summer of 1328, he found the diocese in a deplorable condition, in part no doubt because of the anarchy following the assassination of Walter Stapeldon in 1326 and the unexpected death of James Berkeley in 1327. The episcopal manors had been plundered, all of the accounts were in a state of confusion, and there were payments demanded of this bankrupt diocese by the Crown, Canterbury, and the papal court itself. In addition, Grandisson was appalled by the lack of books and vestments, not to mention that in Exeter he was confronted with a half-finished cathedral. Fortunately the thirty-six-year-old primate was a man of enormous energy, and he set to work immediately to gain control over his diocese.

One of the first major enterprises of the new bishop was to conduct a complete visitation of the county of Cornwall, which he describes as "a foreign land, adjoining England only along its eastern boundary, being surrounded on every other side by the sea," and he finds that his diocese includes "a group of islands [the Scilly Isles] on which his predecessors had never set foot." Writing to some friends in Avignon he says (Grandisson's *Register*, I, 98, translation in Preface, III, xx):

> I am not only set down in the ends of the earth, but in the very end of the ends thereof. My diocese, which embraces Devon and Cornwall, is separated from the rest of England, and, except on one side only, surrounded by seas so

tempestuous that they can scarcely be called navigable. The people of Corn-wall speak in a tongue which is unknown to the English, and only known to Bretons (*Lingua, eciam, in extremis Cornubie non Anglicis, sed Britonibus, extat nota*).

For a sense of how Cornwall was viewed by the good bishop, we can do no better than to follow in outline his visitation of Cornwall as set forth in his *Register* for the years 1328 to 1336.

On 10 September 1328, Bishop Grandisson entered Cornwall for the first time and spend about two months there. His tour included visits at Launceston, Southill, Menhenyot, Bodmin, Tywardreath, St. Breoke, and Lanner, finally reaching Penryn (Glasney College) on 1 November. Then came a stop at the Priory of St. Michael's Mount on 4 November, followed by an ill-fated effort to visit the Collegiate Church of St. Buryan, where the dean and prebendaries attacked the bishop's messenger and apparently wounded him seriously. When the bishop arrived and excommunicated the offenders by name, eighteen people came forward, confessed, and took the oath of obedience; but for years to come St. Buryan proved a thorn in the bishop's side, claiming exemption from his jurisdiction on the ground that their church was a Royal peculiar, despite the concessions that Bishop Stapeldon had obtained from the Crown. Grandisson proceeded from St. Buryan to St. Gwennap and on to Truro on 6 November, resting for a time at his manor of Lanner; then on to the priory at Tywardreath on 11 November, Lanteglos by Camelford, Stratton, and Hartland Abbey, missing an intended visit to the Collegiate Church of Crantock, perhaps because of the onset of winter weather. He thus concluded an initial tour of the county by the middle of November 1328. Circumstances prevented further visits until nearly two years later, when he spent over two months there.

In September and October 1330 he visited Launceston, Padstow, Penryn (for about a week), St. Probus, and Bodmin, where he stayed at Glynn, a manor of the Carminowes, arriving on 7 November. He then returned by way of Launceston and was out of the county before the end of the month. Another brief visitation occurred in early November 1333, when he dedicated the high altar of St. Sampson's Southill, and included in his circuit Launceston Priory, Kilkhampton, and Hartland Abbey.

A final and most interesting visitation, which concluded the bishop's initial efforts to gain control of the county, occurred in the summer of 1336. Stopping first at Cotynbeke near St. Germans on 26 June, he proceeded on 1 July to visit St. Veep (between Lostwithiel and Fowey) and came to Fowey on 3 July. Thence he continued westward to Gulval, Paul, Penzance, and on to St. Buryan, where he finally succeeded in establishing his authority. This last swing included St. Just (in Penwith), St. Madron, St. Ludgvan, St. Colan, and thence back to Launceston on 31 July 1336, thus finally completing his circuit of the county, in the course of which he probably confirmed or admitted to the first tonsure in many places.

The editor of Grandisson's *Register*, F. C. Hingeston-Randolph, points out that the register of the bishop's ordinations, referred to in the *Register* itself ("in Regestro de Ordinibus," II, 820), is missing, which means that much valuable information about the visitations is not available to us. Fortunately, however, the account of Grandisson's appearance in St. Buryan on 12 July 1336, with much pomp and circumstance, is preserved in the *Register* proper (perhaps because it was such a triumph), and gives us an indication of what this tour of Cornwall was really like (*Register*, II, 820; translation in Preface, III, xliii f.):

> The parishioners assembled in the Church in large numbers to meet him, and he spoke to them by an interpreter, Henry Marsley, Rector of St. Just-in-Penwith; for with the exception of the higher classes, who were educated men, they understood only their own Cornish tongue (*qui linguam dumtaxat noverunt Cornubicam*). . . . All submitted, and quite unanimously; the principal inhabitants speaking in English or French, and the others in their own language (*qui linguam Cornubicam tantummodo noverunt*). . . . The sermon was in Latin, the interpreter afterwards reciting the substance of it to the congregation in their Cornish tongue. Many of the younger parishioners then came forward and received the first tonsure at the Bishop's hands; and children, almost more than could be numbered (*puerosque quasi innumerabilis*), gathered from all parts of the large parish and its dependent chapelries, were confirmed.

On some such occasion as this, perhaps, in subsequent decades, John Trevisa may have first caught sight of the famous bishop of Exeter.

At the time of Trevisa's birth, the archdeacon of Cornwall was the Venerable (in more than one sense) Adam de Carleton, appointed in 1307 and serving until Grandisson arranged a transfer for him in 1346. The transfer was requested by Adam himself, who by this time was advanced in years; and the bishop preserved in his *Register* a copy of

Adam's letter proposing an exchange with John de St. Paul, rector of Brington in Huntingdonshire, which had apparently been the archdeacon's original home. In his letter, Adam complains of the hardships involved in his office: he had to cover the entire county of Cornwall, and attempt to discipline a people whose very language he could not understand (*Register*, II, 958; translation in Preface, III, liv):

> I have never got on well with these Cornish folk, for they are a truly wonderful race, of a rebellious temper, unwilling to be taught or to submit to correction (*populus in illis partibus est valde mirabilis, rebellis, et difficilis ad informandum et corrigendum*).

The archdeacon concludes by urging the exchange with John de St. Paul, pointing out how he could then manage his duties in Brington without the fatigue of long journeys, and would be surrounded by old friends who could speak to him in his own language. It is satisfying to know that this exchange was effected in 1346, thus giving Adam de Carleton a well-deserved rest.

This glimpse of Cornwall through the eyes of the bishop of Exeter and his *Register* shows us a county that was almost viewed as a foreign land, perched on the edges of civilization, and occupied by a people whose reputation for reasonableness and conformity was not the best. From this unpromising home we shall next follow the progress of Trevisa to Oxford. But it is well first to summarize what we know or can infer about the first twenty years of his life.

John Trevisa was born in Cornwall about the year 1342, probably at *Trevisa* in the parish of St. Enoder, land which was part of the manor of Tygembreth (Degembris) belonging to the Berkeley family and may have been inspected personally by Thomas III, Lord Berkeley, from 1326 to 1361. Evidence of the presence there of a Trevisa family begins with John (1328–33) and continues with Ralph (1351–71). Since the parish of St. Enoder was appropriated to Glasney Collegiate Church, it is possible that Trevisa began his education at this college, where he could have achieved in 1360 the status of clerk of the second form, for which the minimum age was eighteen. Finally, when he was about twenty years old, and with the help of an influential patron, perhaps one of the Berkeleys, he entered Exeter College, Oxford, early in the year 1362.

2

OXFORD

We now turn our attention to the period from 1362 until 1387, a quarter of a century during which Trevisa was almost continuously resident in Oxford. It will be best to consider first of all the evidence for his presence preserved in the college accounts and then to reconstruct as far as possible what was going on in the University during his stay by calling the roll of the colleges in existence at that time. In the following discussion I am very much indebted to A. B. Emden, whose three-volume *Biographical Register* (Oxford, 1957–59) contains an alphabetical listing of persons connected with Oxford from its beginnings to the year 1500, together with a compact summary of what is known about each individual. When no other work is mentioned, it should be understood that this important reference is the primary source of my information on Oxford students. When it comes to Trevisa himself, of course, we must go beyond the documentation in Emden; but my debt to him is nevertheless very great in the following effort to reconstruct Trevisa's life at Oxford in the latter half of the fourteenth century.

Evidence of Trevisa's sojourn in the University is confined almost entirely to the financial records of the colleges to which he was attached. Thus the rector's accounts (*compoti*) for Stapeldon hall (Exeter College) attest Trevisa's presence there from 1361–62 until the spring of 1369, and similar records in the archives of the Queen's College indicate his more or less continuous presence there from May 1369 until perhaps the summer of 1387. Since these records are all we have in the way of documentation, it is needful to coax as much information from them as their routine nature will permit.

A closer look at the Exeter accounts, which are virtually complete for Trevisa's period, will illustrate the kind of information that such records can provide. These *compoti* were kept in separate rolls (still preserved in the College Library) for periods that correspond closely to the academic terms of study observed by the modern University. In most transatlantic institutions these would be the fall, winter, spring, and summer quarters or semesters; in Oxford they are respectively Michaelmas, Hilary, and Trinity terms plus the Long Vacation. In the Exeter *compoti* the demarcation of these four academic periods falls on the following days: the feasts of St. Denys (9 October), the Nativity (25 December), Easter (a movable feast), and the Translation of St. Thomas à Becket (7 July). Looking backward, beginning the academic year with the feast of St. Denys reminds us of Rashdall's conviction that Oxford's traditions were originally patterned after those of Paris in the twelfth century. Looking forward, it is intriguing to see that the modern schedule of studies at Oxford is very close to that of Exeter College in the fourteenth century, taking as our example the academic year 1982–83: Michaelmas Term, 10 October to 4 December; Hilary, 7 January to 25 March; Trinity, 20 April to 6 July; and then the Long Vacation runs through the remainder of the summer until the next Michaelmas Term begins, precisely on the feast of St. Denys, Sunday, 9 October 1983.

The most common type of entry in the *compoti* is that which records payment of allowances to each of the fellows. Account is thus rendered in the *compotus* of Exeter College for Hilary Term 1361–62 for the allowances of John Trevisa (*pro dietis Johannis Trevyse*), who came into commons on Sunday of the same week, in the amount of eight pence. Similar entries for Trevisa occur in 1362 during Long Vacation (twice), 1364 in Trinity Term and Long Vacation, 1365 in Long Vacation and Michaelmas, 1366 in Michaelmas (twice), 1367 in Long Vacation (twice), 1368 in Michaelmas, and 1369 in Trinity Term. This is a very full record, and it is remarkable, after over six hundred years, to discover that, for the period represented above, only three Exeter accounts are missing, all for Michaelmas Term in the years 1362, 1364, and 1367.

From the list of payments I have recited, there may appear to be gaps, but it is not easy to argue the absence of Trevisa from Oxford by the silence of the *compoti*, since allowances do not seem to have been paid in every term. No payment of allowances for Trevisa is recorded, for example, in the year 1363; hence we might conclude that he was not in Oxford, except that there is a special payment of twelve pence for two horses "when the rector (Robert de Clyste) and John Trevisa were at West Wittenham to arrange with the workmen for the building of a barn." The parish church of West Wittenham was one of those whose tithes provided income for the college, and of course the fellows at times had to take a hand in the business of the parish as a part of their responsibilities. There is evidence in the accounts that the fellows of Stapeldon hall took their responsibilities seriously. Thus during Michaelmas 1366, expenses of nine pence are recorded when one of the fellows was at West Wittenham with a "plumber" for repair of the chancel. This suggests that the fellows did not simply demand their allowances from these churches without paying them any other attention "though it rain on their altars" (*Piers the Plowman*, B X 313).

Another kind of expense was incurred by fellows who entertained visiting friends or relatives. Such expenses are recorded for Trevisa in 1362 (Long Vacation), 1364 (Trinity Term), 1365 (Michaelmas), and 1367 (Trinity). The entry in this category for 1364 is of particular interest because of the way it is phrased: payment of three shillings and four pence to sir John Trevisa for visiting friends (*domino Johanno Trevisa ad visitandum amicos*). The use of the term *dominus* here is unique for Trevisa in these accounts, and is perhaps a form of recognition that he has completed his term as a freshman (*bejaunus*). Obtaining a loan from the common fund of the College was not encouraged, but Trevisa appears to have managed this on more than one occasion. The first instance seems unpremeditated, in that his expenses for visiting friends in 1364 (three shillings and four pence) appear to be carried over as a loan of that amount in 1365 and 1366. This apparently caused no problems, however, for a loan of twenty shillings was granted him in Michaelmas 1366 "until the feast of St. Frideswide" (19 October), whether of that year or the next it is difficult to say. In any case, during Trinity Term of 1367 Trevisa is granted a loan of twenty shillings "by the unanimous agreement of the fellows" (*ex unanimi consensu sociorum*).

There remain only incidental expenses associated with Trevisa's room in the college. What appear to be rental payments (*pro pensione sua*) are recorded against his name in the Long Vacation of 1364 (seven shillings and five pence), 1367 (seven shillings and two pence), and 1368 (ten shillings); and a single payment of four pence is made in 1367 (Long Vacation) for a key to the room of John Trevisa (*pro clave camera Johannis Trevyse*). If there is any gap at all in this record, it would be from Christmas 1365 until the beginning of Michaelmas Term in the fall of 1366, during which interval there is no mention of Trevisa. In the *compoti* for Long Vacation 1366 there is what appears to be a complete list of rental payments on behalf of the fellows (ten of them plus the rector), and Trevisa's name does not appear. Otherwise the evidence of the rectors' accounts suggests that Trevisa was at Exeter College virtually without interruption from early in 1362 until May 1369, when, as we shall see, he transferred his allegiance to Queen's.

Before turning to the Queen's College accounts, it is worth noting a final entry in the Exeter *compoti* which, though it does not mention Trevisa, may relate to the fact that he and several other fellows chose to leave their home college and take up residence in Queen's. In Hilary Term of 1366–67, expenses of twelve pence are recorded "for wine and beer (*cervisia*) when Master Henry de Whitfield and Master John Landreyn and many others were here on business of the house." John Landreyn had been a fellow of Exeter as early as 1344, and though he later transferred his allegiance to Oriel in 1358, his continuing affection for Exeter College is attested by the fact that he joined with Whitfield in the purchase of a manuscript for the college library (MS 28, containing commentaries on Boethius's *Consolation of Philosophy* and other works). Henry Whitfield had been elected provost of Queen's College in 1362, but had retained an interest in Exeter College, not apparently from having been a member (Emden, 3:2038), but because he was himself from Exeter diocese. He was at least three times visitor of the College by appointment of Bishop Brantyngham (1371, 1374, 1378), and from this entry appears to have been engaged on business for the College in 1366–67. We may not be too far off the mark to suppose that on such an occasion as this he engaged in a little recruiting among the Exeter students. In any case, two years later John Trevisa left Exeter and became a fellow of Queen's under provost Whitfield.

The Queen's College long rolls preserve accounts that enable us to follow Trevisa's career at Oxford between 1369 and 1387, and they show likewise that he spent two additional years there in 1394–95 and 1395–96. These long rolls are not as consistent as the Exeter records in their divisions of the academic year; hence it will be convenient simply to give the dates of each and cite volume and page numbers from the valuable handwritten copy by C. L. Stainer, *Compoti Collegii Aule Reginae* (10 vols., Oxford, 1906–8) deposited in the College Library. Citation of Stainer's page numbers will have the added advantage of serving as an indication of the thoroughness of record-keeping of the treasurers, which ranges from two pages required for the briefest of the annual accounts, to over twenty pages for the contents of the fullest of them.

The Queen's College long rolls are in general as thorough and reliable as the records we have examined for Exeter. But for the period we are investigating, their integrity is compromised by a controversy that erupted in Queen's in the mid-1370s and continued well into the next decade. On the surface the trouble was caused by the disputed election of a provost, but we will defer consideration of the deeper significance of this controversy as it relates to Trevisa until the later chapter on Trevisa and the English Bible. Suffice it to say here that a schism developed between northern and southern fellows of the College, and the southerners (including Trevisa) were expelled in 1378 by decision of the king. Nevertheless, the matter seems to have been resolved to the point that at least some of the expelled fellows (again including Trevisa) were allowed to return and rent rooms in the College.

Not everyone using the long rolls of Queen's has done so with an awareness of the effect that this controversy had on their reliability. Hence before we try to interpret the evidence they offer about Trevisa, it will be well to take note of the difficulty involved for the years 1369–87. The treasurer of Queen's in 1368–69 when Trevisa arrived was Gilbert Grimsby, but he died before his year was completed and the accounts were taken over by Trevisa, whose *compotus* runs only from 5 May until 28 September 1369 (Stainer, 2:158–70). Thereafter the rolls appear to be in reasonably good shape to 1375, except for the absence of the long roll for 1370–71, possibly because of an epidemic in Oxford during that year (VCH Oxon, 4:19). The average length of each is twelve to fourteen pages in Stainer's copy. The first visible sign of the coming storm can be seen in the way the post of treasurer is filled: in 1369–70, the accounts are kept by the chaplain John Banham; in 1371–72, by the chaplain Adam Skelton; then in 1372–73 and 1373–74 the position of treasurer is filled by no less than four fellows: Robert Blakedon, Henry Whitfield, Nicholas Hereford, and William Middleworth, all southerners including the provost. If the purpose of this multiple appointment was to impart stability to the office, it failed: long rolls for the next three years are entirely missing. And it is difficult to avoid the inference that this lacuna is due to the controversy then raging between the northern and southern fellows.

When the long rolls resume with the academic year 1378–79 (Stainer, 3:235–41C), a northerner (Robert Hodersale) is the treasurer, and he continues in this office for the year 1379–80 (3:242–48). William

Middleworth, one of the southerners expelled along with Trevisa, was pardoned on 1 May 1380, and by October 1381 had resumed residence. Yet the long rolls do not return to normal. The account for 1380–81 occupies only three pages in Stainer (3:249–51), and is unsigned; for a period of a year and a quarter (9 October 1381 to January 1383) the records are kept by William Brigge (3:252–57); from January 1383 to January 1384 the account is again unsigned, and there follows a gap of nine months, after which we find another anonymous account running from 11 November 1384 to 10 November 1385. At this point the new regime in the College seems to have taken a firm grip on things: the treasurer is now assisted by a *camerarius* each year for the remainder of the century and beyond. Thus John Lokesley is treasurer almost continuously from 1385 to 1390, assisted by Matthew Willesthorpe in 1385–86, for example, and by Richard Browne in 1386–87.

We are now in a position to assess the reliability of the long rolls of Queen's College for the period surrounding the controversy there from 1375 to 1385. The accounts for 1375 to 1378 are entirely missing; those kept by Robert Hodersale in 1378–79 and 1379–80 are perhaps somewhat reduced in size, but the mainly anonymous accounts of the period from 1380 through 1385 scarcely fill four pages per year in Stainer's copy (3:249–65). Clearly the record-keeping during this time was perfunctory at best.

Allowing for the state of the long rolls from 1369 to 1385, it would appear that Trevisa was a resident of Queen's almost continuously for that period. His status as a fellow, however, is clear and uncontested only for the period 1369 to 1374, during which time he regularly received his allowances (*liberata*) (Stainer, 2:167, 173, 189, 196–97, 210). One year before the big gap occurs we note that the *compotus* for 1374–75 (2:222–34) is entirely lacking in references to Trevisa, whereas when the record resumes, in the *compotus* of Robert Hodersale for 1378–79 (3:238), we find that eighteen pence is dispersed to a messenger for two trips on Trevisa's behalf (*garcioni transienti pro Trevisa bis*). Moreover it seems self-evident that the strenuous efforts that were made by the northerners to expel Trevisa, ultimately successful in 1379, would have been unnecessary if he had not been on the scene. Hence we may tentatively conclude that while he appears to have been away from Oxford in 1374–75, he is likely to have returned soon thereafter, during the period for which we have no records.

The next entries involving Trevisa, after the *garcio* of 1378–79, appear only after full record-keeping resumes in 1385–86 in the first *compotus* of John Lokesley (3:274), where twenty pence is paid for letters (*pro brevibus*) for Trevisa and Trevelles, the latter a Cornishman who had been a fellow of Queen's in the 1360s. A little further on in the same account, another twenty pence is paid for letters against Trevisa (*pro brevibus contra Trevisa*), and two pence is paid to someone going to London to expedite these letters. Finally in the *compotus* of 1386–87 (3:291), six shillings eight pence is paid in compensation for the letters against Trevisa. These seem to refer to legal proceedings, apparently successful, against Trevisa, the outcome of which was that he was forced to pay the sum mentioned. A final (and important) entry in the *compotus* of 1386–87 (3:291) records payment by Trevisa of three pounds—that is, four marks—for rental of his room for four years preceding (*de quattuor annis precedentibus*). On the back of the long roll in which this entry is found is a note, not entirely legible, which appears to record a protest by Trevisa to the effect that while he is paying this back rent of three pounds, it is not because of any legal obligation (*sed nihil de obligatione*). The sum required represents full rent for four years, and suggests that Trevisa had been resident in Queen's since 1382 or 1383 without paying. This falls, of course, in that period of shoddy record-keeping that we have already noticed, and it is perhaps impossible to know certainly to what four-year period the entry refers (Emden takes it to be 1382–86). I am inclined to think it is for the period 1383–87.

Incidental expenses of Trevisa in the long rolls of Queen's College resemble those we have already observed in the Exeter accounts. Thus in the *compotus* of 1372–73 (2:216), four pence was paid for a key to the door of Master William de Wilton, and for repairing a candle-holder before the door of Trevisa; and eleven pence was the cost of nails used in shingling Trevisa's room. The following year (2:216), eleven pence was paid two roofers for repairing the rooms of Trevisa and Scharpe. As we have seen in the case of Exeter, the Queen's College received support from churches appropriated for that purpose. Two of these were the churches of Sparsholt and Newbold, and it was often necessary for members of the College to visit these parishes. In 1369–70 (2:176), eighteen pence was charged to horses for Trevisa on a trip to Newbold. Again, in 1371–72 (2:183), thirty pence was paid for the expenses of

Middleworth and Trevisa in showing the muniments of the church of Newbold at Strettone, and expenses incurred on the way.

A final type of entry remains to be considered. I refer to those entries in the long rolls which record payments made by Trevisa to discharge an old debt (*in parte solucionis debiti antiqui*). R. H. Hodgkin, in his *Six Centuries of an Oxford College: A History of the Queen's College, 1340–1940* (Oxford, 1949), observes (pp. 37–38):

> It was an unkind fate which had decided that Trevisa in his first year at Queen's should be made treasurer, to clear up the mess in the college accounts made by the chaplain Grimsby and that as Grimsby's executor an old debt should be entered up against Trevisa in the bursarial rolls for the rest of the century, in spite of occasional efforts to pay it off.

When Gilbert Grimsby died in May 1369, Trevisa not only became treasurer in his place, he also acted as Grimsby's executor, and as such assumed the burden of his debts, which appear to have amounted to the sum of four pounds (2:179, 207). This sum is carefully distinguished from Trevisa's own debts (*debiti sui proprii*, 2:191), and is eventually repaid in installments spread over the last ten years of Trevisa's life. The first payment of twenty shillings was presented to the treasurer (William Dyer) by John Coby, a servant of Trevisa's, on the feast of St. Mark, 25 April 1393 (2:366, 369, duplicate entries), Trevisa at that time being fully occupied as vicar of Berkeley in Gloucestershire, as we shall see. The final four payments were made by Trevisa himself, two of them during his years of residency, 1394–96 (4:381, 400), and the other two in the period 1398 to 1400 (4:437, 453). The debt was thus paid in full two years before his death. Not all executors in Trevisa's day were as conscientious as this: in *Piers the Plowman* some false executors were said to "suffer the dead in debt to the day of doom" (B XX 291).

Having spent seven years in Exeter College and some eighteen years in and out of Queen's, what was the extent of Trevisa's scholastic achievement in Oxford? That he emerged from Exeter with the degree of master of arts is clearly indicated by the fact that he is called "master" in the long roll that he kept as treasurer of Queen's in 1369: *Compotus Magistri Johannis Trevisa* (2:164). No doubt it is on this basis that Emden refers to him as "M.A." In the absence of other documentation, perhaps we must agree with Emden that Trevisa did not incept in theology during his years at Queen's. The only evidence to the contrary that I know of is the statement of John Shirley (BL Add. MS 16165, fol. 94r, ca. 1425): "maystre Iohan Trevysa Doctour in theologye." On balance, it seems we should conclude that though Trevisa may have aimed for the doctorate at Queen's, his many interests (as we shall see) took him farther and farther away from the completion of his theological degree. But since John Shirley was a near contemporary, and had ties with the Berkeley family (see Hanna 1989, p. 902 and n. 58), we should for the present leave open the possibility that he knew what he was talking about. In the beginning of his anthology (MS 16165, fol. 2a), Shirley wrote a versified table of contents, from which I quote his description of *Nicodemus* (Hammond 1927, p. 195):

> þe passyoun þanne / of Nichodeme /
> fful wel translated shul ye seen /
> þe whiche of Berkeley / lord Thomas
> whome god assoyle / for his grace /
> Lete oute of latyn / hit translate /
> By *Johan Trevysa* / þat hit made
> A maystre in Theologye /
> Appreued clerk / for þe maystrye /
> Thankeþe þe lord / and þe Clerk /
> þat caused first / þat holy werk /

The University

In the dialogue prefixed to his translation of the *Polychronicon* (1387), John Trevisa presents a list of famous translators, including King Alfred, "that founded the universite of Oxenford" (BL MS Harleian 1900, fol. 43r). This belief in the antiquity of the University was no doubt widely held in the fourteenth century, and has only been finally discredited in modern times. The association of Alfred with the foundation of the town itself is not impossible, though its existence is not documented before the early tenth century in the Anglo-Saxon Chronicle. The fact is that when Trevisa entered Exeter College in 1362, the University (as an association of colleges) was scarcely one hundred years old, though the development of its schools came gradually in the course of the twelfth century. It will assist in our understanding of Trevisa's life there if we now review briefly the history of the University before turning to a consideration of the major persons and events belonging to the period before and during Trevisa's residency.

The schools that came into being in Europe in the twelfth century were the creation of the Church, and for this reason it is well to keep in mind the various branches of that enormous institution, and to observe how these were involved in the development of the University of Oxford. There were two main bodies of clergy in the medieval Church. One consisted of the seculars, or priests assigned to parish churches whose vineyard was the world (*saeculum*); the other body comprised the regulars, those living apart from the world in a community governed by a rule (*regula*), who led disciplined lives and offered prayer and praise to God.

Until the twelfth century, when the universities first began to take shape, the intellectual life of the Church centered in the great monastic houses; and in England, as elsewhere, the Benedictine Order was supreme, maintaining its sense of purpose against a strong tide of monastic decline. To combat the slackness that was afflicting the Benedictines, new orders were also being founded, notably the Cistercians and the rapidly growing communities of Austin Canons. In view of the prestige of the venerable monastic tradition, and the excitement that accompanied monastic reform in the twelfth century, it should not come as a surprise that the monks and canons comprising the regular clergy of the English Church were in no hurry to associate themselves with the University of Oxford, a newfangled institution that owed its impulse to the secular clergy.

Tension between the seculars and regulars even predates the establishment of the University itself. According to Emden (3:1754), Theobaldus Stampensis (Theobald of Étampes) may have been responsible for laying the foundation of the Oxford schools. Theobald came to Oxford from Normandy about A.D. 1100, and during the first quarter of the twelfth century lectured on theology to large groups of clerics. Toward the end of this period he wrote an impassioned defense of secular canons as against monks, which elicited an emphatic and lengthy reply from an anonymous Benedictine. This little flurry, as we shall see, was but a sign of things to come. R. W. Southern dismisses Theobald's claim, and suggests Robert Pullen as Oxford's pioneer in the years 1133–38 (*HUO*, 1:5–7). But in neither case do we have anything approaching the establishment of a university.

Church reform took a dramatic new turn in the early thirteenth century with the establishment of the fraternal orders. The friars technically belong with the regulars, but in fact they represented new wine in old bottles: they lived under a rule (*regula*), but they worked in the world (*saeculum*). The four orders with which we will be concerned developed almost simultaneously in the first half of the thirteenth century: Franciscans, Dominicans, Carmelites, and Augustinians, known respectively as the Grey Friars, the Black Friars, the White Friars, and the Austin Friars, the first three for their style of dress, and the last in reference to St. Augustine of Hippo, whose teaching provided the basis for their rule. Such discriminations in outlook among the four orders as need to be made can be deferred unless or until they become relevant to our purpose; for the moment it is sufficient to say that the mission of the friars was to take the message and ministry of the Church to the people. The rapidity of their spread is illustrated in the fact that by 1250 most of the orders had houses in all the major cathedral cities and market towns of England, and had penetrated deeply into the parishes of Scotland, Ireland, Wales, and Cornwall.

The popes who presided at the birth of this movement, beginning with Innocent III, were enthusiastic in their support, and granted the friars considerable freedom from episcopal control, a feature which freed the followers of St. Francis for deeds of charity in the beginning, but led to jurisdictional disputes later on, when the bloom of the movement was gone and the spread of the friars into the parishes of the secular clergy began to look more and more like aggression. But the point that needs emphasis here is that, unlike the monks, whose initial reaction to the University was one of suspicion, the friars at a very early stage enthusiastically embraced university studies and saw them as important for the development of their own communities. Even the Franciscans, whose founder had left them with an ambiguous attitude toward learning, arrived in Oxford by November of 1224, and five years later were listening to the lectures of Robert Grosseteste. In summary, the rise of the fraternal orders marked a new phase in the history of church reform, and exerted tremendous moral pressure on all those clergy of the Church, whether regular or secular, who had become at ease in Zion.

With these ecclesiastical developments in mind, we are now in a position to observe the growth of Oxford itself during the two hundred years preceding Trevisa's arrival. By the beginning of this period the ancient monastery of St. Frideswide's had been refounded (in 1122) as an Augustinian priory. The Austin Canons were now on the crest of a wave of monastic reform, establishing over a dozen major houses in England in the first third of the twelfth century. In Oxford, in addition to refounding St. Frideswide's, they established Oseney as a priory in 1129 to the west of the town, and by 1150 had acquired the collegiate church of St. George's in the castle, which had been founded in 1074 and was the locale of the lectures early in the following century by Theobald of Étampes already mentioned.

The rising prosperity of the town itself, based largely on its trade in cloth and wool, was sufficient to stimulate the multiplying of parishes to accommodate a growing population. Before the conquest of 1066, the major parish churches were St. Martin's, St. Mary the Virgin (later to become the University church), and St. Peter-in-the-East; but other preconquest foundations were also represented by St. Ebbe's, St. Michael at the Northgate, St. Mildred's, St. Edward the Martyr, St. George in the Castle, and, outside the city walls, St. Mary Magdalen. The twelfth century saw the raising of several new churches: All Saints, St. Michael at the Southgate, St. Giles (in the fields north of town), St. Budoc, and, after the turn of the century, St. John the Baptist.

The emergence of the Oxford schools in the twelfth century can only be inferred, since there is no real documentation of their existence until 1209, when the murder of an Oxford girl, allegedly by students, led to rioting and the abrupt departure of three thousand scholars. Such town and gown conflicts continued for a century and a half, reaching a climax in the violence of St. Scholastica's Day, 10 February 1355, when the forces of church and state aligned with the University were powerful enough to settle the case decisively in favor of the scholars. This was a turning point: henceforth Oxford was a university town, and a disturbance of this magnitude directed against the scholars was never again possible.

Meanwhile, with the center of the town fully occupied by scholastic halls and rooms, the new wave represented by the fraternal orders had to seek living quarters on the fringes of Oxford. The Franciscan friary rose midway between the south and west gates of the city, while the other three orders were forced to locate well outside the city walls: the Dominicans to the south, west of Grandpont; the Carmelites (who moved from Stockwell Street in 1318) to the north, just west of St. Giles, in the king's houses; and the Augustinians to the northeast on lands that eventually became the site of Wadham College. With the arrival of the Austin friars in 1268, all four orders were represented by friaries to the north, northwest, southwest, and south of the city.

The monastic orders, as we have seen, were in Oxford before the University was born, although the only major foundation inside the city walls was the venerable St. Frideswide's, on lands later to be used for Christ Church. Outside the walls to the west stood Oseney Abbey (1129). These two establishments of the Austin Canons never became a part of the scholastic life of the university in the way that other religious houses did, but both of them profited greatly as landlords in and around the town. Slowly, however, and after the friars were solidly entrenched, the monastic orders recognized the significance of Oxford as a center of learning by establishing residences there for studious members of their own communities.

The proud Benedictine abbeys of England could not agree on a single arrangement for all the monks in their order, with the result that separate houses were established, the first known as Gloucester Hall because of the initiative taken by the Benedictine Abbey of Gloucester. In little more than a decade the original connection with Gloucester was severed, and Gloucester College became the primary residence of more Benedictines than any other Oxford house established by the order. Meanwhile the black monks of Durham founded Durham College in 1280 on lands now occupied by Trinity College north of Broad Street (Canditch in the fourteenth century). These Benedictine houses were wealthy, and conditions in Durham College and the Augustinian Friary, virtually adjoining each other on either side of what is now Parks Road, must have presented a study in contrast. Durham did not have many monks in residence as students, but did have a staff of secular clerics to serve the few monks who were there. It is not difficult to imagine how this looked to the secular masters in the schools.

The most prestigious of the Benedictine foundations was that of the cathedral priory in Canterbury, yet despite sporadic early gestures toward an Oxford house, this great community did not really become established there until 1361, and even then the initiative was taken by a secular archbishop of Canterbury, Simon Islip. The presence of this college just north of St. Frideswide's Priory survives in the name of Christ Church's Canterbury quadrangle. It is interesting that Islip, in founding Canterbury College, envisioned a mixed community of seculars and regulars, an idealistic arrangement that would perhaps bring an end to the kind of master-servant relationship established by Durham. Unfortunately this did not prove to be a workable arrangement, and in 1365 the archbishop reacted by making Canterbury an entirely secular college, with John Wyclif as warden. But Islip died the next year and the new archbishop, Simon Langham, a Benedictine, secured a reversal of this policy, and the College became substantially restricted to monk-students from the Cathedral Priory of Canterbury. Wyclif appealed in 1367, but the new statutes were confirmed by papal decision in 1370, and the reformer was forced to look elsewhere for an academic home.

Our review of the Oxford houses of the regular clergy is completed with mention of Rewley Abbey, a Cistercian monastic house with facilities for the maintenance of monk-students of the order, founded about 1280. This community was never prominent in the intellectual life of the University, and lay at some remove west of the town on lands beyond the Thames.

Meanwhile, as if in reaction to the growing number of regular communities clustered around Oxford, the main body of secular students within the walls of the town began slowly forming communities of their own that would eventually become the secular colleges of the University. What was then known as "Great University Hall" had a statutory existence in 1249, although it did not become a college in fact until about 1280. Balliol is next in order of establishment (ca. 1261–66), followed by Merton, the greatest of the early colleges, founded both de jure and de facto in 1264. Of these three, only Merton was then well enough endowed and organized to acquire a home on a site with features recognizably Mertonian, perhaps in part because of the early appropriation of the church of St. John the Baptist, which may have provided a focal point for the physical deployment of the college buildings. Even in Trevisa's time the properties of University and Balliol were too scattered to provide an architectural presence that would be distinguishable from other houses in the town; and Merton was only then, in 1375, beginning the construction of its magnificent library, completed in 1378.

In the fourteenth century appeared Exeter College, founded in 1312 by Bishop Stapeldon for students from Exeter diocese, as we have seen. Oriel's foundation is dated 1324, and by the time Trevisa arrived it was probably located on its present site. The statutes for the Queen's College were drawn up by Robert de Eglesfield in 1341, and the land he gave in the parish of St. Peter-in-the-East has remained the home of the college ever since, although its room for expansion to the north was lost in the sale of lands to William of Wykeham for the site of New College, founded in 1379. The bishop was engaged in buying up land in Oxford through the 1370s, and in 1378 a jury reported that a thirteen-acre site to the north of Queen's was nothing but "a dump for filth and corpses, a resort of criminals and prostitutes, and it was felt that the building of New College there would be an advantage to the whole town" (VCH Oxon, 4:16). By the time Trevisa left Queen's in 1387, he may have been able to look over his shoulder and see the walls and towers of the first Oxford college built entirely according to plan. But Wykeham's triumph left Queen's forever cramped between New College and the High.

From the survey just completed we may now see the rough outlines of Oxford as it existed when Trevisa arrived there in 1362. There were six secular colleges: University, Balliol, Merton, Exeter, Oriel, and Queen's; the four convents of the fraternal orders; three Benedictine colleges: Gloucester, Durham, and Canterbury; and the home of the Cistercians in Rewley Abbey. There were, of course, in addition, scores of students in rooms with no particular college affiliation, almost exclusively members of the secular clergy, and many of them on leave from the parishes that they served. With this picture of the University before us, we may now undertake a roll call of the colleges in order to become acquainted with some of the students who were there before and during Trevisa's residency.

Colleges of the Secular Clergy

Of the six secular colleges then in existence, Merton, Exeter, and Queen's will demand most of our attention for obvious reasons. Rather surprisingly, University College, the earliest foundation, seems to have attracted a rather small number of fellows, who, if not actually quiescent, at least seem to have done nothing in particular to distinguish themselves in this period. William de Wilton stopped there briefly in 1360 on his way from Balliol to Queen's, where, after completing his doctorate in theology, he was elected chancellor (1374–76). William de Wymondham, physician to Edward III, may have been a fellow at the same time as Wilton. Otherwise University College graduates seem not to have made the headlines.

Balliol must be recognized above all for having been the home of Richard FitzRalph, whose sermon against the friars, *Defensio Curatorum* (1357), was translated into English by John Trevisa. FitzRalph was an Anglo-Irishman from Dundalk, County Louth, Ireland, whose life has been recently and impressively set forth in a study by Katherine Walsh (1981). He may have come to Oxford as early as 1315, and received his M.A. in 1325. By 1329, as a bachelor of theology, he lectured on the theology of the beatific vision, a subject on which his opinion was later required at the papal court. Having incepted in theology at Oxford in 1331, he was elected chancellor for 1332–34, during which time he had to deal with the disruption of the Stamford schism, when northern students threatened to pull out of the University and establish their own school at Stamford in Lincolnshire. According to Walsh, it was Bishop John de Grandisson of Exeter who "smoothed the path of Fitz-Ralph's rise" in the church, granting him first an annual pension until he could obtain a satisfactory benefice, and officiating at his consecration as bishop of Armagh in Exeter Cathedral on 8 July 1347.

On several occasions after leaving Oxford, FitzRalph traveled to Avignon. In the final year of the pontificate of John XXII (1316–34), he was asked to give his opinion on the theology of the beatific vision, a subject dear to the heart of that remarkable pope, who died 4 December 1334. At that time the pope's idea of a vision of God immediately after death was regarded as eccentric. But Walsh argues persuasively that, whatever one might think of it as theology, it may have been a practical consequence of the pope's interest in a dialogue with the Eastern churches, a possibility which seems to put the pontiff's opinion in an entirely different light. And it is certainly true that the dialogue between East and West remained a serious concern of the successors of John XXII. For later glimmerings of this controversy at Oxford in *Piers the Plowman*, see below pp. 54–55 and also Appendix II, p. 242, Oxford XIII 21–214 (William Jordan vs. Uthred de Boldon).

As dean of Lichfield, FitzRalph became involved in litigation that sent him again to Avignon, where he remained for seven years (1337–44) in the service of two popes, Benedict XII (1334–42) and Clement VI (1342–52). While there, he preached a number of sermons, at least one of them in the private chapel of Benedict XII. After his return to England and promotion to the see of Armagh, FitzRalph was commissioned by Edward III to return to Avignon to seek the jubilee indulgence of 1350 for England and Ireland. His discussions there with envoys of the Armenian church prompted him to resume work on the *Summa in Quaestionibus Armenorum*, completed in 1352. FitzRalph had been consulted as an expert in negotiations of the Curia with Armenian representatives, and in this great treatise he sought to reconcile the differences of doctrine between East and West that these negotiations had disclosed by a powerful appeal to Scripture as the common basis for the faith of all Christian churches. It is interesting to see the emergence here of the appeal to *sola scriptura* in this context; later, in the hands of Wyclif and his followers, it will be invoked for entirely different purposes. Little wonder that a favorite authority cited by the Lollards is "Armachanus," who in his arguments from Scripture is adamant in his rejection of "glosing," and firm in his insistence on a literal reading of the text as alone providing the intention of the sacred author (Minnis 1975). But FitzRalph's horizon was much greater than that of the Lollards: books XVIII and XIX of the *Summa* contain an elaborate theological appeal to Saracens and Jews.

Students of FitzRalph have disagreed on when he began to turn against the friars. On several occasions in Avignon he was invited to preach in the Dominican church there, and seems to have been on friendly terms with all the orders, complimenting especially those friar-missionaries whose preaching in pagan lands he had heard about while serving as a papal commissioner. It seems most likely, following Walsh, that it was FitzRalph's experience as archbishop of Armagh in Ireland that affected his attitude toward the friars. His flock was divided, one part English settlers and the other Irish natives. Such was the hostility between these two groups that FitzRalph could not even enter the Gaelic area except in risk of his life. Although himself one of the *Anglicos*, the bishop made a strenuous effort to work toward the unification of these two cultures as members of one Christian community. He was not hesitant in denouncing injustice when he saw it, as in the racial policies of the Anglo-Norman trade guilds, but he soon discovered that the friars in his diocese were going to be a major problem. In their favor it should be said that the friars had penetrated the racial boundaries of the see and were in close touch with all of the people, whether English or Irish. But FitzRalph found that they were unwilling to acknowledge his jurisdiction, and, worse, that in their role as confessors they tended to take the side of the race in whose territory they were assigned by their order. This practice seriously undermined his efforts to effect a reconciliation of the two nations.

Conditions in the see of Armagh amounted to nothing less than civil war, and advocates of violence on both sides invoked the law of the frontier as an excuse for murder, theft, and arson. FitzRalph denounced this excuse at every opportunity, calling the so-called law of the frontier the law of the devil (*legem marchie sive dyaboli*), but he did not limit his efforts to sermons on the subject. His intention was clearly to use the power of the confessional to compel a resolution of the conflict. He reserved to himself the power to absolve crimes of violence against persons or property, with the intention of compelling the sinner to make restitution as a condition of absolution. If anyone failed to confess and be forgiven, he would be refused communion. FitzRalph estimated that he had two thousand subjects in his diocese who were murderers, thieves, or incendiaries, while scarcely forty of these in any given year came to him or his assigned penancers; and yet all the rest came forward to receive the sacraments, claiming that they were absolved, having confessed to the friars. The implication is clear: the friars not only undermined the bishop's authority, but they did not exert the moral pressure that FitzRalph wished to bring to bear in the confessional; rather they seemed to acquiesce in the law of the frontier. No doubt friars on the other side of the racial boundary were simultaneously granting the same easy confessions, in the opposite cause. However conscientious individual friar-confessors may have been in that strife-torn diocese, the overall effect of the presence of the fraternal orders there seems to have created in FitzRalph a sense of outrage.

A conflict between the secular clergy and the fraternal orders was not a new thing, as evidenced by repeated reissuing of the bull *Super Cathedram* in the second quarter of the fourteenth century. But the involvement of a distinguished theologian and bishop raised the issue to a new level of discourse. When FitzRalph crossed over to England in 1356, he had put the finishing touches on *De Pauperie Salvatoris*, in which he advocated the complete dissolution of the fraternal orders. While in London in the winter of 1356–57, he was invited by the dean of St. Paul's, Richard de Kilvington, to deliver a series of sermons at St. Paul's Cross on the subject of the friars. In the controversy that resulted, FitzRalph found the mendicants thoroughly capable of defending themselves. Planning to take his case against them to the papal court, he found that the friars had persuaded the king to issue a mandate prohibiting his departure from the country. But the bishop managed to cross the channel despite the royal order, and reached Avignon, where on 8 November 1357 he preached his famous sermon *Defensio Curatorum* before Innocent VI and his cardinals in consistory. For three years FitzRalph pressed his case against the friars in the papal court, but he was fighting a losing battle. The bishops did not unite in support of him, while the friars raised large sums in the defense of their own existence, as may well be imagined. Whether it is true that FitzRalph lost his case for lack of funds, as has been alleged, the fact is that he made little headway against the onslaughts of such dedicated defenders of mendicancy as Roger Conway and William Jordan, fresh from the Oxford convents of the Franciscans and Dominicans respectively. The death of Archbishop FitzRalph on 10 November 1360 finally brought this unequal struggle to an end.

The aftershock of FitzRalph's crusade was still being felt in the halls of the University when Trevisa arrived in 1361–62, less than two years after the bishop's death in Avignon. Already in 1358 the University had passed a statute forbidding the friars to recruit anyone under the age of eighteen for membership in the University, a practice specifically condemned by FitzRalph in 1357; and in the books of the chancellors and proctors this is followed by additional legislation directed at the orders in general and also against certain individual friars who in some way offended against the spirit or letter of University regulations (*Munimenta Academica*, Rolls Series 50, 1 [1868]: 204–12). The regular business of the University—the lectures, disputations, and the granting of degrees—no doubt continued routinely, but such collegiality as had been established between the seculars and regulars in Oxford over the preceding century was severely impaired, and would never be the same again.

On this ominous note we turn now to a consideration of the fellows of Merton College, where, by my count, no less than forty students came and went during Trevisa's residency in the University. For our purposes, and indeed perhaps from any angle, the superstar in this scholarly community was John Wyclif, who arrived in Oxford in midcentury, though his presence is first recorded as a bachelor of Merton in 1356. But for whatever reason, Wyclif never stayed long in one academic home. From Merton he moved to Balliol, where he became master in 1360. After an interval as rector of Fillingham, Lincolnshire, he was granted license to resume his studies at the University, where he rented a room in Queen's

College for two years (1363–65). In 1365 he was appointed warden of Canterbury College, at a time when, as we have seen, Simon Islip was attempting to reconstitute this mixed community of seculars and regulars as a purely secular society; but when the Benedictine Simon Langham became archbishop on the death of Islip, Wyclif and his three secular colleagues were ordered expelled in 1367, and, though this was appealed by the seculars, the order was confirmed by the pope in May 1370.

Where Wyclif stayed until the completion of his doctorate in 1372 or 1373 is not clear. He may have remained in Canterbury College for a time while opposing his removal as warden in 1367; in the following year he exchanged his appointment as rector of Fillingham for that of Ludgershall, Buckinghamshire, only sixteen miles from Oxford, and he may have spent some time there between extensions of his license to study. After completion of the doctoral degree by 1373, Wyclif resumed his residency in Queen's College. Emden reports his rental of a room there in 1374–75 and 1380–81, but in view of the missing long rolls (as we have noted) it seems safer, with Hodgkin (1949), not "to multiply the changes of residence beyond necessity" (p. 32), and to assume that Wyclif was in Queen's more or less continuously from 1374 to 1381. The one exception to this would appear to be a brief period in the summer of 1377, when as a result of Benedictine pressure on Pope Gregory XI, Wyclif was placed under house arrest in Black Hall. Five years later the Black Friars Council marked the end of his academic career, although Wyclif had already left Oxford in 1381, and spent his final years in Lutterworth, where he died 31 December 1384.

Since Trevisa was involved in the controversy between northerners and southerners in Queen's that occurred during Wyclif's stay there, we may conclude that the two men knew each other and that to some extent their periods of residence coincided. More to the point is that as a fellow of Queen's, Trevisa belonged to a society that had been infiltrated by scholars strongly under the influence of Wyclif, himself perhaps one of these. But such matters can be deferred until we come to consider the membership of this college in its proper place. Meanwhile, we must see what other scholars associated with Merton have a claim on our attention.

Quite apart from having been Wyclif's home in his early years at Oxford, Merton College overshadows all others in its involvement in University life. In the final thirty-five years of the century Merton supplied at least six chancellors and ten proctors, and could point with pride to several distinguished graduates. Simon Bredon was a learned physician and astronomer who died in 1372, and John de Wyke, physician to Richard II in 1385, was still a fellow of Merton when Trevisa entered Queen's in 1369. One of the most interesting, as well as famous, of the fellows was Ralph Strode, well known as a logician in Italy as well as England. Geoffrey Chaucer called him "philosophical Strode," and it is tempting to suppose, though without sure evidence, that under the latter's influence Chaucer may have studied at Oxford in the 1360s, a much more plausible supposition than the assertion of the sixteenth-century antiquarian John Leland in his *Commentarii de Scriptoribus Britannicis* (pp. 419–21) that the poet sat at the feet of the friars John Somer (Franciscan) and Nicholas of Lynn (Carmelite), though both are mentioned in Chaucer's *Treatise on the Astrolabe*.

Ralph Strode and John Wyclif probably came to know each other when both were fellows of Merton. In any case, the two later engaged in friendly controversy, Strode questioning some of Wyclif's conclusions in *De Civili Dominio*, probably about 1378, since in replying Wyclif seems to refer to the papal schism which began in that year. Two other fellows of Merton who knew Wyclif in the early years were William de Barton and Richard Benger. Barton, like Wyclif, was a fellow in 1356 and a doctor of theology in 1380, by which time he had disputed with Wyclif in his determinations for the degree. If, as Workman (1926) suggests, this experience turned him against his colleague, his chance for revenge came when he was elected chancellor of the University in 1379. In the following year he appointed a committee of twelve doctors to consider Wyclif's teaching on the sacrament of the altar: six of the twelve were friars, two were monks, and only four were seculars. This did not bode well for Wyclif, and he himself reports that he was defeated by a vote of seven to five. As a former chancellor, Barton was also involved in the later stages of the Black Friars Council in 1382, of which more will be said later.

Wyclif's other Merton colleague was Richard Benger, who followed him to Canterbury College and became embroiled in the conflict that developed when Islip tried to turn the college into a secular society in 1365. As warden of Canterbury, Wyclif appointed Benger to conduct the appeal against Langham's decision in 1367 to make the college exclusively a home for the cathedral priory of Canterbury. As we have seen, this appeal was unsuccessful, but before Benger could secure papal provision of his appointment in 1374 as rector of Donington, Berkshire, Wyclif and Strode had to act as guarantors in chancery that he would not prosecute any suit overseas.

Because of Merton's traditional involvement in the administration of the University, some fellows who arrived after Wyclif himself was no longer there were drawn reluctantly into the plans of outside authorities to bring Wyclif under control. Such was the case, as we shall see, with Robert Rygge, who became chancellor in 1380 and was pulled inexorably into the conflict that culminated in the Black Friars Council; Thomas Brightwell, whom Rygge took with him to London to face Archbishop Courtenay; and Thomas Hulman, a reluctant member of that Council. But it is also interesting to note that certain fellows of Merton who came after Wyclif's time were drawn to him, in one way or another, as if his former residence there somehow continued to exert an influence. One of these was John Aston, who held out against the threat of Black Friars longer than anyone except Nicholas Hereford; another was William Middleworth, who had come to Merton from Exeter College, but abruptly left to follow Wyclif, first to Canterbury College and then to Queen's in 1369. William James, a fellow of Merton in 1376, was suspended some years later because of his profession of Lollardy, his fellowship not being reinstated until his release from prison in 1399; and he was still under suspicion of Lollardy as late as 1420. Even Robert Stonham, who did not enter Merton until 1384, the year of Wyclif's death, may have come under his influence. When Stonham died in Italy in 1409, he had with him copies of Wyclif's polemical works and his response to Master Ralph Strode. So much, then, for the influence of Wyclif in Merton after his departure.

We now come to Exeter College, Trevisa's home in Oxford from 1362 to 1369. In his first year there he may have learned of the death of William de Polmorva, the most distinguished alumnus of Exeter from Trevisa's home county of Cornwall. Polmorva had entered the college in 1333, served as rector in 1336–37, and become a fellow of University college briefly in 1340. In 1341 he was nominated by Eglesfield to be one of the first fellows of Queen's, and he was later elected chancellor of the University for 1350–52. Among other positions in his professional career he was confessor to Queen Philippa in 1361, and he died the following year. Whether Trevisa had ever met him in person, he must have known him by reputation. Of the fellows who were there when he arrived, Robert Rygge and Thomas Swyndon (alias Styve) claim our attention, Rygge because of his involvement as chancellor of the University in the crisis over Black Friars, and Swyndon as one of the commissioners appointed to investigate the controversy at Queen's in which Trevisa was involved. Both of these men left Exeter in 1365 and became fellows of Merton.

Wyclif, as far as we know, never set foot in Exeter College, but could his influence have been felt there? There is some evidence that it was, if the shifting allegiances of its members are any indication. Four of those who were fellows during Trevisa's residency ended up, like Trevisa himself, in Queen's College, where Wyclif had a room, as we have seen, between 1374 and 1381. Middleworth left in 1365 to join Wyclif in Canterbury College, and when it was clear that this was a lost cause, he moved to Queen's, as did Trevisa, in 1369. Three years later came another influx from Exeter: Robert Blakedon, William Frank, and, shortly thereafter, Robert Lydeford. To some extent this migration to Queen's may be attributed to the recruiting efforts of the provost, Henry Whitfield; yet it is difficult to explain the particular path taken by William Middleworth other than in terms of his desire to follow Wyclif. In all probability Trevisa, too, was attracted to Queen's in part for the same reason; but, as we shall see in subsequent chapters, the extent of Wyclif's influence on Trevisa can be measured only by recourse to his writings.

As we take our leave of Exeter College, a single enigma remains: did Trevisa encounter William Courtenay there? As Emden observes, there is no reason to suppose that the future archbishop, who was destined to shake Oxford to its foundations, was ever a fellow of Exeter. But he was born in the city of Exeter about 1342, an exact contemporary of Trevisa, and though he probably had private quarters in Oxford while studying law, he may well have had occasion to visit his colleagues from the southwest in their hall, or at the very least he would have come to their attention when he was elected chancellor of the University in 1367. His rapid rise in the Church, from bishop of Hereford in 1369, to bishop of London in 1375, to archbishop of Canterbury in 1381, may even have been regarded with a certain regional pride; but if so, the attitude of Trevisa and his colleagues toward Courtenay must have changed profoundly during the course of events in London and Oxford from May to November of 1382.

It is a curious fact that Oriel, fourth in line of the secular colleges, midway between the founding of Exeter in 1312 and Queen's in 1341, seems to have attracted fewer students than any of the colleges except University. Its most distinguished graduate in Trevisa's time was Thomas Arundel, who became archbishop of Canterbury on the death of Courtenay in 1396. Trevisa did not live to experience his visitation of Oxford in 1411, a low point in the history of the University. The only fellow of Oriel that Trevisa is likely to have known was the Cornishman John Landreyn, doctor of medicine, whose appearance with Henry Whitfield in Exeter College as a guest of the house we have found recorded in the treasurer's accounts for Hilary Term, 1366–67.

The statutes of Queen's College stipulate that the number of fellows shall not exceed forty, but the foundation provided by Eglesfield fell far short of providing financial support for that number. In fact, during the fourteenth century there were never more than seven fellows at any one time, and the recurrence of the Black Death over the first sixty years of the college's existence often reduced that figure even more. When Henry Whitfield assumed the office of provost in 1361, he presided over a nearly empty house. Polmorva had left Oxford, John de Hothom had just died, and Nicholas de Aston was fully occupied with his duties as chancellor of the University. Despite the return of the pestilence in that year, Whitfield was able to make three appointments: Henry de Hopton and William de Wilton from University College, and William Trevelles, a Cornishman whose previous affiliation is not known. All three came to Queen's with M.A. degrees in hand, and all had surrendered their fellowships by the end of the decade, Trevelles having received the doctorate by 1368, and Wilton by 1374. Wilton then served as chancellor of the University, 1374–76. The appointment of Thomas Carlisle as a fellow in 1366 brought the number up to five, and there things stood until the influx of 1369.

In 1369 came Middleworth, Trevisa, and a new man, Nicholas Hereford, whose prior life remains a mystery, except for the fact that he came from Hereford diocese. These three fellows proceeded to enter the priesthood in lockstep, and were ordained by Simon Sudbury, then bishop of London, on 8 June 1370, thus conforming to Eglesfield's intention that the fellows take holy orders within a limited time. The presence of these three in the college must have left the northerner Thomas Carlisle feeling very much a minority of one in a college founded especially for students from his homeland. The appointment of John de Stokesley (York diocese) in 1371 may have been intended to redress the balance, but he died prematurely in 1375, and by that time Blakedon, Frank, and Lydeford had come over from Exeter, as well as Richard Thorpe, whose previous college is unknown. At this point it is likely that Carlisle determined to issue a legal challenge to such a packing of the house. The resulting controversy and what it tells us about Trevisa will be deferred to a later chapter. Suffice it to say here that when the dust had settled, all the southerners were expelled or departed, and the new provost Carlisle had made six new appointments, only one of them a southerner, Richard Browne, who moved over from Exeter College in 1379. Since, as we have noted, Trevisa did return to the college and rent rooms, it is not surprising to find that among this later generation of residents he counted some new friends, notably Robert Hodersale, admitted as a fellow in 1378, and William Farington, who rented rooms there along with Trevisa in the 1380s. Not being a fellow, Wyclif was not affected directly by the controversy; he probably departed from Queen's (and from Oxford) late in 1381. His colleague from Canterbury College, William Selby, likewise rented a room in Queen's for the year 1380–81, returning there twice during the decade before he died in 1392.

With Queen's we have finished our circuit of the secular colleges, leaving room for little more than the mention of some of the many secular students who studied at Oxford in this period but who are not known to have been affiliated with any particular college. These tended to be wealthier students, whose income disqualified them as fellows, and in particular many of them seem to have been students of canon and civil law, perhaps forced outside the precincts of the colleges by statutory restrictions on the number of fellows allowed to study law in any one community. Some of the nation's greatest bishops belong in this category: Walter Stapeldon, Richard de Bury, John de Grandisson, Simon Islip, John de Thoresby, William de Whittlesey, William Courtenay, Thomas Brinton, and John Trevenant, most of whom studied law at Oxford and were predecessors or contemporaries of Trevisa's. It may be significant that the greatest bishop of them all, Robert Grosseteste, was not a lawyer but a doctor of theology, though his degree may have come from Paris rather than Oxford. Still, it is certain that he studied at

Oxford, served perhaps as its first chancellor, and was a powerful force for good, as bishop of Lincoln, in the development of the University. The opportunity for England to have another great doctor of theology as primate was tragically lost in 1349 when the Oxford scholar, Thomas Bradwardine, died of the plague soon after assuming office as archbishop of Canterbury. Not all were wielders of power: Geoffrey of Monmouth, John of Garland (who taught at Paris), and Richard Rolle all made their mark in different ways. We conclude our list with the mention of John Cornwall and Richard Pencriche, two humble Oxford masters from the southwest, who were singled out by Trevisa as innovators in their use of English to teach grammar to children (*Poly.* ii. 159, 161).

Colleges of the Regular Clergy

We now turn our attention to the communities established in Oxford by the regular clergy: the Benedictine colleges of Gloucester, Durham, and Canterbury; the home of Cistercian students in Rewley Abbey; and the convents of the four orders of the friars. An introduction to some of the students of these colleges will put us in a good position to understand the meaning of events leading up to the Black Friars Council and Archbishop Courtenay's visitation of Oxford in the summer and fall of 1382. John Trevisa was deeply concerned about these developments and the issues they raised, and we will need to consider these events and issues in order to understand the attitudes that he later expresses in his writings.

The constitutions of Benedict XII in 1336 for reform of the monastic orders made Gloucester College, in theory at least, the home at Oxford of all the Black Monks in England. But two of the largest and most distinguished of the houses, Durham and Canterbury, continued to stand aloof, and the college never achieved the stability or organization of the secular colleges. It became, in the words of David Knowles, "a collection of 'staircases'" (1957, p. 16). The interest of the house that gave it its name had long since evaporated, so that in Trevisa's time not a single monk from Gloucester lived as a student in Gloucester College. Malmesbury had the office of landlord, maintaining the fabric, but the abbot of Abingdon had effective control over the house and appointment of its prior. Neither of these communities seemed to have much interest in the college as a place to send students, although Roger Tame, abbot of Abingdon, intervened with others (as we shall see) to prevent one of his monks (Henry de Wodhull) from incepting under a secular doctor. This kind of meddling probably did little to improve the secular faculty's opinion of the notorious abbey to the south of Oxford. One is reminded of the famous prophecy in *Piers the Plowman* (B X 317–27) which concludes with a warning that the abbot of Abingdon shall have a knock of a king, "and incurable the wounde" (Isaiah 14:4–6).

Where, then, did the monk-students of Gloucester College come from? The largest single contributor, in terms of numbers, was Westminster Abbey in London, which sent eight by my count during this period, followed by St. Albans with five, and Worcester Cathedral Priory and Glastonbury Abbey with three. One student each came from Norwich Cathedral Priory, Bury St. Edmunds, St. Augustine's Abbey, Canterbury, Ramsey Abbey in Huntingdonshire, and Muchelney Abbey in Somerset. Though we can't be sure in every case that these monks actually lodged in the college, we can be reasonably confident that these numbers generally reflect the interest of the various houses in university study. But when we look to see just who these students were, it soon becomes evident that the best scholars did not always come with the largest numbers.

Westminster Abbey, for example, with its eight students, produced only one doctor of theology, Thomas Merks, who received his degree some time before 1395. Simon Langham, later the archbishop of Canterbury, did not complete his studies (and probably did not live in the college), perhaps because of the eruption of the Black Death in 1348–49. Norwich and St. Edmunds are a disappointment, in view of their strong scholastic traditions, but Norwich made up for its lack of numbers by producing Adam Easton, doctor of theology (ca. 1365), renowned as a scholar by the time of his death in 1397. John de Gosford, the lone student from Bury St. Edmunds, was admitted as a bachelor in theology in 1375–76 but never completed his studies, perhaps in part because he got swept up into the politics of his community in 1378–79, and the defense of its property when the abbey was attacked by the peasants in 1381.

The position of Adam Easton as the one monk-scholar of Norwich Cathedral Priory is instructive. While Easton was a student at Oxford, Archbishop FitzRalph passed through the county and delivered his sermons against the friars before departing for Avignon. With the consciousness of the orders thus raised regarding the claims of the mendicants, Easton's superiors recalled him from Oxford to preach in their cathedral in place of some of the friars who had been carrying out that function. This stratagem is eloquent testimony to the shortage of monks qualified to preach in the cathedral. After the completion of his degree, Easton was drawn into papal politics, with consequent appointment as cardinal of England or Norwich in 1381, and with risk to life and limb in the custody of a jittery and embattled Urban VI in 1385. But before the time of the schism, even though out of England, he managed to keep up with what was going on in Oxford, and was probably part of that Benedictine influence in Avignon which led Gregory XI in 1377 to condemn certain of Wyclif's tenets. But Easton was not just an opponent of Wyclif; in his *Defensorium Ecclesiasticae Potestatis*, dedicated to Urban VI, he defended the highest claims of the papacy against the radical views of Marsilius of Padua and William of Ockham, as well as Wyclif himself.

We should note in passing the appearance of John Preston from St. Augustine's Canterbury, a doctor of theology by 1391; William de Shepton from Muchelney, who did not receive a degree; and John Welles from Ramsey Abbey, Huntingdon, doctor of theology in 1376. Preston is notable for the large number of books that he acquired for the abbey library. But John Welles especially claims our attention for two reasons: he was a strong opponent of Wyclif's opinions; and he appears to be the earliest identified owner of a copy of *Piers the Plowman*. (For Trevisa's possible authorship of the B and C versions see Appendix II.) As regards the first point, it may be that Welles felt, as prior of the students in Gloucester College, that he should take the lead in opposing Wyclif's attacks on the "possessioners"; in any case he was able to get Wyclif's attention, since the latter, according to Workman (1926), refers to him as "a certain black dog of the order of Benedict" in one of his sermons (2:123–24). Certainly Welles must have voted with the majority of regulars on the committee of twelve appointed by Barton in 1380 to condemn Wyclif's teaching, and, as we shall see, Welles was a member of the Black Friars Council in the summer of 1382.

The manuscript of *Piers the Plowman* associated with John Welles is Bodleian 851 (S.C. 3041), and the version of the poem that it contains appears to be a composite (as is the case with many manuscripts of this work), the latter part copied from a later version; but the original text that may have belonged to Welles is a corrupt copy of the earliest known form of the poem composed in 1362, and it has been argued that Welles was the owner of this much of the poem (the *Visio*), in a copy dating perhaps as early as 1380, before a continuation was added to his text in the fifteenth century, long after his death. Because of the complexity of the different states of this manuscript, it is understandable that Emden in 1959 should doubt that the inscription could refer to this John Welles, who died in Italy in 1388, after a vain effort to obtain the release of Adam Easton from papal prison. But A. G. Rigg (1978) has argued for a date in the early 1380s for the first part of this copy of the poem (Bodley 851, fols. 124–39), and I was able to elicit an opinion on this question from Neil R. Ker (in his letter of 20 January 1981):

> So I think that ff. 5–139 belonged to the John Wells who died in 1388 and that ff. 1–4 and the rest of Piers Plowman were added later: presumably the manuscript was rebound when these additions were made. The flyleaves show that it was bound at Ramsey.

Caution on this point is advisable, however, since in a forthcoming article in *The Yearbook of Langland Studies*, Ralph Hanna will argue that the earlier *Piers* text (fols. 124–39) should be dated later than 1388, and therefore could not have been a part of this manuscript before the death of John Welles. The reason for my inordinate curiosity about this matter springs from a belief that the poem did indeed circulate in Oxford, and that the B and C versions may have been composed there (see Appendix II). But while it still seems possible to me that John Welles may have possessed a copy of the earliest version of *Piers the Plowman* while he was prior of Gloucester College in Oxford in the early 1380s, we must give serious consideration to Hanna's evidence, which would locate the work of expansion in Ramsey Abbey rather than at Oxford, and at a time later than 1388.

Despite the temptation to think of the monks of Glastonbury in this period as engaged in cultivating their legends and their wealthy lands, it is a fact that two of the three students they sent to Oxford incepted in theology and received their degrees by 1360. The first of these, John Seen, was an opponent of the friars, probably during the controversy that arose in the wake of FitzRalph's visit in 1357; the second was Roger Swyneshed, learned author of treatises in logic and physics, all suggesting that his academic career may have preceded his entry into the Benedictine Order at Glastonbury. The third Glastonbury man was

Richard Hounsworth, whose presence in Oxford seems to have been brief and uneventful.

The one house that could be said to perform as expected was St. Albans, which sent five monk-students to Gloucester College in our period, three of them gaining the doctorate in theology. Even the least known of these, William Wyntershulle, is described as *eruditissimus* in the annals of his house; and of course Thomas Walsingham, though he did not stay for a degree, is famous as author of the great St. Albans chronicles. Among the three doctors, William Binham seems to have been a friend of Wyclif's during their studies for the degree, but turned against him after inception and was bested by Wyclif in the second chapter of his *Determinatio*. Binham's *Contra Wiclivi propositiones*, mentioned by John Bale in his *Scriptorum Illustrium Maioris Brytannie* (1:458), does not survive. Both Nicholas Radcliffe and Simon Southerey, the other two doctors, are described in the annals of St. Albans as opponents of Wyclif, perhaps because Radcliffe certainly, and Southerey probably, served as members of the Black Friars Council in 1382.

Our final source of students for Gloucester College is Worcester Cathedral Priory, and it is a bit disappointing that such a fine house supplied only three students in this period. One of these, John Green, got his start in a secular college, but probably joined the Benedictine Order before undertaking theological studies: he is recorded a fellow of Merton in 1365, and was a doctor by 1381. John Hatfeld was a scholar of Gloucester College in 1355–56, and again in the 1370s, but it is not clear that he ever completed the course for the doctorate. The third and most interesting monk from Worcester is John Malverne, whose greatest claim to fame is the fact, confirmed by John Taylor (1966, pp. 122–23), that he wrote a continuation for the years 1348–77 to Ranulph Higden's *Polychronicon*, the universal chronicle translated by Trevisa in 1385–87. Perhaps on the strength of this, plus his faithful service to the house as precentor, chamberlain, and sacrist after returning from Oxford, he was elected prior of Worcester in 1395, and held that office until his death in 1410. Even more interesting is the probability, according to Stephen L. Forte (1947), that Malverne is the compiler of the academic notebook preserved in Worcester Cathedral Library manuscript F.65 (Forte, pp. 10–12). We shall return to this notebook after we have completed our circuit of the Oxford colleges.

Crossing over from Gloucester College toward the east across St. Giles, we find a disappointingly small number of monk-students in Durham College. A certain hostility toward northerners had led to the Stamford schism in 1333–34, as we have noted, but conditions were much improved in the university in the second half of the century, when we might expect a northern resurgence in Durham such as occurred, for example, in Queen's. But such is not the case. Of the four students for this period that I find listed in Emden's *Register*, only two are doctors: John Aclyff, who incepted in 1377, and Uthred de Boldon, who incepted in 1357. Aclyff was preparing to oppose Wyclif, probably in connection with his inception as doctor, but was discouraged from doing so by the prior of Durham. Uthred was senior to Wyclif and was able to dispute with him on equal terms. Of these two, Uthred has a special claim to our attention, not only because of his reputation as one of the greatest monk theologians of the century, but also because of the controversial nature of some of his teachings and the consequent attention that he attracted while at Oxford in the 1360s. It has even been suggested that one of his opponents, friar William Jordan, is satirically depicted in *Piers the Plowman* (B XIII 1–178), although it should be added that this is one proposal of a connection between the poem and Oxford University that does not originate with the present author, the suggestion having come long ago from M. E. Marcett (1938).

Uthred de Boldon was born at Boldon in the county of Durham, but moved south at an early age and began his studies at Oxford as a secular in 1338. In August 1341 he entered the Benedictine Order at Durham as a novice, and in 1344 was ordained priest at Stamford Priory, a dependency of Durham. He was admitted to Durham College, Oxford, in Michaelmas Term 1347, and by 1350 had been named warden, a position he apparently held until his departure from the University in 1368. During this period he was licensed to oppose on 25 February 1353, admitted as a bachelor of theology in 1355, and incepted as doctor 13 October 1357. Most of his professional career was spent alternating between Finchale, another dependency of Durham, where he was prior, and Durham, where he was subprior, but his later life was not without its moments of drama. He is said to have been consulted by the Black Prince in 1373 regarding the pope's demand for a subsidy, and was subsequently sent by Edward III to Avignon to negotiate in this matter. While abroad he was captured and imprisoned, but was released and returned to England in 1374. Uthred seems to have made one return visit to Oxford in 1383, but otherwise remained in the north, where he died in his priory of Finchale on 28 January 1397.

Uthred's conflict with the friars took place during that turbulent period which as we have seen followed FitzRalph's visit in 1357. The controversy began about 1360 and lasted until his departure from Oxford in 1368. The friars were defending themselves vigorously against the criticisms of FitzRalph and his allies, and one form that this defense took was a sharp attack on the monastic orders or "possessioners." Naturally Uthred rose to the defense of his order, emphasizing the superiority of the spiritual over the temporal power, and the lawfulness of church endowment. He also criticized the Franciscans in particular for their interpretation of evangelical poverty, and rebuked the friars for attacking the endowments of Holy Church. But Uthred was vulnerable personally because of some theological opinions that he had aired in earlier debates, notably his thesis of the clear vision of divine truth at the moment of death, enabling a final choice of each human being of salvation or damnation. His chief opponent, the Dominican William Jordan, seized on this and other doctrines and drew up a list of errors which he called to the attention of Archbishop Langham, with the result that the errors were censured in November 1368, though Uthred was not mentioned by name. Whether coincidence or not, it was at this same time that Uthred was recalled from Oxford by his order, and his stay at the University was thus brought abruptly to an end. In view of the growing power of the friars and their desire to dominate the University, it is very likely that the seculars on the arts faculty, including Trevisa who was at this time a fellow of Exeter, would be emotionally on the side of Uthred and against the fraternal orders. The Benedictine took no part in the condemnation of Wyclif, though later on he did write in defense of orthodoxy in relation to some of Wyclif's opinions, for example on the Eucharist and on predestination, and he composed an eloquent defense of the monastic tradition against contemporary attacks, mainly those of the friars. As Knowles (1951) points out, he was not capable of looking to the future, but he was a strong defender of monasticism at a time when that institution was in deep trouble.

Inside the city walls of Oxford Canterbury College, academic home of monks from Christ Church Cathedral Priory, Canterbury, was taking shape on a plot of land just to the north of St. Frideswide's. We have already touched on the efforts of Archbishop Islip to establish Wyclif as warden of the college and the appointment of Benger, Middleworth, and Selby as secular fellows. Although from time to time seculars were residents, as when Robert Rygge and Thomas Swyndon moved there from Merton in 1379, Canterbury College was primarily a community of monks after the expulsion of Wyclif and his colleagues was confirmed in 1370. Approximately three decades were left for the growth of the society in the fourteenth century, and during that time at least a dozen monks were sent by the Cathedral Priory to study at the University. This group produced three doctors of theology and one of canon law. Henry de Wodhull had incepted as doctor of theology in 1361, before the college came into being, and was its first warden in 1365, when he was replaced by Wyclif. After the order expelling the seculars in 1367, he was reappointed warden by Archbishop Langham, and remained so until 1371. Other wardens were John Bydenden, William Richemond, Thomas Wykyng, and John Aleyn, the last incepting as doctor in 1381–82. William Gillyngham was a bachelor of theology in 1382, when he was present in the chapter house, Canterbury, at the examination of Thomas Hulman of Merton, who was suspected of Wycliffite sympathies; Gillyngham incepted in 1395, thus becoming the third theological doctor of the college in our period. The one doctor of canon law was Thomas Chillenden, perhaps the most prominent and active member of the group, who studied for at least a year (1378–79) in Rome, and received his degree at Oxford by 1383, remaining at least until 1385. Elected prior of Christ Church, Canterbury, in 1391, he became, according to Leland in his *Itinerary* (4:41), the greatest builder that community ever had, and also saw to the rebuilding of Canterbury College. He died in 1411.

Before departing Canterbury College, we should take note of the circumstances of Henry de Wodhull's inception as doctor of theology, if only because it sheds an interesting light both on the relationship of the seculars and regulars, and on town and gown. Henry was ready to incept in 1360, and sought permission from his superior, the abbot of Abingdon, Roger Tame, and from the University, to do so under a secular doctor, William de Whittlesey, then archdeacon of Huntingdon and later archbishop of Canterbury. The opposition to this seemingly innocuous proposal was immediate and decisive, because the abbot and the proctors of the University were united against it. One suspects professional jealousy in the abbot, but the proctors, Richard Tonworth of Merton and Robert de Derby of Oriel, were prompted by the people of the town (*per communitatem excitati*) to oppose the idea because, among other reasons, it was only fair that those who had benefices should spend their money in Oxford for the good of those who worked there for the honor of the Church. Evidently the lobby of local merchants had its effect on the proctors, whose other reasons for denial of Henry's request seem more like afterthoughts: it was unprecedented, and no undue expense would be incurred by following the usual practice, although it was admitted that less money would be spent at the inception than had customarily been the case. Could Wodhull have been trying to cut down on expenses by incepting under a secular, or did he sincerely want Whittlesey to be his sponsor? It is difficult to tell, but the arguments do seem to indicate that a monk's graduation was accompanied by much more spending of money than was the case with a secular. The chancellor of the University, Nicholas de Aston, whom we have seen to be a secular fellow of Queen's in the early days, sided with Wodhull, and made plans to get approval for his inception under Whittlesey by a vote of the congregation, where Aston's influence was very great, by seeking the support of Archbishop Islip in the matter. But one of the proctors went to London, managed to persuade the council of regents there to block the chancellor's efforts, and even forestalled the intervention of Islip, with the result that Wodhull was forced to incept in the usual way.

An amusing postscript to this story concerns the energetic proctor who succeeded in thwarting Henry de Wodhull's efforts to break with tradition. Each candidate, when he incepted, was required by custom to present each of the participating regents with a gift of some kind. Henry presented each of his regents with a robe—except for the proctor who had opposed him. Then this man, assisted by his friends, once more tried to block the inception, but Henry appeared before the chancellor and took an oath, in the presence of Lewis Cherletone and Richard de Tynebury among others, to the effect that he several times sent his servant to deliver the robe to the proctor while he was absent in London. Hearing this he heartily forgave him, and the incident was no doubt closed with the delivery of a robe to the victorious proctor.

We have noted that Rewley Abbey was more monastery than college, in that it was a community existing in its own right, serving incidentally as a home for Cistercian students. It is therefore difficult to know surely which were simply monks and which were monk-students. Of the eight I find in Emden for our period, four were either very inactive or perhaps did not consider themselves students at all: Thomas de Adyngton, Richard Asshton, John Chiselhampton, and John Hildesleye. The other four are listed as doctors of theology, some with very sketchy information. David Gotray is said by Bale to have been a follower of Wyclif, but nothing more of him is known. Richard Lincoln, abbot of Louth Park, 1349–60, was an opponent of the friars at Oxford about 1360; better known is William de Rymington, chancellor of the University in 1372–73, who disputed Wyclif's opinions, even after the latter's death in 1384. This leaves only the maverick Irishman Henry Crumpe, probably regent master of the Cistercian students, who managed to alienate nearly everyone he encountered. He was an early opponent of Wyclif, first in a sermon in about 1376, probably also as member of Barton's committee in 1380, and again at Black Friars. For calling Wyclif's followers "Lollards" he was suspended by Rygge in June 1382, only to be reinstated by instigation of Archbishop Courtenay on 14 July. On returning to Ireland, Crumpe got involved in controversy with the friars, and was condemned for heresy in 1385. Back in Oxford about 1391, sounding now very much like Wyclif on the sacrament of the altar, he was suspended again until he cleared himself in March 1392. The following May he was tried in Stamford, Lincolnshire, before the archbishops of Canterbury, York, and Dublin, and condemned. Returning to Ireland once more, he again ran afoul of the friars, and, when last heard from in 1401, he was living under threat of excommunication.

By way of concluding our survey of monastic students at Oxford perhaps a word should be said about the Austin Canons, founders of St. Frideswide's and Oseney Abbey. While it is true that they acted mainly as landlords in this period, an occasional student of their order did enter into the academic life of the University. One of these was William de Cloune, a student well before Trevisa's time, abbot of Leicester from 1345 until his death in 1378. Another was Philip Repyngdon, doctor of theology in 1382 and determined follower of Wyclif until his recantation on 23 October of that year. He became abbot of Leicester, 1394–1404, bishop of Lincoln, 1404–20, and he died in 1424. These two Austin Canons are a study in contrast. Cloune was a typical abbot, said to have been the model for Chaucer's monk in the *Canterbury Tales*. Repyngdon began as a hot-eyed radical, but on his conversion became a dedicated spiritual leader, administrator, and eradicator of heresy in his diocese. It was as if the Austin Canons no longer molded men, but simply served as the home for clerics of all persuasions, whose doctrinal aberrations were controlled not by the order but by bishops like Courtenay and Arundel, and eventually even like Philip Repyngdon himself.

Convents of the Fraternal Orders

To begin our visitation of the Oxford friaries, it may be helpful, by the use of round numbers, to suggest first how they compared with each other in size during the second half of the fourteenth century. The two largest communities, of course, were the Franciscans and the Dominicans. If we say that these two admitted thirty students each during our period, then by comparison it could be said that the Carmelites had fifteen and the Augustinians ten. About half of the Franciscan and Dominican students completed their doctoral degrees in theology, while the completion rate for the smaller communities of the Carmelites and Augustinians was much higher, the former with twelve doctors out of fifteen, and the latter with ten out of ten, although the higher percentages can be explained in part by the fact that some of these degrees were granted by special dispensation and not at Oxford.

The academic prestige of the two major fraternal orders was still very great at the time of Trevisa's arrival in Oxford in 1362, and this can be sufficiently indicated by prefacing our review of their students with the names of some of the major scholars who had been there before them. The Franciscans could take pride in the achievements of Bartholomew de Glanville (Bartholomaeus Anglicus), whose encyclopedia *De Proprietatibus Rerum* was translated by Trevisa in 1398. Emden is wary of Leland's claim that Bartholomew studied at Oxford, since evidence of his period of residence in Paris is much more substantial, but R. J. Long (1979, p. 3 and n. 16) inclines to the opinion that Bartholomew's interest in the physical sciences as an aid to biblical study reflects the direction of thought at Oxford under the influence of Robert Grosseteste. A similar opinion is expressed by J. A. Weisheipl (*HUO*, 1:453), while the editors of Trevisa's translation of *De Proprietatibus Rerum* place Bartholomaeus at Oxford in 1214–20 when Grosseteste was there as master of the schools (Seymour 1992, p. 10 and n. 48).

Another student of Grosseteste's was Adam Marsh, later a very close friend of the bishop, who bequeathed his books to the Oxford Grey

Friars in Adam's memory. Marsh was the first Franciscan lector at Oxford, elected in 1247, and he died in 1258. Perhaps it was the influence of Adam Marsh that led John Pecham, great reformer and archbishop of Canterbury (1279–92), to enter the Franciscan Order in Oxford; later he moved to Paris, where he was lector of the Franciscan convent for a year or two. On his return to Oxford he was appointed lector about 1272, and there completed his doctorate in theology, before taking up his duties as archbishop.

The greatest of the Franciscan schoolmen was John Duns Scotus (John Duns, the Scot), who entered the order at Dumfries Convent in 1278 and went on to study in Oxford and Paris. Returning to Oxford by 1300, he lectured on the *Sentences* of Peter Lombard for two years before resuming his studies at Paris, where he incepted as doctor of theology, probably in 1305. His achievements in philosophy and theology are justly famous; and it is daunting to think what greater heights he might have attained were it not for his premature death in 1308. The other great philosopher produced by the Franciscans who studied at Oxford was William of Ockham, admitted as bachelor of theology about 1317, but apparently without ever incepting as doctor. Opposition to his interpretation of the doctrine of the Eucharist had reached Avignon by 1325, and Ockham had to spend the next three years there defending himself and composing his *Summa Logicae*. Having taken sides against John XXII on the issue of evangelical poverty, he was forced to flee Avignon, was excommunicated by the pope in 1328, and spent the final two decades of his life in the Munich Convent, supporting the cause of Louis the Bavarian against the papacy in his polemical writings. One of Trevisa's translations is the *Dialogus inter Militem et Clericum*, an anonymous work formerly attributed to Ockham. Though it is clear that Ockham's ideas remained a controversial topic at Oxford, he was ably defended in his absence by a devoted follower, Adam de Woodham, lector of the Franciscan Convent (ca. 1339–41), who incepted as doctor of theology probably in the year of his election. Though he could not rank with Ockham as a thinker, he was the author of several commentaries. By midcentury he is likely to have left Oxford, and may have died before Trevisa's arrival.

When we turn our attention to those friars in the Franciscan Convent who were Trevisa's contemporaries, we find that they are not readily characterized in simple terms. Of all the four orders, the Franciscans present the most complex picture, probably because of the controversy surrounding their doctrine of evangelical poverty. Even Ockham did not escape the threat of excommunication in 1328, as we have seen, when he defended the doctrine against John XXII; and other Oxford Franciscans at that time, like the lector Robert de Leycester, were just as deeply involved. The memory of those days must still have been vivid in the latter half of the century among the Grey Friars in Oxford, and they must still have felt like an embattled community.

As in every flourishing order, there were a few "noble posts," as Chaucer would call them, who worked quietly as students or administrators, in some cases serving as provincial minister. Such were Thomas Kyngesbury, who encouraged his colleague, the astronomer John Somer, to compose a calendar; the musicologist Simon de Tunstede; and John Welles (not to be confused with the Benedictine monk from Ramsey Abbey), who had his degree conferred at the University of Florence in 1368 by papal mandate, thus cutting the red tape in which he had been bound by the secular officials of the University of Oxford. Every order should have its eccentric, and the Franciscans had Reginald de Lambourne, who entered the University in 1353 as a secular fellow of Merton; joined the Benedictines as a monk of Eynsham Abbey, where he speculated on the meaning of eclipses of the moon in 1364, and on the conjunctions of Saturn, Jupiter, and Mars in 1367; moved to St. Mary's Abbey, York, where in 1377 he appealed to the pope to defend him from attack by enemies; and thereafter he entered the Franciscan Order at Oxford, removing finally to Northampton, where he died.

As we have seen, the Franciscans were under attack from all quarters since the time of John XXII, so that inevitably much of their time during our period was taken up with self-defense. Roger Conway and John Mardeslay took up the battle against FitzRalph in 1357, while in 1360 John Hilton and Richard Trevytlam replied to the monks who had attacked the order in the wake of FitzRalph's visit. Trevytlam composed a Latin poem, *De laude Universitatis Oxoniae*, defending the friars and attacking the possessioners, notably the Benedictines John Seen and Uthred de Boldon, and the Cistercian Richard Lincoln, while at the same time commending the learned Roger Swyneshed of Glastonbury.

The attitude of the Franciscans toward Wyclif must have been ambivalent, for reasons already evident. To the extent that they still maintained the views of St. Francis on evangelical poverty, Wyclif was their ally. But

61

these views had become increasingly difficult after the adverse decision of Pope John XXII in 1323, so that Wyclif's real affinity was with the Spiritual Franciscans, who were well on the road to heresy. But the memory of the founder's teaching was still strong enough, even among the orthodox, to make the Franciscans reluctant to attack Wyclif. This is evident in the fact that whereas the Dominicans, as we shall see, opposed Wyclif in substantial numbers, only two relatively undistinguished members of the Franciscan Convent, Thomas Bernewell and Hugh Karlell, represented them at Black Friars in 1382, and only two others disputed Wyclif's opinions sufficiently for there to be a record of the fact.

It is likely that the Franciscan William Woodford disputed with Wyclif in the normal course of events, since both were lecturing on the *Sentences* of Peter Lombard in fulfillment of the degree requirements. In any case, they seem to have had a friendly exchange sometime before 1373, and it was not until later that Woodford began to write extensively against Wyclif's opinions. It is interesting moreover that Woodford did not attend Black Friars, where his presence would certainly have added to the scholarly standing of the council. The only other Franciscan to speak out against Wyclif was John Tissington, lector of the Oxford Convent in 1380, and member of the committee appointed by Barton in that year to deal with some of Wyclif's opinions. When Wyclif issued his *Confessio* as a response to the committee's adverse judgment in May 1381, Tissington composed a determination against him that by special order was preserved in the University archives. But the general response of the Franciscans to the challenge represented by Wyclif was low-key, and it was left to the Dominicans to lead the charge against the heresiarch.

In the late thirteenth and early fourteenth centuries the secular faculty of the University of Oxford passed a series of statutes designed to ensure their continuing control over academic affairs, and these statutes were directed mainly against the mendicants. The strongest in defense of the four orders were the Dominicans. Hence they became the focal point of the hostility of the seculars, which reached a high pitch in the expulsion of Hugh de Dutton, lector of the Dominican Convention in 1311–12. The controversy was settled by arbitration in 1314, though the efforts of the Dominicans to continue the struggle by seeking the intervention of the pope lasted until 1320, when they made an unconditional submission to the University. As a result of all this, the Dominican presence in

Oxford suffered more than the other fraternal orders, and their list of distinguished Oxford scholars is certainly not as impressive as that of the Franciscans.

Nevertheless, the Black Friars could look with pride to the achievements of Richard Fishacre, the first Dominican to incept in theology at Oxford, who became a doctor in 1244, was the author of several commentaries and tracts, and whose influence was notable in both Oxford and Paris. Another early Dominican was Robert de Kilwardby, most of whose studies were carried out at Paris; he became a regent master of the Oxford Convent in 1256, and provincial prior of the order in England, 1261–72. In his capacity as archbishop of Canterbury (1272–78) he struck a blow in 1277 against the growing Aristotelian influence in the University by condemning theses similar to those condemned by Bishop Tempier in Paris that same year. In some ways the most learned, and certainly the most prolific, of the Oxford Dominicans was Nicholas Trevet (or Trivet). According to Leland in his *Commentarii de Scriptoribus Britannicis* (pp. 326–28), he joined the order in the London Convent, while his presence at Oxford is first recorded in 1297, and he may have remained there until 1307. For the next seven years, during the time of the most intensive conflict between his order and the University, Trevet studied at Paris, returning to Oxford only after the settlement of the dispute in 1314. He wrote commentaries on both the Bible and the classics, and in his later years turned to the writing of chronicles in French and in Latin.

Trevet was followed in the first half of the fourteenth century by two eminent theologians and preachers, Thomas Waleys and Robert Holcot. The academic progress of Waleys was interrupted because of the quarrel of the Dominicans with University authorities, but he was finally admitted as a bachelor about 1314, and incepted four years later. As a critic of the pope's doctrine of the beatific vision he endured ten years' imprisonment, but was finally released about 1342 and returned to England to spend his final years. A remarkable knowledge of the classics is exhibited in his commentaries and in his treatise on the art of preaching. His younger colleague Robert Holcot, who incepted as doctor of theology about 1332, had similar interests and was a protégé of Richard de Bury. His commentaries, especially on the wisdom literature of the Bible, were famous, and he also composed a book of moralizations with sermon outlines for the use of preachers. His commentary on

Ecclesiasticus was interrupted by his premature demise in the first wave of the Black Death in 1349. For a detailed and fascinating study of these and other scholars, see Beryl Smalley, *English Friars and Antiquity in the Early Fourteenth Century* (1960).

We conclude this roll call of early Oxford Dominicans with one who could not be called a scholar, but who proclaimed the faith in foreign lands: the kind of missionary-friar that Richard FitzRalph admired. He was John de Stanes, in the Oxford Convent about 1318, perhaps the Dominican of that name who was given safe-conduct for three years on 8 October 1320 to go with two other friars to preach to the Saracens in the Holy Land. This man had no quarrel with the University, but represented an emerging Dominican enthusiasm that should be given due recognition.

The most active of the Dominicans at Oxford during Trevisa's stay in Exeter College was undoubtedly William Jordan, who had received the degree of doctor of theology by midcentury, and was then elected vicar general of the English Province. We have already noted his role as a defender of the Dominican Order against FitzRalph before Innocent VI in 1358, as an opponent of the monk Uthred de Boldon at Oxford in 1366–68, and as the object of satire in *Piers the Plowman*. Bishop Bale attributes to him a tractate *Contra positiones Wiclevi*, but the University records are silent on Jordan after 1368, leaving his whereabouts and even the date of his death a matter for speculation.

Although we tend to think of a Dominican community in this period as organized and disciplined, at least comparatively speaking, the Oxford Convent did have its problems. Richard Leomynstre, who was granted a doctorate in theology in 1359 at the request of the Black Prince, with the understanding that he was not to be required to lecture, is cited in the Oxford statutes as a notorious example of what was called a "wax doctor" (someone who advanced himself to a degree by currying favor with the great, who thus sent letters, sealed with wax, to ensure the granting of the degree whether the candidate was qualified or not). Hugh of Stamford, on the other hand, alleged in 1363 in a petition to the pope that he was well qualified for the doctorate but had been prevented from receiving it because of the multitude of candidates in the Convent waiting their turn for inception; the pope therefore granted him permission to have the degree conferred by a member of his order.

The presence of foreign students in the Dominican Convent seems to have been the source of some discord. Miguel di Polo, a Spanish friar who was appointed to lecture on the *Sentences* at Oxford, was forced to leave town because of discord among the students there, and was reported wandering around the country "to the peril of his soul and the scandal of his Order" (CPR 1364–67, p. 278). A much larger problem arose in 1370 after a visitation by the prior provincial of the order, William de Bodekesham, who was forced to obtain a royal mandate in order to subdue seventeen unruly members of the friary. Of the seventeen students named, six were foreigners, though they may not have initiated the rebellion. Only two members of this group seem to have been successful students: John Lindlow was admitted as a bachelor in theology in 1382, and John Chesham completed the doctorate by 1380. The very presence of most of the others in Oxford would not be known if their names had not been included in the mandate.

The Dominicans were strong in their opposition to Wyclif, although they did not have anyone for the task as distinguished, for example, as the Franciscan William Woodford. William Brunscombe, John Chesham, and John Wolverton were chosen by Barton for his investigation of Wyclif in 1380, and no less than six Oxford Dominicans were present at the Black Friars Council of 1382, half of whom were doctors. We may say in summary that while the Order of Preachers in Oxford was active during our period, it did not turn out scholars as distinguished as the Franciscans, nor even of the caliber of Trevet, Waleys, or Holcot, earlier representatives of the Dominican Order itself.

Although Knowles (1957, p. 145) reports that there were some sixty Carmelites in the Oxford Convent in 1377, there was no disruptive incident such as we have noted in the Dominican house that might have preserved for us an extensive list of names. Of the group of about fifteen that I have gleaned from Emden, at least twelve were doctors of theology. The Carmelites did not have the strong scholastic tradition of the Franciscans and Dominicans: perhaps only John Baconthorpe in the first half of the fourteenth century could be cited as a distinguished alumnus of the Oxford Convent, and much of his period of study was spent in Paris. One other member worthy of mention is John Titleshale, chosen to defend the order against FitzRalph, whose *Proposicio* of 5 July 1350 represented the first public airing in Avignon of his antimendicant views. But the English Province by now was the largest of the entire

Carmelite Order, and during the time of Trevisa's residency their Oxford house was flourishing. Nicholas of Lynn, the astronomer, stood alone in his scientific interests; the others were theologians, and they were united in their opposition to Wyclif.

It comes as somewhat of a surprise that the Carmelites sent ten representatives to the Black Friars Council, outstripping even the Dominicans in this respect. Of this group John Loneye had already served on the Barton committee in 1380, undoubtedly voting with the majority. Three other Oxford Carmelites—Richard Lavenham, Thomas Lombe, and John de Marre—are said to have written in opposition to Wyclif, and of course the battle continued against the Lollards into the next century under the leadership of the distinguished Carmelite Thomas Netter of Walden, author of the *Doctrinale Antiquitatum Fidei Catholicae Ecclesiae*, a highly respected defense of the Catholic faith against the Wycliffites and Hussites (1420–30). The more accomplished of the delegates to Black Friars were Robert Ivory, whose doctorate was awarded by papal mandate in Avignon, 1374; John Kynyngham, skillful opponent of Wyclif in the University, who was elected provincial prior in 1393; Richard Maidstone, translator of the penitential psalms; Stephen Patrington, who may have collected the materials on the early days of Wycliffism later used by Thomas Netter; and Peter Stokes, who was called "white dog" by Wyclif, and worked as the unofficial agent of Courtenay in the crisis of 1382. Thus the Carmelites may have been slow in their development at Oxford, but in the second half of the fourteenth century they reached full strength, and used their power effectively in opposition to the threat represented by Wyclif and his followers.

We complete our circuit of Oxford with the friary of the Augustinians, or Austin Hermits, to the northeast of the city on land now occupied by Wadham College. Like the Carmelites, the Austin Friars developed slowly, no doubt because of their eremitical origins, but entered into a period of growth in the later fourteenth century. The most distinguished scholar of their order was an Italian, Giles of Rome (Aegidius Romanus), whose *De Regimine Principum* was translated by Trevisa. Among the Augustinians of Oxford in Emden's *Register* perhaps the most distinguished are Geoffrey Hardeby, who opposed FitzRalph in 1357, and John Waldby, author of a collection of popular sermons, whose relative, Robert de Waldby, received his doctor's degree in Toulouse, and later became archbishop of York (1396–98). A German student who spent some time in the Oxford Convent in the 1350s was Johann Klenkok, who while a bachelor of theology lectured on the *Sentences* and disputed with Uthred de Boldon.

The Hermits sent four representatives to Black Friars, but their stand against Wyclif was not as firm as that of the Carmelites, and in fact resembled the wavering of the Franciscans. John Bankyn de London seemed to have favored Wyclif in 1371 when he and Thomas Ashborne presented articles to parliament favoring partial confiscation of the Church's wealth, yet in 1382 both men attended Black Friars; and Thomas Winterton was said to have been on friendly terms with Wyclif until the latter issued his *Confession* in May 1381, after which Winterton wrote in opposition to him but without bitterness. Clearly the common opposition of Wyclif and the Hermits to "possessioners" made parting difficult. One of the Augustinians was unable to dissociate himself from the Wycliffite movement: Peter Pateshull addressed a gathering of Lollards in London, presenting charges against members of his order, when he was confronted by some of his brethren who by interrupting him nearly caused a riot. For this disturbance Peter's arrest was ordered by the king on 18 July 1387. When last we hear of this renegade he was nailing a copy of his charges against his own order to one of the doors of St. Paul's Cathedral.

The Curriculum

A modern educator transported back to fourteenth-century Oxford would likely be struck by the emphasis on disputing in the educational process, and the absence of such a sharp distinction between faculty and students as exists in a modern university. All those who went to Oxford then did so to prepare themselves in theology, law, or medicine, a division of knowledge reflected to this day in the old library of Merton College. When they entered the University they were apprentices or, in our sense, students; if successful, by the time they left they were regent masters, or what we would call faculty. To visualize this in today's terms we might imagine a modern university with the permanent faculty removed, and the teaching done by graduate students at the dissertation stage. But this would not be enough: we would have to picture several intermediate stages in which students disputed with each other and also attended the disputations of their colleagues. Such encounters, monitored by the more advanced students, more than lectures delivered to passive audiences, were the heart and soul of the educational curriculum.

One of the points insisted on by the secular faculty at Oxford was that every candidate for an advanced degree in one of the three major areas must first complete a seven-year course in the arts, beginning with grammar. The friars, impatient with such a delay and anxious to direct their young candidates straight into theological study, would often seek to evade this requirement, thus bringing them into conflict with the University authorities. Trevisa, we know, passed through the arts course in the minimum period of seven years in Exeter College, 1362–69, emerging with the degree of master of arts. Like all the others, he must have begun as an "artist" with responsions, a sort of entrance examination in which he would dispute with a sitting master in grammar or logic—something like a tutorial except that the student had to stand. As a "questionist" he was examined by a committee of four regent masters (our graduate students serving as examiners), after which he was qualified to "determine," or enter into debate as a bachelor with students of lower status, and to lecture to them, perhaps on certain books of Aristotle. Then after two or three years of this, the candidate was invited to dispute on a subject of his own choice, called a "quodlibet"; if successful, he was licensed to incept as a master of arts within the following year.

When Trevisa moved to Queen's College, it was undoubtedly with the intention of going through the course required for a doctorate in theology, which we have seen to be the expectation of the founder, Eglesfield, as expressed in the statutes. We do not know whether he actually completed the course (Emden thinks not), though he seems to have been in residence long enough to do so. The requirements for the doctor's degree were demanding and time-consuming, and it would be a rare candidate who could complete the work in less than ten years. Trevisa was in Queen's from 1369 to 1387, a period of eighteen years, but with some interruptions of uncertain duration.

The first four years of progress toward the doctorate would be taken up hearing lectures and disputations on the Bible and on the *Sentences* of Peter Lombard, the former in the morning by masters and the latter, called cursory lectures, in the afternoon by bachelors who had reached the lecturing stage. The *Sentences* of Lombard presented to the student a doctrinal synthesis, a summary of church teachings that he must know and be able to discuss intelligently. The interplay of the authority of the Bible and the instructional character of church doctrine was thus a vital feature of the lectures and disputes that took place in the University. This provided the candidate's grounding in the basic knowledge required for the degree.

The main change that occurs after the first four years is that the candidate now had an active role in the educational process, first by opposing in a disputation (presumably the easiest to do) and then by responding to the opposition of others. This system of employing students to instruct each other was not only efficient, when controlled by a skillful regent master, but it also utilized the desire to perform well in public as a powerful motive in the student's quest for knowledge of the Bible and the doctrine of the *Sentences*. No doubt Chaucer's famous description of the clerk of Oxford in the *Canterbury Tales* reflects this system of education: "Gladly wolde he lerne and gladly teche." Students in the University were expected to do both.

After seven years, the candidate applied for admission as a bachelor, and a license to lecture on the *Sentences*. These would be the cursory lectures that the candidate had encountered on the way up, only now he would be doing the lecturing himself to young would-be bachelors. He would also be disputing with fellow students (*socii*) who were sententiaries (lecturers on the *Sentences*) in that same year. After three terms devoted to the *Sentences*, the bachelor was required to lecture for at least a year on the Bible, although he must confine himself to textual matters, since theological questions were permitted only in magisterial lectures. On completion of the two years' lecturing, one on the *Sentences* and one on the Bible, the bachelor was ready for the responsions and opponencies that precede and accompany inception as a doctor.

The inception process was very elaborate, combining what we would call examinations, graduation, and apprenticeship, all in a series of ceremonial acts. The inceptor preached twice, once in the church of the Dominicans (according to the compromise of a dispute between the friars and the University) and once on Sunday before inception in the University Church of St. Mary's. To be licensed for inception the candidate must have the approval of the chancellor and all regent masters, who must be assured that he had completed his lectures, responsions, and opponencies, that he had delivered his sermons, and that he was living a good life and had no deformities. One negative vote could inhibit the further progress of the candidate.

When all requirements were completed and the candidate was licensed for inception, he consulted with the senior master, setting date, time, and place for inception, and the subject to be disputed. It is interesting that what we would call "graduation" was very much an individual matter for the doctorate, and that the ever-popular disputation was the centerpiece of the graduation "exercises." Even by Trevisa's time, of course, the number of doctors incepting in a given year was large enough to require the scheduling of more than one inception at the same time, with the result that friends of the candidate engaged in recruiting students and masters to attend his inception, perhaps with hints to the effect that their candidate's inception feast was to be the most sumptuous Oxford had ever seen.

The inception process extended over several days, beginning with the sermon by the candidate on Sunday in St. Mary's, followed by the Vesperies on the eve of inception, and then the inception itself the following day. The Vesperies included preliminary disputes, but the main occasion was the inception. In the inception the candidate disputed first with the next bachelor in line for inception, then he argued the opposite view with a new regent master who had not previously acted as respondent, or, if none was available, he argued with the senior master. Finally the ceremony concluded with the candidate's restatement of the positive argument in support of his own solution to the problem. No doubt such shifting of sides in an argument was a common exercise in the schools. An amusing example of this occurs in Trevisa's *Dialogue on Translation*, in which he assigns all the positive arguments to Lord Berkeley, and gives himself (the clerk) the role of devil's advocate.

The doctor's degree, as the name implied, was simply a general license to teach (*jus ubique docendi*), and the new doctor was required to spend at least one year after conferral as a regent master, lecturing on the Bible and in general exercising leadership in the training of younger students. No doubt some regents took these duties more seriously than others. It is said of FitzRalph, for example, that he plunged into the debates of his juniors with skill and enthusiasm, presenting determinations on arguments that interested him and in general ensuring a lively year for the students then passing through the system. As we have seen, he also was elected chancellor and had his hands full dealing with the Stamford schism.

To the best of my knowledge, no record of Trevisa's disputations in Oxford survives, so we must rely on examples of arguments by his contemporaries to get a sense of what was going on in the classroom (*studium*) during his time. Fortunately some students kept notebooks (*reportoria*) which in varying degrees preserve for us some of the lectures and disputations that they attended, usually as nonparticipating juniors. Those that survive for our period were mainly the work of monks, sent by their order to acquire knowledge and teaching skills, so they could go back to their house and teach the brethren what they had learned. Unlike the secular masters, the monks did not generally move from one place to another, and probably for that reason more of their notebooks survive to the present day. Such indeed is the case with Worcester Cathedral, where several of these student *reportoria* are still a part of the library. One in particular, Worcester Cathedral manuscript F.65, belongs in our period, and has been the subject of an excellent dissertation by Fr. Stephen L. Forte (1947).

Manuscript F.65 is not signed, but it is certainly the work of a Worcester Priory monk-scholar, very likely John Malverne, who was at Oxford between 1355 and 1372. Before looking at an example of the kind of thing recorded by him, we should note the names of those whose arguments are preserved in his notebook. One might expect a monk to show a preference for monastic lecturers, but Malverne's choices indicate a balance in this respect, perhaps reflecting the fact that the University tried to limit inceptions to one per year for each secular college and each order. Nine scholars are identified by name in his *reportorium*; of these only one, Botilston, cannot be identified as to college or order. If Botilston was a friar, however, then it can be said that the nine scholars consist of three seculars, three monks, and three friars.

In our review of the colleges and convents, we have already met most of these scholars. Of the seculars, Nicholas de Aston was at Queen's, and incepted in 1358; Adam Tonworth apparently was not a fellow of any college, incepting about 1366; and William Trevelles was a fellow of Queen's, incepting in 1368. Of the monks, Uthred de Boldon was the warden of Durham College, incepting in 1357; Adam Easton was at Gloucester College, and incepted about 1365; and Nicholas Radcliffe, also of Gloucester College, was a bachelor respondent at the Vesperies of

Easton, and probably incepted himself the following year, 1366. Of the friars, John Titleshale was a Carmelite from Norwich, chosen to defend the order against FitzRalph in Avignon about 1350; but little is certainly known of John Acton, except that he was a Dominican. Botilston, as we have noted, is not identified beyond the bare name.

In the disputations, determinations, lectures, and arguments of these scholars preserved in the Worcester notebook, many of the doctrinal questions that spring naturally from a reading of the *Sentences* are represented. Most frequently discussed are grace and free will, God's foreknowledge, the part played by God in the actions of every creature, justification, and predestination—the last no doubt owing to the influence of the late Bishop Thomas Bradwardine. The controversy over Uthred's theory of the clear vision of God is reflected in four questions, three of them by John Acton, and one by Uthred himself. Uthred's arguments against mendicancy are also included. Example: mendicant poverty is sometimes the occasion of theft, perjury, and forgetfulness of God, since "the lack of things necessary for life drives man to these vices" (Forte, p. 145). On this point compare Need's argument in B passus XX of *Piers the Plowman*. (See Appendix II: Bible PP B XX, 1–50.)

Most interesting of all for present purposes, however, are two determinations on the infallibility of scripture by the Cornishman William Trevelles, colleague of Trevisa's in Queen's College. It is quite possible that Trevisa, who would have been no more than a bachelor when Trevelles was a regent master, may have listened to these determinations as they were being delivered in the *studium*. The first one takes up the question whether the prophecies and sayings of sacred scripture concerning the day of judgment and the coming of Antichrist are true and to be infallibly asserted (fol. 5). Trevelles begins by dealing with apparent contradictions. That the day of judgment will come appears from Acts 17:31, where the apostle says that God "hath appointed a day," as well as in more detail in Luke 17:22–37. And yet it would seem that nothing will come to pass that is not known by Christ, who is both God and man, and scripture (Mark 13:32) says that this day is not known to the Son. According to Ambrose, this knowledge is withheld only so that men should not know the day; Augustine says that the Son does not know because the body of the Son, which is the Church, does not know. But it would seem that if the head of the Church knows, which is the Son, then the whole body should know. Gregory says that the Son knows, but not through his humanity. On the other hand, Peter Lombard in his *Sentences* (III, d.14, Ch. 1) asserts that Christ in his spirit knows all; and if he knows it in spirit, he knows it according to his humanity. But since the evangelist says that only the Father knows when the day of judgment shall be, it follows that the Holy Spirit does not know; and if the Holy Spirit does not know, then that day shall not be.

The evidence of scripture is examined by Augustine (*City of God*, XX, 19), who cites 2 Thessalonians 2:3 to show that the day of judgment shall not take place unless Antichrist first come (for Vulgate *discessio* Augustine has *refuga*). The time fixed for the judgment is referred to when Daniel hears someone ask the angel concerning the duration of that persecution, and the angel replies that it will be three and a half years (*City of God*, XX, 23; Dan. 12:6–7). Therefore, the day of judgment will come in a limited period immediately following the coming of Antichrist. For the apostle tells us (2 Thess. 2:8) that Christ will destroy him immediately following these signs: hence after the death of Antichrist shall be the day of judgment. The time of enduring mentioned by the angel (Dan. 12:12) is understood by Chrysostom, Jerome, and Ambrose to be a period given to men to repent, after which the day of judgment shall come.

But all those signs that should precede that day were manifested before the fall of Jerusalem: hence it would appear that it has passed. But so far no Antichrist has fulfilled in himself all of those signs. Thus Gregory, in his *Morals on the Book of Job*, comments on 41:13b (AV 41:22b): *egestas precedit faciem eius*, "want (or need) goeth before his face," by saying that before the coming of Antichrist the power to work miracles shall be withdrawn from the Church, but this has not yet occurred.

At this point in the determination, the monk's notes are a bit disconnected, but it would appear that Trevelles wanted to explain, perhaps in answer to a question, how a good prophet could speak a prophecy in error and be corrected by God (e.g., Isa. 38:1 and 38:4–5), citing by analogy the Mosaic law which asserts the power of a man to revoke the vow of his wife or daughter (Num. 30:4–16). He then returns to the issue of Christ's knowledge of the day of judgment, and settles the matter by explaining that Christ had three kinds of knowledge: first, the knowledge of God himself; second, that which he had as the Word; and third, that which he had through the operation of the senses. By the first two he knew the time of judgment, but not by the third. Scripture itself provides no certain evidence of when the final judgment will be, but from the sayings of the saints and scripture we may deduce that it will occur forty (five) days after the death of Antichrist (the "five" is inserted above the line). He cites no authorities here, but one wonders if the forty-five days may not have been derived by subtracting 1,290 days from 1,335 days as stipulated by the angel in Daniel 12:11–12, a passage discussed earlier in this determination. On the variation 40/45 days, see Lerner (1976, p. 108, and 1985, pp. 183–84n).

Another matter that Trevelles takes up is the identity or nature of Antichrist himself. This is an issue of some interest because even to-day scholarly opinion is divided on the question. "By the fourteenth century," says R. W. Frank (1957, p. 112), " 'Antichrist' had become a mere term of abuse," and this leads him to conclude that the final vision in the B version of *Piers the Plowman* is *not* a vision of the Last Judgment. Others (including the present writer) are not so sure. The question as it applies to the poem of course cannot be settled by an appeal to general usage; but for our purposes it is interesting to observe what was being taught on the subject at Oxford in Trevisa's generation. Trevelles says: "Many heretics and persecutors of the Church that scripture calls 'Antichrist' have come and gone, but the Antichrist concerning whom the writing of the apostles and Paul and Daniel speaks either now is living or will come in the future." Having thus settled all the relevant issues, the master delivers the final conclusion of this determination: the prophecies and sayings of holy scripture concerning the day of judgment and the coming of Antichrist are true and are to be infallibly asserted.

The second determination of Trevelles on the infallibility of scriptures (F.65, fol. 25vb) is related to the first, and takes up the question whether all the sayings by John in the Apocalypse (Revelation) and the other prophets in holy scripture are, were, or will be true. On the affirmative side he cites as his authority Armachanus (Richard FitzRalph), but for the contrary case gives examples of prophets who speak falsely: Nathan (2 Sam. 7:3), Micaiah (1 Kings 22:15), and the anonymous prophet of Bethel (1 Kings 13:18), who is explicitly said to have lied. Hence in this respect there need be no distinction between good and evil prophets, and we thus are not bound to believe all the sayings of the prophets. Nor does innate ability or solemnity of life render the prophecy more credible: David was no more inspired by the Holy Spirit than was Balaam (Num. 22–24).

There is a distinction to be made, however, between the true and the false prophet. The true prophet is one who proclaims, has proclaimed, or will proclaim mysteries supernaturally revealed to him by God or by another good spirit. The false prophet, on the contrary, speaks in a deceiving spirit and for an evil purpose. The true prophet can be distinguished from the false in four ways: the first is sanctity of life; the second is fulfillment of all those prophecies not later retracted; the third is retraction of all that was wrongly stated; and the fourth is recognition by the Church, since even as the Holy Spirit inspires the prophet, so it inspires the Church and its pontiff, who themselves approve and conserve the sayings of the prophets as authentic. Another response is that all prophecies are received with the understanding that they are subject to change by the supreme Judge, as evident in the example already referred to from Numbers 30:4–16, in which the vows of wife and daughter do not hold unless husband and father approve. Hence the first conclusion is that all prophetic utterances are subject to the providence of the supreme Judge. Second: all prophecy truly uttered is, was, or will be true. Third: the gift of prophecy may even be found at times in someone in a state of mortal sin.

What we miss in these notes, of course, is the excitement of the preceding disputation. But enough is preserved to convey some notion of the flavor of lectures on the Bible that Trevisa may have heard in his early years as a student in theology, before trying his hand (as will be conjectured) at biblical translation.

The Crisis of 1382

The conflict between the seculars and regulars at Oxford which we have seen to be developing steadily since the time of FitzRalph reached its climax in 1382 when the University came under the scrutiny of William Courtenay, the new archbishop of Canterbury replacing Simon Sudbury, who was assassinated by a mob in the Peasants' Revolt of June 1381. The violent death and beheading of the prelate who ordained him priest in London eleven years earlier must have been a considerable shock to Trevisa. Much worse in the long run must have been the realization that Courtenay, in an alliance with the fraternal orders, intended to conduct an unprecedented search for heresy among the scholars at Oxford in the summer and autumn of 1382. At the center of this conflict, of course, was John Wyclif, the most accomplished and talented Oxford scholar of his generation, but also a blunt and outspoken proclaimer of unorthodox beliefs. Though not mentioned by name, he was the object of Courtenay's inquisition.

We have already noted Wyclif's progress from Merton to Balliol to Canterbury Hall and his subsequent rental of a room in Queen's during Trevisa's time there. Looking now at his academic progress we see that he was a bachelor of arts by 1356, and a master of arts by 1360. He seems to have begun the course in theology in the fall of 1363, become a bachelor by 1369, and incepted as doctor in 1372 or 1373. By the time of his inception he had virtually completed his scholastic, noncontroversial writings. Thereafter, as he turned from philosophy to political theory, his work began to move in new directions. Viewed philosophically, Wyclif was not a radical; indeed he often showed himself to be in reaction against the moderns, such radical "possibilist" theologians as William of Ockham, those that he called "modern Averroists" and "pagan philosophers." Instead Wyclif reached back to FitzRalph, Grosseteste, and even St. Augustine for a realism that some of his contemporaries found very appealing: solid ground in a sea of "possibilities."

It would be interesting to know how Wyclif's thought might have developed if he had stayed out of politics, but this was not to be. He was used by the court as an intellectual opponent of papal authority, and then discarded when in 1375 the exigencies of an uncertain government policy required an aboutface. At that very moment Wyclif was engaged in writing *De Civili Dominio*, in which his attitude toward church and state came very close to "a plague on both your houses." Personal disappointment regarding professional advancement could have been a factor in this attitude, but Wyclif's thought had already acquired a momentum of its own which was not likely to be retarded by a plush appointment. Nor did the spasmodic accommodation of the crown with the papacy survive the hostility of the Good Parliament in 1376. When Courtenay, as bishop of London, procured the citation of Wyclif to appear before Archbishop Sudbury at St. Paul's in 1377, the tension between the duke of Lancaster and the Londoners prevented the hearing from taking place. Later that same year, as we have noted, the lobbying of Benedictines in the papal court resulted in the promulgation of bulls by Gregory XI citing eighteen errors attributed to Wyclif, and requiring his arrest and examination.

At the very time that all this was going on, the government was seeking Wyclif's opinion on the legality of preventing its wealth from going abroad, even if the pope demanded it—and indeed he was doing so at that moment. Wyclif of course affirmed the legality of such a procedure in very strong language. Meanwhile, ecclesiastical efforts to have him arrested continued, and he finally appeared before Sudbury in March 1378, protected by a prohibition from the king's mother against any final judgment in the case, with the result that he was simply told not to express any opinions that might scandalize the laity. This year also marked the death of Gregory XI and the beginning of the great schism, an event which no doubt further weakened the efforts of any pope to make his voice heard in national affairs.

England itself at this time was experiencing a certain turbulence as the result of the collection of two burdensome subsidies inflicted on the disgruntled population by a parliament controlled by John of Gaunt. The unpopularity of the poll taxes was destined to erupt in the riots of June 1381 in London and elsewhere, which were to shake the confidence of the entire nation (Covella 1992, pp. 34–35). But whatever the forces at work nationally, Wyclif himself was now embarked on a course from which there was no turning back. By the time his *De Eucharistica* appeared in 1379, his few supporters that remained among the friars were alienated, and even his colleagues on the secular faculty became alarmed. The following year his old friend from Merton, William de Barton, now chancellor of the University, appointed a committee, as we have seen, to report on his teaching concerning the Eucharist. The adverse judgment of this group, by a vote of seven to five, we have already observed. Wyclif's reply to this judgment, the *Confessio*, was issued on 10 May 1381, and some time thereafter he left Oxford forever and retired to Lutterworth.

The University itself did not experience unrest associated with the Revolt of June 1381, but in its wake came accusations of complicity, the seculars accusing the regulars, in particular the friars, of causing the uprising, and the latter pointing an accusing finger at the heretical teachings of Wyclif condoned by the secular faculty. Considering that Wyclif's protection from prosecution was attributable to the power of John of Gaunt, the friars went so far as to address a letter to the duke, calling attention to the dangers represented by Wyclif and his followers at Oxford. This letter was dated 18 February 1382 and was delivered to Lancaster personally by the Carmelite Stephen Patrington. The friars were particularly anxious to do something about Nicholas Hereford, named in an early manuscript as one of the translators of the Bible, and a committed disciple of Wyclif's. The duke ignored the appeal of the friars, and on 23 February Hereford announced in a sermon that the religious should hereafter be barred from receiving degrees in the University. In March Wyclif himself published *De Blasphemia*, in which the denunciation of ecclesiastical abuses became even stronger, and in May he submitted a sharply worded petition to Parliament urging the rejection of any and all papal assessments, and the taxing of possessioners in England. Meanwhile in Oxford on Ascension Day (15 May 1382), Hereford delivered a sermon in English designed to alienate nearly everyone except the most fanatical of Wyclif's followers.

While all this was going on, the friars, unable to get satisfaction from John of Gaunt, sought the assistance of Courtenay. The archbishop was now established at Canterbury, and was ready to act, being already convinced that the heresy of Wyclif and his colleagues was a clear and present danger that needed immediate attention. In response to the friars he summoned a council of theologians to meet at the convent of the Black Friars in London beginning 17 May 1382. The business of the Council extended over several sessions, and met in different places, but for convenience we may refer to the entire proceeding as the Black Friars Council. The first substantial gathering was on 21 May, the so-called Council of the Earthquake, because the afternoon's deliberations were interrupted by a tremor that was seized on as a sign of divine displeasure, whether against Wyclif or against his accusers being a matter of dispute. Courtenay of course explained the quake in such a way as to enable the proceedings to continue, and secured the condemnation of twenty-four conclusions attributable to Wyclif, although his name is not mentioned in the council proceedings. Courtenay evidently knew how far he could go: laying hands on Wyclif himself would not be permitted.

With as much legal leverage as he could obtain, Courtenay proceeded in his effort to identify and arrest any and all adherents to the twenty-four conclusions. He ordered the condemnation read publicly in Oxford, but this was not easily accomplished. Peter Stokes, another Carmelite opposed to Wyclif, had been given the job of reading the condemnation just before the sermon to be delivered by Philip Repyngdon on Corpus Christi Day (5 June) in St. Frideswide's. The chancellor, Robert Rygge, however, prevented him from doing so, and joined with the largely secular audience in congratulating Repyngdon following his delivery of an eloquent sermon defending the orthodoxy of Wyclif's teachings and beliefs. Stokes reported the failure of his efforts to Courtenay, and was eventually ordered by the archbishop to return to London.

Meanwhile Chancellor Rygge seems to have had second thoughts, or at least to have felt a need to explain his position to Courtenay, for soon after Corpus Christi Day he set off for London, taking with him Thomas Brightwell of Merton and the two proctors, both from Oriel, Walter Dash and John Huntman. This delegation was kept waiting at Lambeth Palace for a few days, and finally instructed to appear at the second session of the Council in Black Friars convent on 12 June. Now beginning to feel more like the victims of an inquisition than a University delegation, Rygge and his colleagues were persuaded to agree to publish the Council's condemnations in Oxford. When this was done on Sunday, 15 June, a storm of controversy arose, with harsh words on both sides; and the obstreperous Cistercian Henry Crumpe was suspended for allegedly calling the followers of Wyclif "lollards," the first known use of the term in that sense.

On 18 June a hearing was held before a committee of the Council, made up mostly of friars, to examine Hereford, Repyngdon, and John Aston. The defendants asked for time to prepare their answers and were granted two days, after which, on 20 June, the fourth meeting of the full synod took place, when Aston was condemned, and judgment on Hereford and Repyngdon was reserved for later. Finally, on 1 July the full Council met for the last time, on this occasion in the chapter house at Canterbury. Hereford and Repyngdon failed to appear, and were excommunicated. The Council had to content itself with examining Thomas Hulman of Merton, a member of the Council suspected of favoring Aston, and under the pressure of this inquiry Hulman recanted. Hereford and Repyngdon appealed to Rome, nailing copies to the doors of St. Mary le Bow and St. Paul's in London. Courtenay brushed aside these appeals and proclaimed their excommunication at St. Paul's Cross with bell, book, and candle on 13 July.

Looking back over the events of this long hot summer of 1382, it is well to consider the makeup of the Black Friars Council: who participated in the condemnation of these twenty-four conclusions? Looking at it first from a hierarchical viewpoint, there were ten prelates including

Courtenay, only one of whom was a theologian, John Gilbert, bishop of Hereford. There were, however, some thirty doctors of theology in attendance at one or more sessions of the Council, about half that number of bachelors, and perhaps fifteen lawyers, including ten doctors of civil law and one doctor of both laws (Ralph Ergum, bishop of Salisbury). It is of interest also to observe that of some sixty-five members, nearly fifty were students or graduates of Oxford, while perhaps ten had come from Cambridge, all of these members of the fraternal orders.

The large Oxford contingent included very few representatives of the secular colleges. Of the seven who eventually answered the call, only two were present from the beginning: John de Waltham of Balliol, doctor of civil law, and John Bloxham of Merton, bachelor of theology. On 12 June two more appeared: John Balton of Balliol, bachelor of theology, and John Landreyn of Oriel, doctor of theology. Another bachelor, Thomas Hulman of Merton, joined them on 18 June in time for the examination of Hereford, Repyngdon, and Aston. The last two seculars, William Blankpayn and William de Barton, both doctors of theology from Merton, attended only the final meeting of the Council on 1 July in the Chapter House at Canterbury. At least two of these seven, Balton and Hulman, were reluctant participants; indeed, as we have seen, Hulman's hesitation to condemn Aston very nearly turned him from a judge into a defendant.

It is remarkable that there were no more than five monks on the Council, four of them Benedictines, and a lone Cistercian, Henry Crumpe, whose suspension by the seculars at Oxford was quickly overruled when Courtenay secured the king's intervention on his behalf on 14 July. Two of the Benedictines were from St. Albans, one was from Christ Church Cathedral Priory in Canterbury, and one was from Ramsey Abbey. All were doctors of theology except William Gillyngham of Canterbury, who attended only the final meeting in the Chapter House there. The monk from Ramsey was of course John Welles, possible owner, as we have noted, of a copy of the A version of *Piers the Plowman*, and persistent opponent of Wyclif who also had served on the Barton committee the previous year. Why were more monks not attracted by this opportunity to strike back at this scourge of the possessioners? Perhaps the answer is simply that there were not enough of them academically qualified in theology or law for the Council. We may wonder at the absence of William Binham, now prior of Wallingford;

but not many other doctors come to mind who might have participated but did not.

In contrast to the monks, the fraternal orders formed the largest single group at Black Friars: some thirty delegates, twenty-two of them from Oxford. Little wonder that Wyclif called the body "a council of friars." Oxford supplied two Franciscans, six Dominicans, ten Carmelites, and four Augustinians. All but seven of these were doctors of theology, the most distinguished perhaps John Gilbert, bishop of Hereford, whose degree was probably conferred at Paris. Most active of the Oxford group were the Carmelites: Chiseldene, Legat, Patrington, Reppys, and Tomson were bachelors, while Ivory, Kynyngham, Loneye, Stokes, and Maidstone were doctors. Patrington and Stokes were particularly effective in alerting Courtenay to the situation in Oxford leading up to the Council. Thus we see that the best-qualified members of the Council were also the most committed opponents of Wyclif and the seculars. Therefore it is not difficult to see that the condemnation of Wyclif was regarded by many of the arts faculty of Oxford as an attack on themselves and ultimately on the freedom of the University.

But the most humiliating phase of the archbishop's campaign was his visitation of Oxford in November 1382. The technical nature of the occasion was a Convocation, with Courtenay presiding as Visitor. The actual purpose was to stamp out any fires of opposition that might still be smoldering after the condemnation. This was rather easily done. Laurence Stephen (alias Bedeman) had already submitted on 18 October, and Repyngdon and Aston were induced to recant publicly before Courtenay left Oxford. The instrument for facilitating the accomplishment of this purpose was a committee appointed by the archbishop to investigate the Oxford faculty to discover whether any of them still adhered to the condemned conclusions. No transcripts of the committee's hearings survive, so we are spared the sight of Oxford scholars who had been supporters of Wyclif coming before this committee and swearing that they no longer believed his teachings. If Trevisa was a witness to these proceedings, he must have watched in dismay as many a wise teacher fell, wounded by hypocrisy (*Piers the Plowman*, B XX 299–301).

The investigative committee was carefully selected by Courtenay for balance, prestige, and cooperativeness. There were six members: three prelates and three Oxford scholars, all seculars. They were Thomas Brinton, a Benedictine and bishop of Rochester; Ralph Ergum, bishop of Salisbury and doctor of both laws; John Gilbert, a Dominican, bishop of Hereford and the only friar on the committee; Robert Rygge, the now repentant chancellor and fellow of Merton; William de Barton, also of Merton, and chosen perhaps because of his earlier opposition to Wyclif when he was chancellor in 1380; and John Middleton (alias Vyneter) of Oriel, virtually unknown except for his appointment to this committee. Was there a single member of this group who, in the eyes of the embattled Oxford seculars, ought to be ashamed for lending his prestige to this humiliating investigation of the Oxford faculty? Undoubtedly such a person was Bishop Brinton, renowned preacher and opponent of corruption in church and state. It must have seemed deeply distressing to many scholars like Trevisa that this man should not only lend his support to the Black Friars condemnations, but should now take a leading role in the examination of Oxford teachers for heresy. One can't help feeling that the poet had Brinton especially in mind when he urged that "correctors" (i.e., bishops), before they undertook the correction of others, should correct first themselves (*Piers the Plowman*, B X 284). Any internal conflict that Brinton may have felt about his role as an inquisitor on this occasion must remain a matter of conjecture. But it is a fact that very soon afterward he was apparently stricken by a lingering illness from which he never fully recovered in the seven remaining years of his life.

The extent of John Trevisa's agreement with the teachings of Wyclif must remain uncertain. But it may be suggested at this point that he probably agreed with many of the reformer's ideas, particularly in the political sphere, as expressed in the *Complaint* which Wyclif offered to Parliament in May 1382. This petition emphasized four points: the first was that members of the religious orders should be allowed to leave them, since "private rules" must give way to "the rule of Jesus Christ"; second, possessioners should be relieved of their temporal goods, and even priests should be deprived if they do not properly discharge their responsibilities; third, the appropriation of livings by monasteries must cease, a reform suggested long ago by that great clerk Robert Grosseteste; and fourth, Christ's teaching concerning the Eucharist should be taught openly to all Christian people. Of these points, Trevisa might have hesitated over the fourth, since he almost certainly would not agree with Wyclif on what the teaching about the Eucharist should be. But he would no doubt strongly endorse the other three, as we shall have occasion to observe. And when we remember that he translated FitzRalph's sermon against the friars, we may well conclude that to John Trevisa the victory of the friars over the seculars at Oxford in 1382 was a cataclysmic event, with apocalyptic overtones that may have led him to see in it the triumph of Antichrist, and the coming of the latter days.

3

BERKELEY

The remainder of Trevisa's life—about a quarter of a century—was taken up primarily with his duties as chaplain and man of letters to Thomas IV, Lord Berkeley, in Gloucestershire, on the banks of the Severn estuary. Exactly how long he was associated with this family has been a matter of some uncertainty. We have noted how Caxton's erroneous date for completion of the *Polychronicon* translation (1357 instead of 1387) has left a trail of error in accounts of Trevisa's life down to modern times. In particular this led John Smyth to suppose that he was at Berkeley by midcentury, and that he may have been the author of the Latin pedigree roll (Jeayes, Select Roll 102) which Perry (1925) lists under Trevisa's "original writings." Because his thinking was dominated by this chronology, Smyth inserted the account of Trevisa in his biography of Thomas III, lord of Berkeley from 1326 to 1361. It is indeed possible, as we have seen, that this lord "discovered" Trevisa during a tour of his properties in Cornwall, and arranged for him to be subsidized at Oxford when he came of age, but we should bear in mind that the young Cornishman was probably not quite twenty years old when Thomas III died in 1361.

Documentary Evidence

The earliest documented connection between Trevisa and Berkeley is his dedication of the translation of the *Polychronicon*, completed on 18 April 1387, to Thomas IV, lord Berkeley. We do not know that he was physically in Berkeley at that time, because he does not mention his whereabouts; if the four years' back rent that he paid the treasurer of Queen's College was for the period 1383–87, he may be presumed to have completed this work at Oxford, where in any case most of it would have been accomplished between 1385, when he was still translating book one (*Poly.* ii, 161), and April 1387, the date of completion.

The first record that testifies to Trevisa's presence in Gloucestershire comes in the form of an ancient petition, in which it is alleged that Trevisa participated in a series of attacks on the petitioner in 1388 and 1389 (PRO SC 8/148/7355). The incident involves a dispute over Trevisa's right to an appointment as canon of the Collegiate Church of Westbury-on-Trym (near Bristol). To this matter we shall return later.

In the preceding chapter we had occasion to note, in the long rolls of Queen's College, the entries showing that Trevisa spent at least a portion of the years 1394–95 and 1395–96 at Oxford. The normal rent for one year seems to have been fifteen shillings: for the former year, he paid eleven shillings eight pence; for the latter, thirteen shillings four pence. Perhaps already he was beginning work on his most voluminous project: the translation of Bartholomew's great encyclopedia, *De Proprietatibus Rerum*. Trevisa gives the completion date at the end of his translation of Bartholomew, and also tells us that he finished work on it at Berkeley:

> Endless grace, bliss and thanking to our Lord God all-wielding. These translations ended at Berkeley the sixth day of February the year of our Lord 1398, the year of king Richard the second after the conquest of England two and twenty, the year of my lord's age Sir Thomas lord of Berkeley, that made me make this translation, seven and forty.

Trevisa's other known translations, the *Gospel of Nicodemus, Dialogus inter Militem et Clericum, Defensio Curatorum*, and *De Regimine Principum*, are entirely lacking in indications of either place or date of composition.

For the sake of completeness we may take note here of the documentation of Trevisa's death, which occurred sometime before 21 May 1402, when John Bonjon was instituted vicar of Berkeley in his place. This institution is recorded in the register of Richard Clifford, bishop of Worcester 1402–7 (fol. 14d–15a): later in this chapter we shall have occasion to examine this entry more closely. Meanwhile, having reviewed the slim documentary evidence of Trevisa's life in Gloucestershire, we are now in a position to consider some matters for which documentation is lacking. Thus we do not know, for example, when he first went to Berkeley, nor do we know (a most regrettable lacuna) when he was instituted vicar of the parish church there. The pursuit of these questions will have an intrinsic interest, but will also provide an opportunity to learn more about his patron Thomas IV and the importance of the Berkeley family in the life of the community and the nation. For a much fuller picture of this Thomas as a patron, see the important and informative essay by Ralph Hanna (1989).

85

The Lords of Berkeley

The Berkeley family traces its origin to the twelfth century, when Henry II rewarded his supporter Robert FitzHarding with the Berkeley lands and even arranged for the building of the castle that remains standing to this day. A series of resolute lords of Berkeley presided over these lands and served their kings during the thirteenth century, reaching a kind of climax in the fourteenth century with the long reign of Thomas III, lord of Berkeley from 1326 to 1361, whom John Smyth calls "Thomas the Rich" (I, 279). The lords of Berkeley prided themselves in their service to the monarchy, but they were not subservient; and John Smyth, perhaps under the spell of the Tudor myth, is reluctantly driven to tax them with disloyalty on occasion. Their record, however, is not readily faulted: the two kings that they rebelled against were John Lackland and Edward II, while under almost every other monarch through our period (except Richard II) they were intensely loyal servants of the crown.

For the first few years of his lordship, Thomas III lived under suspicion of involvement in the death of Edward II in Berkeley Castle; and, as Smyth shows, this suspicion was well grounded. But his trial in 1330 was inconclusive, and he was finally acquitted in 1337, when his services were soon to be required by the king for the conflict in France which later generations would call the Hundred Years' War. Thomas III fought for Edward III on many fronts: in Scotland, in France, at sea against the French fleet off the coast of Flanders, and on the home front, where he held an important post in the defense of the west country. He was a leader of the army that overthrew William Douglas in 1342, and four years later fought in the battle of Crecy and the siege of Calais, where his brother Maurice died. In 1349 he took part in a cloak-and-dagger operation with the king and the Black Prince to thwart the betrayal of the English garrison at Calais, an event dramatically recounted by the chronicler Froissart (1:336–40). The climax of his military career was the battle of Poitiers on 19 September 1356, at which time this lord Berkeley was over sixty and had fought in battles under two kings over some forty years.

It should be emphasized that Thomas III's activities were by no means limited to war. He rebuilt, beautified, and enlarged Berkeley Castle, and repaired other residences, notably his house at Wotton-under-Edge; he kept close track of the livestock and produce of manors extending from Oxfordshire to Cornwall; and he acquired a well-deserved reputation for hospitality, clothing and feeding a household of some three hundred attendants, esquires, officers, and servants. But his interests were not purely temporal: perhaps more than any lord of Berkeley since Robert I, he concerned himself with spiritual matters.

Simultaneous with the establishment of the Berkeley family itself was the founding of the house of Augustinian canons in Bristol known as the Abbey of St. Augustine. Traditionally the canons looked back to Robert I as their founder and chief benefactor, and the relations between the abbey and the Berkeleys remained very close apart from occasional periods of friction such as occurred, for example, in the time of Maurice I (1170–89), son of the founder. Among the endowments granted to the abbey by Robert, and confirmed in his time by Maurice, was the parish church of Berkeley, which stood just north of the castle. As it happened, Maurice was engaged in strengthening his fortifications, and in doing so made a ditch on the north side which cut into the grounds of the church. This led the abbot and convent to harass Maurice with ecclesiastical censures until he asked pardon and made further grants of land by way of recompense in Berkeley and other parishes, much to the indignation of the family historian (Smyth, 1:66–68).

Thomas III confirmed the ancestral grants of his family to the abbey, but he did much more than that. He subsidized "hopeful scholars," paid taxes of the fraternal orders in Bristol and Gloucester, and made perpetual grants of wax and wheat to Berkeley church. Above all, Thomas was a prolific founder of chantries for the singing of masses for the souls of his ancestors and himself and family after death. Four of these were instituted under the name of his receiver and priest, William de Syde: in the church of Syde (Parigate Hundred), and in the chapels of St. Katherine, Cambridge (within the parish of Slimbridge), St. Maurice, Newport (Berkeley parish), and St. John the Baptist, Wortley (Wotton-under-Edge). In his own name Thomas founded chantries in the chapel of Over (Almondsbury) and in the abbey of St. Augustine itself. Nor should we overlook his gifts to chantries already in existence in the abbey, the church of Berkeley (St. Mary's), and the chapel of Sheppardine (Rockhampton).

The family historian, John Smyth, was a product of the Reformation, of course, but he was deeply impressed by these testimonials to the spirituality of Thomas III (1:338):

> And pardon mee, Oh my god, in my overflowing affection to this lord Thomas, If I break out in prayer before thee, to remember the dust of this thy honorable servant, resting in Berkeley Church, in the travells and pious ways wherein hee walked; And forget not (lord) thy doctrine taught him by thy learned servant his Chaplen, John Trevisa, vicar of the same Church, whose bones rest there alsoe; That though his Ancestors guifts to Abbyes in old time, and some of his own, bee more wasted in gluttony pride and outrage of the owners, then in sustenance and need of men and guests, yet the givers shall not lose theire mede, for their will and intent is weyed in thy ballance, and their good deeds shall follow them, with the reward of glory and immortality.

Of course Smyth in this passage was thinking of Trevisa as a contemporary of Thomas III, which we have seen to be a mistake derived from Caxton; but the point is an important one, which may well apply, as we shall see, to Trevisa and Thomas IV (1368–1417).

Thomas III died old and full of days, having reigned thirty-five years as lord of Berkeley. His death occurred on 27 October 1361, and it is tempting to wonder if Trevisa was in Berkeley at that time. His arrival in Oxford in Hilary Term, the winter of 1362, is an unusual time to begin one's studies at the university, and it seems possible that his plans may have been to enter Exeter College in Michaelmas Term (autumn) of 1361—plans that had to be changed because of the final illness and death of his patron. Thomas was buried in an impressive tomb in the south aisle of Berkeley church, where some twenty-five years later his second wife, Katherine, was likewise interred, during Trevisa's tenure as vicar of Berkeley.

That the lady Katherine and Trevisa were acquainted seems an entirely reasonable assumption. While her husband was alive she was fully occupied with giving birth to and rearing four children, but after his death she emerged as a person of significance in her own right. Two years after her loss she embarked on a pilgrimage abroad, and thereafter resided for the most part in Wotton-under-Edge until she died 24 March 1386. Two years before her death, however, she founded the chantry of St. Andrew in Berkeley church, and established a grammar school for a master and two poor scholars in Wotton (Wakefield's Register

#556–62). Trevisa would necessarily be involved in the establishment of the chantry, but it is also possible to suppose, though without evidence, that he had a role in her decision to establish the grammar school, which has become her greatest claim to fame in modern times.

The next lord, Maurice IV (1361–68), was the son of Thomas III by his first wife, Margaret. He was born in 1330, and, at the age of seven, when his mother died, he was placed under the tutelage of his father's trusted priest and receiver, William de Syde, in whose name four of the six chantries of Thomas III were to be founded. In that same year, his father took Maurice with him to Scotland—perhaps, as Smyth surmises, to help ease the grief of the loss of his mother at so early an age. In the following year was formalized the marriage of Maurice and Elizabeth, daughter of Hugh lord Spenser when both were eight years old. It may be, as Smyth suggests, that Thomas III deliberately sent his son to Spain for a couple of years in 1342 to keep him away from his young bride; in any case, on his return he was quickly swept up in the preparations for war with France, and was attendant on the Black Prince in the battle of Crecy (1346). No doubt this great English victory made a deep impression on Maurice, who was then only sixteen.

Nearly ten years later, Maurice and his father went with the Black Prince to spend the winter of 1355–56 in Gascony and Aquitaine. At the end of the following summer, on 19 September 1356, they participated in that final English victory at Poitiers. At that time Thomas III was over sixty, and probably occupied himself more with field command than with actual fighting. But Maurice, now twenty-six, took an active part in the battle. Indeed, the skirmish in which he received the wound that was to shorten his life is recorded by Froissart, who perhaps understandably confuses him with his father, but otherwise seems to preserve a faithful account of the action (1:337):

> The same season there was in the felde the lorde Bercle of Englande, a yong lusty knyght (*un jeune et appert chevalier*), who the same day had reryd his baner: and he all alone pursued the sayd Johan of Helenes, and whane he had folowed the space of a leage, the sayde John tourned agayne and layed his swerde in the rest instede of a speare, and so came ronyng towarde the lord Bercle, who lyft up his swerde to haue stryken the squyer: but whan he sawe the stroke come, he tourned fro it, so that the Englysshman lost his stroke and Johan strake hym as he past on the arme, that the lorde Berclees swerde fell into the felde. Whan he sawe his swerde downe, he lyghted sodaynly of

89

his horse and came to the place wher his swerd lay, and as he stouped downe to take up his swerd, the Frenche squyer dyd pycke his swerde at him, and by happe strake hym through both the thyes, so that the knyght fell to the yerth, and could nat helpe hymself.

It was one of those ironies of warfare: the English had won the day, and Maurice was wounded by a cast that John of Helenes probably could not have duplicated (using his sword like a javelin) if he had tried it again a dozen times. As a result, young Maurice was taken prisoner, and eventually his father had to pay six thousand nobles for his release. The money he could afford, but the sight of his wounded son, returning home after more than a year's recuperation in Picardy, must have been very grievous indeed.

Four years after his return from captivity, his father died, and Maurice IV entered upon his brief seven-year tenure as lord Berkeley. In May 1360 Edward III signed a treaty at Bretigny waiving his claim to the French throne, with the result that the land rested for a few years from the demands of war. Maurice's wife, Elizabeth, bore him four sons and three daughters, and when he died in 1368 she, like him, was only thirty-eight years old. She survived him twenty-one years, dying in 1389 in London, where she was buried in the parish church of St. Botulph.

Perhaps because of his early death, a result of the wound he received at Poitiers, Maurice founded no new chantries in the manner of his father, but he did contribute to the upkeep of some already in existence. It is of particular interest here to take note of the papal bull he obtained in 1364 granting forty days' pardon to all who heard masses in the two chapels of Berkeley Castle, one dedicated to St. John the Baptist in the keep, and the other to the Virgin at the upper end of the great hall stairs. The latter chapel is the one to which Trevisa refers in the *Dialogue* prefixed to his translation of the *Polychronicon*, on the walls and roof of which were inscribed passages from the Apocalypse in Latin and French.

Since Trevisa was at Oxford almost continuously during the time of Maurice IV, it is unlikely that he was in any sense a member of that lord's household. We know of at least three men who received grants from Maurice for service in some capacity as his chaplains: Walter Rope, Richard March, and William Winchcombe. The latter received in 1366 a house before the gate of St. Augustine's monastery, Bristol, especially to pray for the soul of Maurice's mother, the lady Margaret (Smyth, 1:372). Two years later, Maurice died after a lingering illness on 8 June

1368, in Berkeley Castle. He was buried in St. Augustine's, Bristol, beside his mother, who had died when he was but seven years old.

Maurice's eldest son was thus the heir of the Berkeley estates at the age of fifteen. Since he was a ward of the king (although the actual wardship was held by his father-in-law, Gerald, Lord Lisle), he did not enter upon possession of his lands until 5 January 1374, when, at the age of twenty-one, he became Thomas IV, Lord Berkeley. We look in vain for evidence that his father made any arrangements for his education, as Thomas III had done in turning Maurice over to William de Syde. If Trevisa was indeed at Berkeley for the funeral of Thomas III, he would no doubt have seen young Thomas, then some eight years old, but would not have realized that in seven short years, while he was at Oxford, this boy would inherit the Berkeley lands. Trevisa was perhaps nineteen at the time of the death of Thomas III, and would have made a good tutor, but we have no way of knowing how often he was in touch with young Thomas before he became vicar of Berkeley.

A year before his death, Maurice arranged an early marriage between Thomas, then fourteen, and Margaret, then seven, daughter of Gerald Warren, lord of Lisle. She was to remain at least four years with her father because of her tender age, whereas in fact the lord Lisle did not bring her to Berkeley until 1382, when Thomas was twenty-nine. By this time, in keeping with the military tradition of the Berkeleys, Thomas had been to war in France and Spain between the years 1375 and 1380, and was destined to go to Scotland in 1384. Apart from the wars, Thomas IV was living in turbulent times. He was one of many lords commissioned to investigate and punish the malefactors responsible for the Peasants' Revolt of June 1381, and no doubt he viewed with alarm the unsteady leadership of Richard II. He entertained the king at Berkeley Castle in 1386, but seems to have avoided as far as possible the gamesmanship of court politics until his hand was forced, as we shall see, in the crisis of 1399.

Thomas seems to have survived the wars unscathed; the real tragedy of his life appears to have been the death of Margaret in 1392, soon after she had given birth to their only child, Elizabeth. Thomas was then still in his thirties, and the family historian wonders why he never remarried, why he threw away an opportunity to provide the male heir who would have precluded the turmoil that in fact arose, after Thomas's death, over the division of the Berkeley estates. It may well be, as Smyth suggests, that the pilgrimage abroad undertaken by Thomas IV soon after his wife's death is evidence of the profound grief he was experiencing. This seems more plausible than the alternative explanation of the journey as a device for escaping involvement in the controversies of the royal court.

As one reads the *Lives of the Berkeleys* it is impossible to avoid the impression that the history of this family reached a peak in the time of Thomas III. His son Maurice, as we have seen, did not live long enough to do more than make use of the momentum bequeathed by his father. But in Thomas IV we find a man who, though undoubtedly talented, nevertheless lacks, for whatever reason, the exuberance of his most distinguished ancestors. The early death of his wife and the lack of a male heir no doubt had some effect, but there remains a kind of caution or hesitancy that strikes us as a new thing in the history of the Berkeleys. Unlike his grandfather, he was not a farmer, and he relied much more heavily on the income from rentals than from any husbandry of his own. There may have been occasional great entertainments in the castle during his reign, as when he hosted the king in 1386, but there is little evidence of the colorful household of three hundred maintained by his magnanimous ancestor. Indeed Thomas IV seems to have been restless, even before the death of his wife, moving from Berkeley to Wotton, to Portbury, to London, and perhaps back to Syde or another of his numerous manors. It may be, as Smyth suggests, that this peripatetic life was much in vogue, or it could be that it was simply a means of economizing. No doubt the castle at Berkeley was expensive to maintain, but to those who remembered the days of Thomas III the austere lifestyle of the new lord must have left something to be desired (*Piers the Plowman,* B X 94–100):

> Ailing is the hall each day in the week
> Where the lord and the lady liketh not to sit.
> Now hath each rich a rule to eat by himself
> In a privy parlour, for poor men's sake, [i.e., to avoid eating in the
>   company of poor men],
> Or in a chamber with a chimney, and leave the chief hall,
> That was made for meals, men to eat in:
> And all to spare to spill that spend shall another.

The tenure of Thomas IV as lord of Berkeley lasted some forty-three years or, if his minority be included, nearly a half-century during which the estates were under his name. Hence it is not, as in the case of Maurice, a lack of opportunity that prevented him from adding his share of new chantries or chapels to the list of his grandfather's foundations. To be sure, monasteries in general were coming under public scrutiny during this period, as we have seen in earlier references to the quarrel at Oxford between the seculars and the possessioners. But it is tempting to suppose that Trevisa, fresh from the scene of these quarrels, with a definite view of his own, may have influenced Thomas IV away from making further gifts to local monastic houses.

Concerning the bequests of Thomas IV, Smyth reports as follows (2:19):

> I find not any one act of devotion which he performed to any monastery chantry or order of religion, nor ought else which was done for his wives soule after her death, as by all their ancestors had been accustomed for their predecessors, until I come to this lords will made the second of February in the year 1415. . . .

In this will Thomas leaves modest sums (usually forty shillings) to each of the churches in the neighborhood, and some vestments, a missal, two chalices, and a pair of cruets to the chapel in Berkeley Castle. Among his other bequests one would like to know more about the glossed psalter (now MS Bodley 953, for which see Hanna 1989), and "the legends of Saints in English" bequeathed to the sisters of Mary Magdalen hospital in Bristol, but otherwise we find mostly conventional gifts to the Cistercian abbey of Kingswood (near Wotton) and to the church of Portbury, including for the latter a copy of the psalter. Ten marks were designated for each of his household chaplains to pray for his soul. Thomas IV died 13 July 1417, fifteen years after the death of John Trevisa, and was buried beside his beloved wife, Margaret, in Wotton-under-Edge parish church, where their tomb may still be seen.

The Date of Trevisa's Institution

Having been introduced to the three lords that Trevisa may have known, we need now to come to grips with a most difficult question: the date of his institution as vicar of Berkeley. We are alerted to the danger of relying on Smyth, but do not as yet have an alternative estimate of the date of his appointment. For several years I thought that it may have come much later, perhaps as late as 1390 (Fowler 1971), but my conclusion was based on misinterpretation of an entry in what is known as the second volume of the register of Reginald Brian, bishop of Worcester in 1352–61. It seemed that there were later decrees bound in this volume that belonged to the time of Bishop Henry Wakefield (1375–95), and one of these, beginning with a salutation by "Henricus etc.," addresses a dispute between Master David, perpetual vicar of Berkeley, and Walter Oldland of that church over the mortuary fees of Richard Rivers. The dates of entries preceding and following suggested that this dispute belonged to perhaps the year 1389, making it unlikely that Trevisa could have been vicar before 1390, when, as we shall see, he is so identified in an order dated 5 November of that year. But it has been demonstrated clearly by Roy M. Haines (1975) that *Register Brian 2* is a precedent book prepared during the episcopate of Wakefield, based mainly on cases of much earlier date. My reaction to this discovery was divided: I was glad to know the truth of the matter, but regretted that the problem of Trevisa's institution as vicar was now back to square one.

The Master David referred to in the register is David of Melksham, and it seems best to begin our reappraisal of the situation with him, since, as far as we know, he was Trevisa's predecessor as vicar of Berkeley. David was ordained to the priesthood in 1349 and simultaneously installed as vicar of Berkeley owing to the death of the previous incumbent, Matthew, who was probably a victim of the plague. Berkeley church, it will be remembered, was appropriated to the canons of St. Augustine's Abbey, Bristol, and the abbey is listed as Master David's patron on this occasion. If the title of master means anything, David must have studied at least seven years at a university, but there is no record of his presence at either Oxford or Cambridge.

The family of Melksham had lived in Stinchcombe, less than four miles from Berkeley, since the time of Edward I, and seems to have been associated with the Berkeleys. In 1338, for example, John de Melkesham was witness to a grant by Thomas de Berkeley (CCR 1337–39, p. 522), and in 1342 his name is mentioned in a suit along with Peter de Veel, another neighbor of the Berkeleys (*Reg. Bransford* #1162). It would appear that David was a local favorite, and with the cooperation of the abbot and convent of St. Augustine, his institution as vicar in 1349 was noted by the bishop (*Reg. Bransford* #1381). In that year he is also listed along with William de Syde and others as licensed to hold the Berkeley estates, a legal device employed by Thomas III to protect his lands from expropriation (CPR 1348–50, pp. 225, 234).

With the aid of various records, we can trace the career of David of Melksham to a certain degree. On 20 November 1350 he was granted an indulgence by the pope to enjoy the fruits of his benefice for three years while studying at a university (CPR/L III, 368), though again there appears to be no record of his attendance at either university in England. In the authentic register of Bishop Brian (fol. 108d) he is mentioned as vicar of Berkeley in 1360, and then among the Berkeley muniments we find two grants, both dated 1364, by David perpetual vicar of Berkeley (Jeayes, unpublished catalogue in the castle, general series, nos. 3550, 3552).

The latest available information concerning the activities of David of Melkesham is contained in the decree already referred to treating the dispute between David and Walter Oldland. Thanks to the researches of Haines (1975), the original entry can be traced to the register of William de Whittlesey, bishop of Worcester from 1364 to 1368 (fol. 31v.). In this document, Willelmus greets his beloved sons in Christ Master Thomas Delany and Robert rector of the church of Uley (the latter probably Robert de Retforde, who resigned as rector of Uley on 29 March 1374: *Registrum Sede Vacante* 302), after which the text follows as in the exemplary copy in *Register Brian 2*. The position of this decree near the end of Whittlesey's register, surrounded by decrees mostly dated 1368, suggests that this entry, though undated, belongs to the final year of Whittlesey's episcopate. If this is accepted, we may then say that we have traced David's career as vicar of Berkeley to the year 1368.

Thereafter the trail of Master David becomes more difficult to follow. Just as we have no record of Trevisa's installation as vicar, so also we have no direct evidence of David's resignation or death. The fact that Trevisa's ordination as priest in 1370 was to the title of "the college of the Queen's Hall, Oxford" proves that he was still without a benefice, and suggests that his predecessor was still in office at that time; but this is merely an inference. The final bit of direct evidence concerning this elusive man shows up in the *Inquisitions Post Mortem*, volume 14 (1952), item 10, which records the death of Thomas son of Robert son of Thomas de Bradeston, writ of devenerunt, 20 May 48 Edward III (i.e., 1374), pages 7–12. Among the properties inventoried is Styndescomb (i.e., Stinchcombe), page 10, where in the list of tenants we find the name of "David de Melksham," and, under place names, "Mayster Davidysacre." At first glance it seemed to me that here was evidence that

David was alive as late as 1374, but through the kind assistance of Dr. R. F. Hunnisett, Public Record Office, I have learned that the original manuscript of the Bradeston IPM (as opposed to the published calendar cited above) "gives him as a *former* tenant, which certainly does not prove that he was alive at the time of the inquisition (1374), although equally it does not prove that he was not" (letter of 29 November 1982).

In reviewing the possibility that David of Melkesham may have moved from his home in Stinchcombe in 1374, we should consider his age, his reason for being there, and where he may have gone. If indeed he had incepted as a master before ordination, he may have been around twenty-eight years of age in 1349, which means that in 1374 he would have been perhaps fifty-three, having served twenty-five of those years as vicar of Berkeley, and having survived three onslaughts of the pestilence, which was especially severe in the west country and southeastern Wales in 1369 (Short 1749, p. 180; Shrewsbury 1970, p. 131). Since the Melkesham family had resided in Stinchcombe from the time of Edward I, I take it that David was living there, because this was his permanent home, less than four miles, as we have noted, from Berkeley church. There seems little doubt but that "mayster Davidysacre" was a parcel of the land on which the beautiful manor house known today as Melksham Court still stands (Overy and Tynsdale 1954), a site that would later be the home of a branch of the family of William Tyndale. As to where David may have moved in 1374, the records are silent. The only subsequent appearances of his name that I can find all refer back to the transaction of 1349, when he acted as one of the receivers of the lands of Thomas III (CPR 1348–50, p. 225).

In view of these considerations, I am inclined to believe that the identification of David in 1374 as a *former* tenant of Stinchcombe means that he was no longer living at the time of the inquisition. If the executors were using an existing rental list of the Bradestons, they may simply have inserted "former" opposite his name on hearing that he was dead. The death of Thomas occurred on 20 May, and it is possible that the vicar's death took place earlier that same year. But before making any more speculations along such lines, we need to approach this matter from the other end, and see how near this date we can come with evidence of Trevisa's possession of the title "vicar of Berkeley."

Having been denied the late date for Trevisa's appointment, as mentioned above, I recently followed the obliging suggestion of Dr. Alison

McHardy of Aberdeen University and began looking for some record of him in the clerical subsidy rolls of the Public Record Office in London. These tabulate payment by members of the clergy of taxes levied by Parliament. Not all of them list individuals by name, but I found one for the archdeaconry of Gloucester with first names provided (PRO E 179 58/5). This roll records the assessment of the clerical subsidy approved by Parliament in the spring of 1379, which was probably collected during the summer of that year. The complete list for the deanery of Dursley, in which Berkeley is situated, will be discussed further below; here I quote only the relevant entry for Berkeley church, using a number I have assigned each name in the list for easy reference:

> 30. Johannes vicarius de Berkeleye cuius beneficium est infra valentiam xx li. . . . . . . v s

One wishes that the assessors had taken the trouble to include last names, but at any rate this entry shows that Master David, at least, was at that time no longer vicar of Berkeley. We should allow for the possibility that some other "John" was vicar briefly between Melksham and Trevisa, but on the whole I am inclined to think, for reasons that will appear, that our evidence shows John Trevisa to have been vicar of Berkeley in 1379, eleven years earlier than previous knowledge would allow.

The consequence of a series of events, which I shall now review, leads me to the hypothesis that John Trevisa was instituted vicar of Berkeley probably in the spring or summer of 1374. I refer to the vacancy of the sees of Worcester and Canterbury, the coming of age of Thomas IV, the probable death of David of Melksham, Trevisa's absence from Oxford, and the declining fortunes of St. Augustine's Abbey, Bristol. No one of these circumstances is decisive, but taken together they strongly suggest that we have now surrounded and perhaps identified the year of Trevisa's institution.

The see of Worcester became vacant with the death of William de Lynn on 18 November 1373, and remained so until 28 October 1375, when Henry Wakefield took up his duties as bishop. Why the chair remained empty so long is not easily explained, but it could well be attributed to the death of the archbishop of Canterbury in June 1374, and the delay in appointing his successor, Simon Sudbury, then bishop of London (*Reg. Wakefield*, p. xxxvii). By virtue of the Boniface composition of 1268, the Worcester chapter of Black Monks had secured the right of automatic appointment of their prior to administer the affairs of the see during a vacancy (Haines 1965, pp. 268–73). This meant that on the death of Lynn, the prior of Worcester, who was Walter de Legh, was the acting bishop. A similar arrangement with the chapter of Canterbury existed in case of the death of an archbishop. This means that in our quest for a record of Trevisa's institution in the two-year period from November 1373 until the end of October 1375 there are at least three places to look: the *Registrum Sede Vacante* (WHS 1893–97) for the period covered by Walter de Legh from 18 November 1373 to 28 October 1375; the unpublished register of Archbishop William Whittlesey in Lambeth Palace Library, a portion of which contains Worcester *Sede Vacante* business from November 1373 until the archbishop's death in June of the following year (fol. 139r-v); and the *Calendar of Institutions by the Chapter of Canterbury Sede Vacante* (KAS/RB 8, 1924), covering exactly the year from 5 June 1374 to 5 June 1375. And since the register of the priory of Worcester itself (*Liber Albus*, the relevant portions of which are unpublished) sometimes contains *Sede Vacante* business (Haines 1965, pp. 274, 294, 314), it should also be considered a possible source of information.

There is unfortunately nothing on Trevisa's institution to Berkeley in any of the above records, even though Walter de Legh's section of the *Sede Vacante* register contains many ordinations and institutions. One might suppose that Trevisa simply was not instituted during this period, but there are other factors that we need to consider before drawing conclusions from the silence of these records. Hence, for the moment, we set this matter aside and turn to a review of the events of the year 1374 mentioned above.

There are four events of concern here to which a definite date in 1374 may be assigned. The first is the coming of age of Thomas IV on 5 January, at which time he received the power to act in his own right, or, more to the present purpose, he was now empowered to act as a patron, to present candidates to vacancies. The second event was the departure of John Trevisa from Oxford University. We saw in the preceding chapter that according to the Queen's College long rolls he was absent for the entire academic year 1374–75. A closer look shows that his expenses for the preceding year are entered for the period from the feast of St. Michael 1373 until the feast of the conception of the Virgin (Stainer, 2:210), which suggests that Trevisa could have left Oxford as early as December

1373. Then on 20 May comes the inquisition into the death of Thomas Bradeston, which we found to present evidence of the departure or death of David of Melksham. The final date, already mentioned, is the death of the archbishop of Canterbury on 5 June, which, it would seem, increased the obstacles to normal record-keeping already present by virtue of the death of the bishop of Worcester.

In light of the above, I offer the following hypothesis. David of Melksham died, sometime during the winter of 1373–74, perhaps near the time of Trevisa's arrival from Oxford. By previous arrangement, or by on-the-spot decision, it was agreed that he would be Thomas IV's choice as vicar of Berkeley to replace the late Master David of Melksham. As indicated earlier, I would suppose the appointment was made official during the latter half of 1374. Trevisa's absence from Oxford in 1374–75 would then be accounted for as the year during which he established himself as vicar, got acquainted with his parishioners, and made the necessary arrangements for a substitute to allow his return to the University. We saw that the long rolls for the next three years are missing, but we also noted that Trevisa's return to Oxford can be reasonably assumed, since he was involved in the disputed election of a provost of Queen's in 1376, and was expelled from the College in 1378. His whereabouts in the years 1378–83 are unknown, but we can be fairly confident that from 1383 through the academic year 1386–87 he was again in the College, these being presumably the four years for which he was charged rent in 1387.

No doubt there are flaws in the above hypothesis: first, it would seem more natural to assume that the silence of the records militates against this being the date we want; and second, since the abbey of St. Augustine's in Bristol was the patron of Berkeley church, the coming of age of lord Berkeley is surely irrelevant. It is my opinion, however, that these two points are related, and that a closer look at the status of St. Augustine's during this period may in itself provide an explanation for the silence of the records. To do this we must briefly review the relations between the Berkeleys and the abbey in the fourteenth century.

For the most part the canons of St. Augustine and the lords of the Berkeleys lived in harmony, with such minor flareups as we have noted between the abbey and Maurice I, when the latter encroached on the grounds of Berkeley church and was forced to grant compensation. Certainly in the time of Thomas III it is clear that relations were exceptionally good, and this lord was not at all neglectful of spiritual matters. The inner health of the abbey itself, however, is a matter less easily determined. In June 1340, Bishop Bransford conducted a visitation there, but the injunctions which he drew up for the abbot and convent after his visit (*Reg. Bransford* #116) are conventional, and it is difficult to say whether he found anything seriously deficient. The fact that Bransford himself was a monk perhaps did not enhance any tendency he may have had to be rigorous in his correction of abuses.

In any case, Thomas III continued, like his ancestors, to involve the canons in the founding of his chantries. Thus in the bishop's confirmation, dated 30 June 1345, of arrangements for the chantry in the chapel of St. James, Over, in Almondsbury parish, it is stipulated that if Thomas or his heirs fail to act within one month to fill a vacancy, the right of presentation is to pass to the abbot of St. Augustine's, and only if he fails to present within a month does the right pass to the bishop, or the prior during a vacancy (*Reg. Bransford* #735). Three years later the identical arrangement is made in the founding of a perpetual chantry in the abbey itself (*Reg. Bransford* #907).

Serious trouble in St. Augustine's Abbey seems to have developed following the election of Henry Shellingford, abbot from 1365 till his death in 1388. On 1 April 1366, Edward III placed the keeping of the abbey in the hands of Maurice IV and three other commissioners, essentially because of what we would call bankruptcy. The king described the abbey as being "depressed by corrodies [i.e., pensions] sold and conferred on persons suspected of ill-fame, and by profitless leases of its possessions, as also by the excessive and fruitless expenses of the presidents thereof, and by the reason of its being burdened with debt" (CPR 1364–67, p. 225). As we know, Maurice had never fully recovered from his wounding at Poitiers, and there is no evidence that he did anything about the abbey before his death in 1368.

It is unlikely that Thomas, during his minority, would have been assigned the task of reforming the canons, though because of his father's involvement it cannot have escaped his attention that the monastery was in trouble. The king's next effort to deal with the matter took the form of a commission on 14 September 1371 to seven men, including John Sergeant (founder of Stone chantry in Berkeley parish), to investigate the depleted condition of the abbey as previously described, to which is added the phrase "by misrule of Henry [Shellingford], now president thereof" (CPR 1370–74, pp. 177–78). The mandate concludes with the observation that the abbey was now so burdened with debts "that divine service there has ceased and alms and other pious works are withdrawn."

Perhaps because of the absence of a mature and experienced lord Berkeley to provide leadership, the king did not put his trust entirely in the seven-man commission, for in the following month he wrote to William de Lynn, bishop of Worcester, urging him to conduct a visitation of the Bristol house and institute necessary reforms (*Reg. Lynn*, fol. 51). Lynn died two years later, apparently without having done anything in response to the king's request. The first effective measures were taken by Walter de Legh, prior of Worcester, acting during the vacancy caused by the death of Lynn, as we have seen. Legh issued a series of injunctions in 1374 for the government of the monastery (*Reg. Sede Vacante*, pp. 318–20). The power of the abbot was limited, and a council or executive committee was formed for the transaction of business. Provision was made for improvement in the quality of bread and ale and an adequate supply of meat and fish. Maintenance of the secular clerks who sang in the Lady chapel was to be restored "as was accustomed of old time," so we may suppose that the priests of the Berkeley chantry, along with the others, now resumed the prescribed masses for the departed members of the family.

And thus we may conclude that the nadir of the abbey's fortunes was reached in the first fifteen years of the rule of Henry Shellingford, from 1365 till about 1380, when the reforms of Walter de Legh began to show results. My impression from a glance through the registers is that ordinations and institutions in the name of St. Augustine's dropped sharply in this period, and first show an upswing with the ordination of four acolytes and a deacon to title of the abbey on 26 March 1379 (*Reg. Wakefield* #876b, e). Institutions are similarly sparse, although William Noble (or perhaps Walter Noble, as in *Reg. Wakefield* #324) is presented by the abbot and convent to the vicarage of Almondsbury on 6 June 1374 (*Reg. Sede Vacante*, p. 307), in the midst of the reforms being undertaken by Walter de Legh, and at the very time that our hypothesis envisions the vacancy at Berkeley—a vacancy it was presumably the duty of St. Augustine's to fill. Not until the 1380s does the abbey reassume its right of presentation to any considerable extent. Ashleworth receives attention in 1383, 1390, and 1391 (*Reg. Wakefield* #252, 540, 642),

Almondsbury in 1385 (#324), St. Nicholas, Bristol, in 1387 and 1389 (#397, 470), and St. Leonard, Bristol, in 1393 (#749).

The next crisis for the monastery came with the death of Abbot Shellingford and the need to elect a new president. The temporalities of St. Augustine's had now been technically in the hands of the king for over twenty years (e.g., CPR 1385–89, p. 219), even though the formulas employed by Wakefield in the above institutions did not always acknowledge this. No doubt the canons hoped that a decisive election might bring them their freedom. Four years earlier, in October 1384, they had been subjected to another visitation, this one by no less a person than William Courtenay, archbishop of Canterbury, less than two years after his triumph at Oxford in November 1382. The reforms introduced by Courtenay as a consequence of his visitation of St. Augustine's in Bristol are recounted by J. H. Dahmus (1950, pp. 37–38). In particular the archbishop established rules governing the administration of finances. When it was later reported that these rules had not been followed, he suspended the treasurer, and ordered him to devote the rest of his life to the divine services of cloister and church.

The leading candidate to replace Shellingford seems to have been William Lane, and, in a letter of 2 December 1388, Archbishop Courtenay commends him to the attention of the canons (*Reg. Wakefield* #796). Bishop Wakefield, however, makes no mention of Lane in his letter, urging the canons only to choose someone that he can approve (#797). The outcome of all this was that the archbishop's nominee was ignored, and John Cernay was elected. What the archbishop evidently did not know, but Wakefield did, was that William Lane had been indicted for ravishing one Iseult, wife of Thomas Irysch, on 16 December 1386 at Stoke Gifford near Bristol, taking away goods and chattels to the value of twenty shillings. Lane received a pardon for this from the king on 7 January 1389 (CPR 1385–89, p. 537), but this seems to have come too late to sway the electorate in his favor.

It is difficult to say whether this incident can be understood as evidence of the continuing laxity of the canons of St. Augustine, or as the aberration of a single individual. The latter alternative seems to me the more likely explanation. Evidently Courtenay's high opinion of Lane's administrative ability was well founded, and, though the order could not bring itself to elect him the next abbot, it did later (in 1392) acquiesce in his appointment as master of the Augustinian house of St. Mark,

Belleswick, Bristol (*Reg. Wakefield*). Declining to exercise their right of election, the canons of St. Mark's allowed the bishop to make the appointment. It seems hard to fault the manner in which this crisis was handled.

The new abbot, John Cernay (1388–93), had only five years to start things on an upward path, but he seems to have done one thing that is of particular relevance to our interests: he elicited from Courtenay— apparently following up on a promise made by the archbishop during his visitation of 1384—letters of dimission dated 6 February 1393, upon proof of the right of St. Augustine's Abbey to the income of churches that had been appropriated to them from time immemorial, including, of course, the parish church of Berkeley. Six years later, in May 1399, Abbot Daubeney obtained from Boniface IX the following affirmation of their right (CPR/L V, 191):

> To the abbot and convent of St. Augustine's, Bristol. Appropriation *motu proprio* of the perpetual vicarage, value not exceeding 43 marks, of the parish church, long held to their uses, of Berkeley, that of the monastery not exceeding 800. Upon the resignation or death of the vicar they may have the vicarage served by one of their canons regular or by a secular priest, appointed and removed at the pleasure of the abbot.

Confirmation of this and other appropriations is contained in a subsequent mandate from the same pope in February 1401 (CPR/L V, 360–61), adding that the abbey need not in future exhibit any other proof of their right than the archbishop's letters. A satiric reference to "princes letteres" occurs in *Piers the Plowman* C X 281 (Skeat) at the end of a long passage which may be a criticism of the policies and practices of Archbishop Courtenay. (See my commentary on Pearsall's edition of the C text in *Review* 2 [1980]: 248–49, under IX.255–81.)

The pope's language is very generous indeed, allowing the canons to present and remove at will, against the hard-won principle of perpetual vicars established by the reform bishops of the thirteenth century. But this may only be an inflation of language consequent on the competition for support between the two claimants to the chair of Peter since the schism in 1378; and the intention of St. Augustine's seems to have been merely to recover the churches that had been theirs for so many years. But why did they feel it necessary to make this claim, particularly in the case of Berkeley, which is singled out in the pope's communication of

May 1399? Obviously, Berkeley is precisely an illustration of their concern, if the presentation of John Trevisa to that church was accomplished without their consent.

We have seen that for the institution of David of Melksham as vicar of Berkeley (*Reg. Bransford* #1381), St. Augustine's Abbey is listed as the patron. If we look ahead now to the ordination of John Bonjon, Trevisa's successor in 1402, we find that once again the candidate for vicar of Berkeley is presented by the abbot and convent of St. Augustine, Bristol (*Reg. Clifford*, fol. 14d–15a). Hence it seems likely that the efforts of the canons to obtain papal support for their traditional right of presentation may be attributed at least in part to their frustration precisely over cases such as the appointment of Trevisa.

Our hypothesis may then be recapitulated as follows. On the death of David of Melksham in 1373–74, the coming of age of Thomas IV, and the return of Trevisa from Oxford in the spring of 1374, Lord Berkeley assumed the role of patron and acted to fill the vacancy in his parish church, sometime just before or after his expedition to France in that year. He probably did this at a time when the sees of both Worcester and Canterbury were vacant, and perhaps more than normally amenable to unorthodox procedures. Distracted as they were by eight years of scandal and seizure, the canons of St. Augustine's either did not know of or were in no position to object to the action of Lord Berkeley at the time. It is even possible that no paperwork was attempted (hence the silence of the records), and that when Bishop Wakefield took over the see of Worcester in late October 1375, he was faced with a fait accompli. If all this is anywhere near the truth, then we can conclude that the finesse of young Thomas IV in this instance may have been only the first sign of an ability that was to enable him later to steer safely through perilous waters during the crisis that reached its climax in the deposition of Richard II.

The Deanery of Dursley

The diocese of Worcester in the Middle Ages consisted of two large subdivisions: the archdeaconries of Worcester and Gloucester, extending from Kidderminster in the north to Bristol in the south. The archdeaconry of Gloucester coincided more or less with the modern county, and in the area south of the town of Gloucester, with which we are concerned, it consisted of the deaneries of Gloucester, Stonehouse,

Dursley, Hawkesbury and Bitton, and Bristol. Our attention focuses particularly on Dursley, in which the parish of Berkeley is located, and we may utilize the clerical subsidy list for this deanery, already referred to, as a means of becoming acquainted with Trevisa's parish in its ecclesiastical setting.

According to the subsidy roll for the deanery of Dursley (PRO E 179 58/5 mm. 2–3), in the summer of 1379 there were sixty-three clergymen in that jurisdiction ranging from rectors or vicars of parish churches to the lowliest clerk. Generally speaking this seems to be a complete and accurate list. The omission of the church of Uley and the chapel of Owlpen could be an indication that these were temporarily vacant, and the Cistercian house of Kingswood near Wotton was either exempt or perhaps counted with the adjoining deanery of Hawkesbury and Bitton. The number of "parishes" in the modern sense is not easily determined, since *parochia* is employed to designate such communities as Nibley and Stinchcombe, which were actually served by chapels of ease. But if those places for which valuation is given are considered parish churches, then the number of parishes in the deanery would appear to be fourteen (counting Uley).

The largest of the parishes is of course Berkeley, employing fifteen clerics, with a taxation of £1 9s. 8d. These include the vicar, four chaplains and two clerks attached to the parish church, the prior of Longbridge hospital and his companion, and chaplains for the chantries of Newport, Stone (two), Hill, and Breadstone (two). Ranking nearly as high is Wotton-under-Edge, with eleven clerics and a taxation of £1 8s. 4d. The church itself has a rector, five chaplains, and three clerks, and chaplains for the chantry of Wortley and the chapel at Nibley. The remaining parishes are much smaller, at least in wealth and appointments. Thornbury has a vicar, four chaplains, a clerk, with a chaplain for Oldbury (15s. 4d.); Cam a vicar, two chaplains, and three clerks, if we count Stinchcombe with Cam (7s. 0d.); Slimbridge a rector (I assume), a chaplain and two clerks, plus a chaplain at Elmcote near Cambridge (14s. 8d.); Rockhampton a rector and chaplain, plus a chaplain and clerk for Shepperdine (6s. 4d.); Beverston has a rector and clerk, as well as a chaplain for Kingscote (7s. 4d.); Dursley has a rector, clerk, and chaplain (4s. 4d.); Frampton on Severn has a vicar, chaplain, and clerk (4s. 4d.); and Howley, something of a surprise, has a rector and one chaplain (4s. 0d.). The remaining four parishes have single appointments representing taxation of two shillings each: Newington Bagpath, Lasborough, Coaley, and Ozleworth.

The valuation of these parishes ranges from (less than) ten, twenty, or forty pounds and, in one case, a hundred marks. The highest evaluation is assigned to Wotton (under a hundred marks), the next highest to Slimbridge (under forty pounds), while thereafter Berkeley, Beverston, and Thornbury are rated at under twenty pounds, and the remaining parishes at under ten. At first glance this does not seem to square with what we know of the size and wealth of these parishes: Slimbridge, for example, seems to be rated higher than Berkeley, and Wotton much higher than both. But such a flat comparison fails to take into account the appropriation of some of these churches by other ecclesiastical bodies.

A glance through the episcopal registers suggests that perhaps nine of the fourteen parish churches of the deanery of Dursley were appropriated to monastic houses in our period. The abbot and convent of St. Peter's, Gloucester, held the churches of Cam, Beverston, Dursley, Newington Bagpath, Ozleworth, and Uley, the largest number associated with a single community. Thornbury was appropriated to Tewkesbury Abbey, Coaley to Pershore in Worcester archdeaconry, Frampton to the alien priory of Clifford in Hereford diocese, and Berkeley, as we have seen, to the abbey of St. Augustine's in Bristol. Three parish churches somehow remained in the hands of the Berkeley family, namely Wotton, Slimbridge, and Rockhampton; this is why the valuation of these is so much higher than we might have expected. It is remarkable that a parish so rich as Wotton had escaped appropriation for so long; and indeed during our period there seems to have been a sort of tug-of-war between Thomas IV and the king for the right of presentation there (*Reg. Wakefield* #414), following the death of Katherine, widow of Thomas III, in 1386. For more on this dispute see Hanna (1989, pp. 888–89 and n. 25).

Since the Dursley assessors listed only the first names, it is difficult to identify individuals, but I find by consulting Wakefield's register that perhaps half of the fourteen parish rectors or vicars can be identified. William Todye (alias Gody) seems to have been vicar of Cam from 1378 to 1385 (#68, 301); John Austyn was vicar of Coaley until 1383 (#248); on the assumption that "Johannes" is our man, we may say that Trevisa was vicar of Berkeley, 1374 to 1402; John Brampton was vicar of Thornbury until his death in 1390 (#516); John Ingryth (alias de Burton) was rector of Rockhampton from 17 April 1379 until 2 July

1382 (#129, 197); Thomas Hockeleye was instituted vicar of Frampton on Severn 27 May 1378; and, if Uley was not vacant at this time, it is possible that its rector was Richard Doynton (alias Bruton) from 23 April 1376 to 13 December 1379.

Some of the lesser clergy also may be identified. The chaplain of the chantry of Wortley in Wotton was Adam Dongurdile, who remained there until 1388 (#460). Three and perhaps even four appointees in Berkeley parish can be traced. The prior of Longbridge hospital was Robert Edmundes until 1387; one of the chaplains in the chantry of Breadstone was John Herebard, instituted in October 1378 (#62); William Harreis was chaplain of Stone chantry from July 1366 (Berkeley muniments, S. R. 138) until April 1388 (*Reg. Wakefield* #439); and it is possible that one of the chaplains in Berkeley church was Walter Oldland, ordained to the first tonsure about 1339, and involved in a dispute with David de Melksham, as we have seen, in 1368 (*Reg. Whittlesey*, fol. 31v). These, then, were some of the local clergy that Trevisa may have known at this time.

Canon of Westbury

Information about Trevisa's official life in Gloucestershire is largely limited to legal documents reflecting controversies that arose during his tenure as vicar of Berkeley. One such controversy involves Trevisa in a clash with Robert Wattes, dean of the collegiate church of Westbury-on-Trym (near Bristol), and with Thomas Cone, a prebendary of that same church. The dispute left a paper trail of at least three documents, one of them discovered many years ago by Wilkins (1915, pp. 79–82), and the other two found more recently by Nigel Saul (1981, p. 166, n. 288, and p. 176, n. 32). Viewed chronologically, the first is a petition by Wattes, the second a petition by Cone (both of these in Norman French), and the third a record in Latin of a hearing before the King's Bench, containing the only statement giving Trevisa's side of the story. Since the originals have never been published, I include all three in Appendix I.

We do not know what precipitated this quarrel, but it seems likely that Robert Wattes in some fashion impeded Trevisa's installation as a canon of Westbury. This appointment may have been intended by his patron as an added source of income that would provide Trevisa with the free time he needed as chaplain to Thomas IV. We have already seen that the

Berkeley appointment was not that of rector (as at Wotton-under-Edge) but vicar, with the bulk of the income going to St. Augustine's Abbey in Bristol, and that Trevisa's budget was already strained by demands such as the provision of a priest for the chapel at Stone in Berkeley parish. Hence it must have been exasperating to Trevisa to discover that the dean of Westbury was seeking to award the prebend of Woodford to his own candidate, Thomas Cone, thus denying Trevisa the income he was counting on to support himself in the carrying out of his duties as vicar and as chaplain to Lord Berkeley.

The collegiate church of Westbury-on-Trym drew income from various Gloucestershire lands granted over the years by local families. Each of the several canons associated with the church drew subsistence from one of these properties, which were known as prebends, and were situated as close by as Henbury (one mile northwest of the church), or at some distance, as in the case of the prebend of Aust (which John Wyclif had held some years earlier), about seven miles to the north, on the Severn estuary. The dispute between Trevisa and the dean, however, was over the prebend of Woodford, located on the main road at least fourteen miles to the northeast of Westbury, or about halfway between Gloucester and Bristol. Moreover, Woodford stands within half a mile of the chapel of Stone, and less than two miles (as the crow flies) from Berkeley Castle. It seems plausible to suppose that this parcel of land was a gift to Westbury from the Berkeley family.

In his petition (SC 8/148/7355), Robert Wattes, dean of Westbury, complains that John Poleyne, squire of Thomas Berkeley, came before dawn to Westbury on the feast of Holy Trinity in the eleventh year of Richard II (25 May 1388) with a great number of armed men assembled in manner of war. They broke down the doors and entered by force into the dean's chamber, took him from his bed, and dragged him from his house into the street, where they assaulted, beat, wounded, and maltreated him until he was in despair of his life. Then they imprisoned him and threatened to kill him, until he promised to make a fine with the squire and surrender all his goods, in order (as he believed) to save his life.

Almost nine months later, according to the dean (in the same petition), when he himself was apparently absent, John Poleyne brought another armed band to Westbury on Monday, 12 February 1389, with the intention of killing the dean. When they were unable to find him, they turned their attention to his servants, whom they assaulted, wounded, and maltreated, carrying with them when they left goods and chattels to the value of forty pounds, and apparently commiting vandalism to the amount of one hundred pounds; for all of which he prays for remedy from the king, "because the said suppliant cannot have justice nor recover against them by the common law because the said John Poleyne is so great a maintainer of quarrels and so much encouraged by the great lords in the aforesaid country." In connection with this second attack, the dean mentions specific individuals (in addition to Poleyne): John Trevisa, John Breton, Richard Curteys, and John Smyth of Westbury are all said to have participated in the attack of 12 February. In the register of Bishop Wakefield there is no mention of John Breton, but Curteys is listed as acolyte on 23 September 1382 (910a) and Smyth as priest to the title of Longbridge hospital (in Berkeley parish) on 2 March 1387 (913a).

The second petition (SC 8/84/4193) is submitted by Thomas Cone, who identifies himself as "prebendary of the prebend of Woodford in the collegiate church of Westbury." He describes an attack on Westbury by Trevisa and Poleyne, along with three hundred armed men, which would appear to correspond to the second one mentioned by Wattes, except that Wattes gave the date as 12 February, while Cone's petition gives the date as 16 February. Both petitions are written in a way that suggests their authors were not present at the time of this second attack, perhaps accounting for the discrepancy as to the date. But whereas Wattes merely mentions injuries to certain unnamed "servants," Cone not only speaks of the beating and wounding of a pair of the vicar's servants (Walter and Thomas), but he also identifies the vicar and two of his men by full name: Robert Banak (Cone's vicar), William Colerne, and John Rothewell. These three, complains Cone, were seized and taken as far as Berkeley Castle (where they were imprisoned overnight), and from there removed to Gloucester, where they were held for at least ten more days until finally freed by brief of the king. Because the wounding of Walter, the servant in the sanctuary, drew blood, the church was closed and divine services ceased.

According to Cone, something else happened that day (16 February): the same hostile force that had broken into Westbury marched north to Woodford and occupied the grounds (corpse) of the prebend, refusing to leave unless ordered to do so by their leader, John Poleyne. Cone concludes by asking the king for damages of five hundred pounds, since he "cannot have justice nor recovery through common law from the said John Trevisa and John Poleyne his maintainer in the said quarrel, because the said John Poleyne is so charged with great lordship and alliance and a common maintainer of quarrels in the above-mentioned land." The third document is in Latin (KB 27/512/Rex m. 17) and is the record of a hearing before the king in Westminster on the first Sabbath after the paschal month (2 May 1389). It is also the only document I have been able to find that tells the other side of the story. This version seems to have been presented originally before Thomas of Berkeley and his associates in county court. It is alleged there that the chaplain, Robert Taillour, along with William Colerne, John Rothewell, and various other persons unknown, did forcibly enter the collegiate church of Westbury, on 23 February 1389, and occupied "the dwelling place of Master John Trevisa, canon of the said church and prebendary of the prebend of Woodford in the same church for a day and a night." Moreover they insulted John Boteller, Trevisa's servant, making remarks about who really had a right to the income of the prebend, and terrorized the people of the neighborhood. It was further alleged that this occupation was instigated by Robert Wattes, dean of Westbury, who supplied the occupants with arms and weapons to the value of five marks, and later recovered and held them in his possession when he petitioned the king. A hearing was scheduled at Westminster before the king on 2 May so that Taillour, Colerne, and Rothewell could tell their side of the story, but at this point the account breaks off abruptly with no response from the defendants.

There is ambiguity in the documents as to where and when these events took place, and precisely who was involved in the conflict. Cone's petition mentions his vicar, Robert Banak, and William Colerne and John Rothewell, who were all apparently removed from the church at Westbury, taken to Berkeley Castle, and then imprisoned at Gloucester, before finally being released. Of the three men mentioned in the Latin document, two are the same (Colerne and Rothewell), but the first man is identified as the chaplain Robert Taillour (instead of the vicar Robert Banak). It is tempting to conclude, given the common first name Robert, that this is merely a clerical error, but we can't be sure. The time discrepancy is odd (February 12, 16, or 23?), unless several attacks were involved. But if Cone's three men were imprisoned for at least eleven days following their capture on 16 February, they could not have done what the Latin text says they did on 23 February. It is perhaps simpler to assume a single series of events taking place on or around the 12th, the 16th, or the 23rd.

Leaving aside the dates, it would appear that the quarrel may have begun with the dean's decision to back Cone and oppose Trevisa's appointment as prebendary of Woodford. This then provoked John Poleyne's attack on 25 May 1388, directed against the dean himself. When the dean proved powerless against the forces of Poleyne, the next move was made by the backers of Thomas Cone in February 1389, when they occupied Trevisa's stall in Westbury for a day and a night, only to be forcibly removed soon after by the large force assembled by Poleyne, who not only took the vicar and his two supporters prisoner but sent an armed band to occupy the grounds of the prebend in Woodford, the source of the prebendary's income located within two miles of Berkeley Castle. This strategy might be faulted as a case of overkill, but it seems to have brought the conflict to a decisive end. In the following year (1390) Robert Wattes gave up his position as dean of Westbury in an exchange with John Menhyr (*Reg. Wakefield* 531) and became rector of Stalbridge in Salisbury diocese.

Nigel Saul (1981) points up the difficulties confronting local law enforcement in these cases: "The Commons understood the helplessness of the sheriff in the face of such violence; for well placed though he was to prey on the weak, he lacked the means to confront the powerful" (p. 166). But what about the king? Should he not back his sheriff? But in fact Richard II knew that Thomas Berkeley represented an important part of the national defense forces in the west country, and that he was (at least to this time) a loyal defender of the king's prerogatives. Hence we see signs that the king chose not even to prosecute the small fry caught in the sheriff's net, as in this order dated 23 March 1389 (one month after the Westbury attack) for the release from prison of John Dyer (CCR 1385–89, p. 665):

> To the sheriff of Gloucester . . . order in favour of John Dyer chaplain, by mainprise of Master Henry Hedlam and John Trevisa clerks, reciting an order to the sheriff to make like proclamation in Wodeforde, Westbury and elsewhere in his bailiwick.

And what about Trevisa's title to the prebend of Woodford? Evidence that Trevisa made good his claim survives in a document in which he arranges for a trip overseas by granting power of attorney to two of his associates in Treaty Roll 75, Public Record Office (14 Richard II, m. 10):

> Master John Trevysa, vicar of the church of Berkeley and canon of the collegiate church of Westbury (who by the king's leave is about to depart to the parts beyond the sea, has the king's letters of general attorney) under the names of Master Robert de Hodersale, clerk, and Master William de Faryngdon, clerk. Witness the king at Westminster the 5th day of November (1390).

Here we have at last full (and royal) recognition of Trevisa's status as vicar of Berkeley and canon of Westbury. We may also see that near the end of the year 1390 he planned to leave on a voyage overseas.

Vicar of Berkeley

Perpetual vicars were required to take an oath of continuous residency, but this did not prevent them from being absent from time to time, and Wakefield's register contains examples of licences granted for the absence of rectors and vicars for various reasons. No such licence is recorded for Trevisa, although we know that he did return to Oxford for a number of years in the seventies and eighties, and later for a two-year period in 1394–96. On the basis of such evidence as we have, I would judge that his times of residency in Berkeley were probably during the years 1374–75, 1387–94, and 1396–1402. Even these may not have been continuous periods. We have seen that he made preparations for travel overseas in 1390, and there may have been other journeys for which there is no such record; he may, for example, have accompanied Lord Berkeley in his travels in 1392 following the death of Margaret. We know that he was in Berkeley on 6 February 1398/9, because the fact is reported in the colophon to his translation of Bartholomew's *De Proprietatibus Rerum*. The only other firm date is 21 May 1402, when his death is reported in connection with the institution of John Bonjon as the next vicar.

A long-forgotten document involving Trevisa was discovered in 1960 by Canon J. H. W. Fisher, then vicar of Berkeley, among the records of Stone chapel near Berkeley. It is an English translation, made at the beginning of the eighteenth century, of an episcopal decree by Henry Wakefield which does not appear in the bishop's register. I am indebted to Canon Fisher for this discovery, and to Mr. Irvine E. Gray of the Gloucester Records Office for providing me with a transcription. Mr. Gray says, in a letter to Canon Fisher of 8 December 1960, "The translation has every appearance of being genuine, and from the writing must have been made about 1700." This date suggests that the transcriber may have been Dr. Richard Parsons, whose *Parochial Visitations of the County of Gloucester* (Bodleian MS Rawlinson B 323) was compiled at about that time. In any case we are fortunate to have this translation, since the Latin original seems to have vanished. The text was published some years ago (Fowler 1962, pp. 308–11).

Since the document is extremely verbose, I shall give here only the essentials of its contents, relying considerably on the kind assistance of Dr. Roy M. Haines, in his letter of 26 December 1969. The text records the efforts of Bishop Wakefield to enforce the settlement of a suit brought by the parishioners of Stone in Berkeley against John Trevisa for failing to provide a chaplain for the chapel of Stone. The plaintiffs are John Sergeant, John Guiliane, Stephen Hikedon, William Chapman, and the inhabitants of the village of Stone. Their argument is that previous vicars of Berkeley have always, within living memory, provided for a chaplain there, as well as a house for him to live in, and they offer to produce witnesses to testify that Trevisa himself had in the past acknowledged his obligation to do so. But since the bringing of this suit (they say) he has refused to act, even after repeated requests. Apart from tradition, they argue that this arrangement is necessitated by the distance of the village from the parish church, so that they are unable because of "the often overflowing of waters . . . without danger of their bodies to goe to the said church of Berkeley in fitt time."

The suit was heard in the consistory court, with the bishop's commissary Robert Crosse presiding in this instance (apparently *not* the bishop's official). Crosse is mentioned only once in Wakefield's register, as witness at an institution in Tewkesbury Abbey (#58). The proctor for the plaintiffs was John Wenden, one of Wakefield's notaries (#298, 851). Trevisa's proctor at the original trial was Richard Glym, and at the hearing later held by the bishop himself his proctor was John the Clerk of Wydryndon. Robert Crosse seems to have handed down a definitive sentence in favor of the plaintiffs, and Trevisa was then cited by the dean of Dursley, but he seems to have taken no action, either to appeal the sentence to a higher court (Canterbury or Rome) or to submit and provide the chaplain. John Sergeant and his colleagues then appealed directly to the bishop, asking him to do something about Trevisa's refusal. In response, Wakefield summoned both parties to appear before him, and this is the hearing that produced the document we are now examining.

The plaintiffs seem to have come before the bishop in person, whereas Trevisa was represented by his proctor, John the Clerk. Wakefield began by reviewing the substance of the case, summarizing the sentence handed down in consistory court, and introducing into the record the certificate of citation of Trevisa by the dean of Dursley. He then explains that this hearing has been called at the request of the plaintiffs, who have asked him to confirm, if he will, the sentence handed down against Trevisa; but he also points out that Trevisa has been summoned as well, so that he can defend himself if he will. Unfortunately, the document concludes with an extended recapitulation of the original charges, and we have no hint of any response by Trevisa, no interrogatories, and no definitive sentence by the bishop himself.

The text has no date, which means that the outer limits must be the period of Wakefield's episcopate, 1375 to 1395. There is some evidence that it may be later rather than earlier in this period. The plaintiffs seem to feel that their suit may have stiffened Trevisa's resistance, and they say so in these words: " . . . Mr. John the viccar did voluntarily acknowledge the same in his time until the time of the plaintiffs suit or contradiction," and they go on to assert that in the past he had acknowledged his obligation to the chapel. This suggests that Trevisa has been vicar for a substantial interval.

The clerical subsidy list already examined records the presence of two chaplains in Stone, William Harreis being the appointee of John Sergeant for the chantry which he founded in 1356, the other William presumably having been appointed to the chaplaincy which is at issue in the Stone document. Unfortunately, we have no means of identifying this William, and no record of the date of his resignation or death. The possibility exists that the vacancy occurred during one of Trevisa's absences, and that the consequent delay in provision of another chaplain led the people of Stone out of exasperation to bring suit as a way of forcing Trevisa to pay attention to the matter. If this be the case, the vacancy may have occurred during the time that Trevisa was translating the *Polychronicon* (1385–87), the suit perhaps being brought against him in 1387. But this can be little more than a guess. For more information on the responsibilities of Berkeley's vicar, provided by an entry in the register of Philip Morgan, bishop of Worcester in 1423 (pp. 178–80), see Hanna (1989, p. 893, n. 37).

The passage of time has left us little means of reconstructing Trevisa's life as vicar of Berkeley. But there is one memorable event that took place there which should not be overlooked, even though his name is not connected with it. Trevisa completed his translation of *De Proprietatibus Rerum* on 6 February 1398/9 at Berkeley, which suggests that he was probably still in residence during the summer of 1399, the year of the deposition of Richard II. In July the fall of Richard was imminent, and the country up in arms, encouraged by the return of Henry Bolingbroke from exile. Many chroniclers record these exciting developments, but only one tells of the momentous meeting in Berkeley church which may have decided Richard's fate. The account is preserved in the *Historia Vitae et Regni Ricardi II* (edited by Thomas Hearne, 1729, and by George B. Stow, Jr., 1977), attributed to the Monk of Evesham, and translated in the sixteenth century by Holinshed in his *Chronicles* (ed. Ellis, 1807–8). We pick up the narrative after Henry duke of Lancaster had landed, and is on his way south toward Bristol, gathering supporters on the way (Holinshed, 2:853):

> From Doncaster having now got a mighty armie about him, he marched foorth with all speed through the countries, coming by Evesham vnto Berkelie: within the space of three daies, all the kings castels in those parts were surrendred vnto him [omitting the monk of Evesham's remark: *Et hoc mirabile in oculis nostris*].
>
> The duke of Yorke, whome king Richard had left as governour of the realme in his absence, hearing that his nephue the duke of Lancaster was thus arrived, and had gathered an armie, he also assembled a puissant power of men and of armes and archers (as before ye have heard) but all was in vaine, for there was not a man that willinglie would thrust out one arrow against the duke of Lancaster, or his partakers, or in anie wise offend him or his friends. The duke of Yorke therefore passing foorth towards Wales to meet the king, at his comming foorth of Ireland, was received into the castle of Berkelie, and there remained, till the coming thither of the duke of Lancaster (whom when he perceived that he was not able to resist) on the sundaie [27 July 1399], after the feast of saint Iames, which as that yeare came about, fell vpon the fridaie, he came foorth into the church that stood without the castell, and there communed with the duke of Lancaster. With the duke of

Yorke were the bishops of Norwich, the lord Berkelie, the lord Seimour, and
other; with the duke of Lancaster were these, Thomas Arundall archbishop
of Canturburie that had been banished, the abbot of Leicester, the earles of
Northumberland and Westmerland, Thomas Arundell sonne to Richard late
earl of Arundell, the baron of Greistoke, the lords Willoughbie and Ros, with
diverse other lords knights, and other people, which dailie came to him from
everie part of the realme: those that came not, were spoiled of all they had,
so as they were never able to recover themselves againe, for their goods being
then taken awaie, were never restored. And thus what for love, and what for
feare of losse, they came flocking vnto him from everie part.

Probably never before or since did Berkeley church shelter so many peers
of the realm at one time. Trevisa then, at age fifty-seven, was nearing
the end of his life. We can only regret that he did not leave us his views
on the significance of this meeting.

Besides being vicar of Berkeley, Trevisa was, to use his own words
from the epistle prefixed to the *Polychronicon*, the "priest and beadsman"
of Lord Berkeley. To what extent was his time divided between his
duties as parish priest and his responsibilities as chaplain to the Berkeley
family? Apart from the known translations dedicated to Thomas IV, we
have very little on which to base our conclusions. The possibility that
he may have been a tutor to Thomas at one time has been mentioned,
but this is nothing more than speculation. There is, however, one bit of
evidence that should be mentioned as this chapter concludes, and that
is the possibility that Trevisa was responsible for the inscriptions in the
private chapel used by the family in Berkeley Castle.

There are in fact two chapels in the castle, one dedicated to St. John
the Baptist in the keep, and the other dedicated to St. Mary the Virgin
occupying the southeast angle of the great court. It is this latter chapel,
known today as the morning room, which contains the inscriptions
referred to by Trevisa in the dialogue on translation prefixed to the
English *Polychronicon*. Here Trevisa defends the need for translation by
having the lord cite precedents such as King Alfred's translation of the
psalter, Caedmon's famous poetic renderings of scripture, and Venerable
Bede's translation of the gospel of St. John. We shall have occasion to
refer to this passage again in another connection; it is of interest here
because of one further example mentioned by the lord:

> Also thou wost whare the Apocalips is ywrite in the walles and roof of a
> chapel, bothe in Latyn and in Frensche.

Over one hundred years ago, J. H. Cooke (1876) examined this chapel and reported in part as follows:

> The roof is nearly flat and covered with lead. It is supported by heavy tile beams, the spaces between which are divided by the purlius and ridgepieces into nearly square panels. On the flat part of the sides of all roof-timbers the inscriptions may be traced. The writing, of which there are generally one or two, but sometimes three or four lines on each beam, is in black on a white ground, the initials in red; the lettering is of the kind most in use in the 14th and 15th centuries. The beams and timbers seem to have been originally painted white, the spandrels being picked out with red, but the whole has been at some subsequent period painted over black and white. Five centuries gradual decay and the scarcely distinctive process of ignorant or careless repair have, however, left the inscriptions legible in very few places.

With his essay Cooke includes tracings of these few remaining inscriptions, the most legible of which is a phrase from Revelation 8:13 in Norman French: "un egle volant" (Vulgate: *unius aquilae volantis*).

When I first viewed these inscriptions in the morning room of Berkeley Castle in 1959, I was ready to believe that they were the work of Trevisa, or at least put there under his guidance. But dating these verses is for all practical purposes impossible. Obviously they existed at the time Trevisa composed his *Dialogue* (1385–87), but how long before that had they been inscribed? Surely it must have been at a time when French was still the preferred language of the English aristocracy, and it is not likely that this preference lasted much beyond the lifetime of Thomas III (1326–61). Trevisa himself points out the shift from French to English in the grammar schools of England at the time of the first occurrence of the plague (1349), in one of his most famous notes to the *Polychronicon* translation (Rolls Series edition, II, 159–61), concluding "also gentlemen have now [in 1385] much left off teaching their children French." Therefore, it seems likely that one of Trevisa's predecessors, perhaps David of Melksham (vicar, 1349–ca. 1374), was responsible for the inscribing of the French biblical verses in the Berkeley family chapel.

4

TRANSLATIONS

A proper study of Trevisa as transla-
tor requires more space than is available in the present volume. Here we
must be content with defining the canon of his translations, establishing
their chronology insofar as that is possible, and placing them in the
context of Trevisa's life in Oxford and Berkeley. This will be followed
by an introductory discussion of each of the translations, including the
nature of the work itself and examples of Trevisa's translation of it.
The major translations (*Polychronicon*, *De Regimine Principum*, and *De
Proprietatibus Rerum*) will receive comparatively brief treatment, since to
give them the attention they deserve would require a separate volume.
To some extent the chronology adopted here is hypothetical, but taken
together the evidence suggests a translator who began at Oxford in the
midst of controversy with a strong polemic intention, but who ended
his career at Berkeley translating orthodox texts in the pursuit of high
educational objectives.

The Trevisa Canon

The fullest and most reliable discussion of the Trevisa canon is to
be found in Perry's *Introduction* (1925). As a consequence of his investigations, we may accept as genuine the following translations: *Gospel
of Nicodemus*, *Dialogus inter Militem et Clericum*, Archbishop FitzRalph's
Defensio Curatorum, *Polychronicon* (with its prefatory *Dialogue* and *Epistle*
by Trevisa), *De Regimine Principum*, and *De Proprietatibus Rerum*. Perry
rejects two translations that have been ascribed to Trevisa at one time
or another. One of these is the *De Re Militari* of Vegetius, which H. E.
Childs (1932) took to be the work of John Walton, on the basis of
a rebus in the colophon. More recently, Hanna (1989, pp. 900–901)
makes a case for the interpretation of the rebus as referring to William
Clifton, master of the grammar school at Wotton in 1416. Whatever
the truth as to authorship, the Vegetius translation would appear to
have been sponsored by Thomas IV. The other translation is Pseudo-
Methodius, *The Beginning of the World and the End of Worlds*, a tract that
is found with Trevisa's genuine translations in British Library MS Harley

1900 and in Huntington Library MS HM 28561 (formerly the Burleigh House MS). Perry finds that the methods of the translator of Methodius are sufficiently different to deny Trevisa any role in this translation.

There are two rather mysterious works that have been attributed to Trevisa. One is the *Gesta Regis Arthuri*, first mentioned by John Bale (1557), and the other is the *Genealogia Davidis Regis Scotiae*, first called Trevisa's by Thomas Tanner (1748). Perry is noncommittal about these two attributions. It is possible that the first is a consequence of Bale's attempted inflation of the Trevisa canon. The *Genealogia Davidis Regis Scotiae*, however, is a false attribution originating in a demonstrable error. Tanner, who lists this work in his *Bibliotheca Britannico-Hibernica* (p. 721), cites as his source James Ussher, *Historia Dogmatica* (London, 1690, p. 123), where we read: "Psalterii magnam partem ab eo ex Latino Anglice conversam esse apud Joannem Trevisam[z] legimus." Turning then to the bottom of the page, we see footnotes *y* and *z* as follows:

[y] In Genealogia Davidis Regis Scotiae MS.
[z] Dialog. praefix. Polychronico a se verso.

Evidently Tanner's eye caught the wrong footnote, and thus another literary ghost was created.

Only two of the six known translations are dated. In a colophon at the close of the *Polychronicon*, Trevisa tells us that his work was completed on 18 April 1387 (he does not say where), and that his patron, Thomas IV Lord Berkeley, who "made me make this translation," was thirty-five years old. A similar colophon concludes the *De Proprietatibus Rerum*, which was "ended at Berkeley" on 6 February 1398/9, Thomas then age forty-seven, and again identified as the instigator of the project. The remaining texts are completely lacking in such colophons, but in one of the three copies of Trevisa's translation of the *Gospel of Nicodemus* (British Library Additional MS 16165, fol. 94r) there is a note by John Shirley (ca. 1425), which reads as follows:

> and filowyng begynnethe the translacion of Nichodeme out of latyn into englisshe laboured by maystere Johan Trevysa Doctour in theologye at the instaunce of Thomae some tyme lord of Berkley.

This tantalizing note is unique, both in its claim of the doctorate for Trevisa, and in the allegation that Berkeley prompted the Nicodemus translation. If we accept it at face value, we could scarcely date the translation of the gospel earlier than 1374.

In view of the uncertain chronology, the only alternative I see is to try to place these translations in the context of Trevisa's life. Those most likely associated with his sojourn in Oxford are the *Dialogus inter Militem et Clericum*, the *Defensio Curatorum*, and of course the *Polychronicon*. The "Berkeley" translations would then be the *De Regimine Principum* and the *De Proprietatibus Rerum*. The latter is, of course, explicitly placed and dated. My reason for placing the *De Regimine Principum* at Berkeley is quite simply a conviction that this treatise on the education of a prince was selected by Trevisa (or his patron) at a time when the rule of Richard II was causing deep concern in baronial circles. On these grounds I would be inclined to date the translation in the period 1388–92.

The *Gospel of Nicodemus* is difficult to place, and remains a problem. What was the nature of Trevisa's interest in this text? We have no real clue. One thinks of Trevisa's possible role as a Bible translator (to be discussed in the next chapter), but *Nicodemus* is extracanonical, and was not included in the English Bible of the fourteenth century. Nor do I see any real likelihood that Lord Berkeley made the choice. The one conviction that I have about this translation—without any real evidence to base it on—is that it is early. For this reason it comes first in the list of works to be discussed in this chapter. Of all the translations, it receives the most attention here, not only because of the difficulty of placing it in the Trevisa canon but also because of its importance in medieval literary tradition.

Gospel of Nicodemus

We need to consider the status of this *Gospel* in relation to the New Testament canon, the forms in which it survives, the chronology of these forms, and, as nearly as possible, the character of the exemplar used by Trevisa in making his translation. But before coming to these issues it is well to have before us the essential narrative contained in the *Gospel of Nicodemus*. When these matters are completed, it should then be possible to consider a few examples of Trevisa's work as a translator, and perhaps glean from them some hint as to the nature of his interest in this remarkable text.

Our story originally consisted of an account of the passion and resurrection of Christ as recorded by Nicodemus, a ruler of the Jews (John 3:1), to which was added an account of Christ's harrowing of hell, reported by two witnesses who had themselves been raised from the dead as a result of Jesus' sacrifice on the cross (Matt. 27:52–53). These two were Karinus and Leucius, sons of the devout Simeon, who had recognized the child Jesus as Israel's messiah (Luke 2:25–35). The *Gospel* thus readily divides into two parts, the first concerned mainly with setting forth unassailable proofs of the resurrection, and the second with dramatizing Christ's redemption of mankind, in particular his victory over death and the rescue of the good souls in hell who would otherwise have been damned forever by the sin of Adam. The two parts, therefore, although originally having different purposes, were skillfully joined together by the author of the addition, so that the harrowing becomes the final and climactic proof of the resurrection, while at the same time it spells out dramatically the theological meaning of that event. Hence we may legitimately regard this *Gospel* in its final form as a unified whole.

Part one opens with accusations against Jesus which the Jews bring before Pilate: he breaks the law by healing on the Sabbath, and casts out devils by the strength of Beelzebub (Mark 3:22). Pilate himself points out the theological inconsistency of this, as does Jesus in the canonical gospels (Mark 3:23–30), but the Jews brush his argument aside and ask that Jesus be summoned to testify. Pilate sends a courier, who surprises everyone by approaching Jesus with great deference, even going so far as to spread a napkin (*fasciale*) on the ground for Jesus to walk on. When asked the meaning of this, the courier explains that he had observed Jesus' triumphal entry into Jerusalem, and was simply repeating what he had seen the multitude do on that occasion (Matt. 21:8).

The pomp and circumstance of Pilate's court come into play when Jesus enters the hall: the Roman emblems atop the staves of banners held by the guards bow down their heads in an attitude of worship as Jesus appears. This is a very popular motif in the New Testament apocrypha, no doubt suggested by such Old Testament precedents as the humble behavior of the Philistine god Dagon in the presence of the ark of the covenant (1 Sam. 5:3). But Jesus' accusers suspect that the guards have done this deliberately, and so Pilate directs them to choose twelve of their strongest men to hold the banners while Jesus reenters. The result, of course, is the same, and the justice himself is in awe of this supernatural manifestation. Moreover, Pilate's wife sends him a message, saying that she has been warned in a dream that he should not do anything to this just man (Matt. 27:19). But the Jews seize upon this as evidence that Jesus is a witch (*maleficus*) with the power to cause such dreams, and then press additional charges: he was born of fornication (Matt. 1:18–19), he caused the slaughter of the innocents in Bethlehem (Matt. 2:16), and his parents fled to Egypt (Matt. 2:14) because they had no faith in the people.

But it is soon evident that those making the accusations do not speak for all Jews. Some of those present deny the charges and, when the accusers call them "proselytes," twelve men come forward and identify themselves by name as "sons of Jews," maintaining that Jesus was not born of fornication. To this the chief prosecutors, Annas and Caiaphas, respond in effect, It is our word against theirs—leaving little doubt as to which side should be believed. In an effort to be fair, Pilate asks the twelve men why the accusers are so intent on slaying Jesus, and they reply that it is because of envy (Mark 15:10). Going out of the hall Pilate addresses the accusers and swears by the sun that he can find no fault in this man (Luke 23:4). But when he suggests that they try Jesus themselves, they point out that only he can impose the death penalty.

The *Gospel of Nicodemus* portrays Pilate as a conscientious judge who is reluctant to put Jesus to death but who is cornered by the skill and determination of his accusers. After a hapless interview with Jesus, ending with the famous question "What is truth?" Pilate once more declares his conviction that Jesus is innocent of wrongdoing. He dismisses the allegation that Jesus claimed to be able to destroy the temple, and takes the Jewish leaders aside in conference, hoping to persuade them privately to drop their charges. But they refuse to back down and reaffirm the charge of blasphemy against Jesus, for which the punishment is death.

At this point Nicodemus speaks in defense of Jesus (John 7:51), arguing in the manner of Gamaliel (Acts 5:34–40) that if he is of God his miracles will prevail, and if not, they shall be of no consequence. But despite this low-key defense, the Jews accuse him of being a disciple and are not dissuaded from their course. Other witnesses for the defense appear: a man cured of the palsy, and others formerly blind, lame, and leprous. Veronica reports being healed of an issue of blood by touching his garment (Matt. 9:20–22), but the accusers, on a point of order, cite their law that a woman cannot be a witness. Some affirm that Jesus is a prophet, and others testify that he raised Lazarus from the dead. Pilate begins to quake from dread, and cries: "What will ye do? Will ye shed his blood that is not guilty?" His effort to free Jesus because of the feast day (Matt. 27:15) backfires when the people call for the release of Barabbas. As in the gospel, Pilate is finally intimidated by the accusation that he is not the emperor's friend if he releases Jesus, who claims to be king (John 19:12). Washing his hands, he declares himself innocent of this man's blood, and the Jews respond: "His blood be upon us and upon our children" (Matt. 27:24–25).

The events of the crucifixion, death, and burial are presented in brief, closely following the canonical narrative. Most of the followers of Jesus hide themselves, but Nicodemus and Joseph appear in the synagogue to speak out against those who had brought about Jesus' death. Nicodemus, a prince of the Jews (John 3:1), is not in danger, whereas Joseph is seized for defending Jesus, imprisoned, and threatened with death. But when the Sabbath is past and Annas and Caiaphas have ordered that Joseph be brought before them, they discover that the cell is empty, though the door is still locked and sealed. While the officials are still reacting to this news, one of the soldiers reports the empty tomb of Christ and the appearance of the angel to the women. Summoning all the soldiers, the Jews question them and rebuke them for failing to carry out their duties. The soldiers reply: "Give us Joseph, whom you locked in a cell, and we will give you Jesus whom we guarded in the tomb." As a last resort, the Jews bribe the soldiers to say that Jesus' disciples stole the body while they slept (Matt. 28:11–15).

At this point the narrative diverges from the canonical gospels in order to follow the efforts of the Jewish leaders first to cover up news of the resurrection, and then, when this no longer seems possible, to try to understand what it means. No sooner have they paid and dismissed the soldiers, than three men from Galilee appear before them and report having seen Jesus alive with his disciples. The priests, elders, and deacons question them and make them repeat their testimony under oath, holding the book of God's law. They swear that they saw Jesus teaching his disciples, after which he ascended into heaven. The leaders give them money and three men to escort them home with instructions not to tell anyone what they have seen. But the growing evidence of the resurrection has its effect on the Jews, who ask: "What is this token that is done in Israel?" Annas and Caiaphas try to reassure them by saying that the soldiers were lying, but cannot explain everything away to the satisfaction of all those present.

In this atmosphere of uncertainty, Nicodemus rises once more to speak, and this time gets a hearing. Reminding his listeners of the precedent of Elijah, who was taken up to heaven in a chariot of fire, and was sought afterward by the sons of the prophets (2 Kings 2:16–18), Nicodemus suggests that men be sent to search the hills of Israel, looking for Jesus. This is done and, though they do not find him, they report having seen Joseph in his own city of Arimathea. It is then agreed that a delegation will be sent to Joseph with a politely worded letter apologizing for having arrested him, in the hope that he may be persuaded to come to Jerusalem and speak with his former captors. Joseph gladly agrees, and recounts the circumstances of his deliverance from prison.

On Saturday at midnight, says Joseph, I was in the prison cell saying my prayers when the house was suspended by the corners and Jesus appeared to me in a blaze of light. I fell to the ground for fear, but he raised me up, comforted me and said, "Fear not, Joseph, it is I: behold thou me." And I said, "Master Elias!" "I am not Elias," he said, "but I am Jesus whose body thou didst bury." "Show me the grave," said I, "where I laid Thee." Jesus led him to the tomb, and showed him the napkin that was about his head (John 20:7). Then Joseph knew that it was Jesus, and worshipped him. But Jesus took him by the hand and led him to his home in Arimathea, where he remained until found by the men who had been sent out in search of Jesus.

The Jewish leaders are astonished at this testimony, and begin to ask each other what it might mean. In response, one of the deacons (a teacher named Levi) suddenly remembers that he had known Jesus' family, and recalls the occasion when they came to the synagogue after Mary's purification to make an offering. Simeon had held the child, praising God and saying: "For mine eyes have seen thy salvation, which thou has prepared before the face of all people, a light to lighten the gentiles, and the glory of thy people Israel" (Luke 2:30–32). Thereafter the three witnesses to the ascension are recalled from Galilee, and reaffirm their previous testimony. Then Annas and Caiaphas put into words the doubt and wonder they all experienced: "We know of the mystery surrounding the departure of Enoch, Moses, and Elijah—whereas this Jesus was crucified, dead, and buried; and yet three men bear witness to us that he appeared with his disciples alive and ascended into heaven!"

In the original form of *Nicodemus* the story end▓▓▓▓with the Jews'
acceptance of the resurrection. But when part two was added, the
attitude of the Jews at this point was shown to be poised (as I have
summarized above) in a state of indecision, so that the events of the
harrowing of hell might be introduced as the final clinching evidence
needed to persuade them of the truth.

Seeing the uncertainty of the Jewish leaders, Joseph of Arimathea
seizes this opportunity to report the resurrection of many men as a
result of Jesus' redemptive act (Matt. 27:52–53), including the two sons
of Simeon: Karinus and Leucius. The graves of these two had been found
open, and they were seen alive in their prayers in the city of Arimathea,
but dumb and still when approached by men. Joseph suggests that they
be conjured to speak, if perchance they may be allowed to relate the
secret experience of their resurrection. When the two men are found
and brought to Jerusalem, they respond to the appeal of the Jews and
call for pen and paper so that each may record in writing his experience.
The narrative which follows is thus the testimony of these two witnesses.

We were with our forefathers in the darkness of hell when there suddenly appeared a great light, shining like the sun (Rev. 1:16), as if it were
the light of a king. Whereupon Adam and other patriarchs and prophets
rejoiced and spoke of this light as coming from God, the maker of light,
who has sent his everlasting son to them that dwell in the shadow of
death (Isa. 9:2). Successive speakers reminded all of us sitting in darkness
of their own predictions of this moment of deliverance: Adam, Isaiah,
our father Simeon, John the Baptist, all reiterated prophecies from the
scriptures, and Seth, at his father Adam's request, related the prophecy
of the archangel Michael concerning the oil of mercy with which the
Lord will anoint all the faithful unto life everlasting. Whereupon all the
patriarchs and prophets rejoiced.

Meanwhile the forces of darkness seek to prepare their defenses. Satan
confidently addresses Hell, telling him to make ready to receive this Jesus
who, though he is God's son, admits that he is afraid of death (Matt.
26:38). Yet at the same time Satan concedes that Jesus has healed the
sick with a word, and even taken back the dead. Who is this, replies
Hell, so powerful of word and yet dreads death? How can he withstand
our power? I believe he is going to take you away and you shall be in
woe forever. Satan protests that he has arranged the death of Jesus, and
that they will be able to make him their captive. True it is, replies Hell,

that others have taken the dead from us, but only through the power of prayer, by which means God brought back the dead (e.g., 1 Kings 17:17–24). But this Jesus takes dead men from me without prayer, hence I suppose he is the one who took Lazarus from me. When I heard his command "Lazarus come forth!" (John 11:43), I trembled for dread, and was unable to hold the dead man: with the swiftness of an eagle he rose and departed from here at the word of the Lord. Do not bring this savior of mankind hither to me, for I fear that he will deliver all the righteous and bring them to eternal life.

Then came a voice of thunder saying, "Lift up your head, O ye gates, and be ye lift up, ye everlasting doors, and the King of glory shall come in" (Psalm 24:7). In the ensuing panic, Satan is cast down from his seat, and Hell orders his officers to close the cruel brazen gates and bar them with iron bars lest all be taken captive. Phrases from the Psalms are effectively employed to dramatize Christ's entry into Hell, with verses being spoken by the Redeemer, the saints, and even Hell himself. David in particular (as the author of the book of Psalms) is anxious to remind the saints of his prophecies concerning the redemption. "Said I not to you on earth while I was alive: 'Praise the Lord for his goodness, and his wonderful works to the children of men, for he hath broken the gates of brass, and cut the bars of iron in sunder'" (Psalm 107:15–16). Similar reminders come from Isaiah (26:19) and Hosea (13:14).

Once more the voice of thunder speaks, demanding that the gates be opened, and Hell responds as though he knew it not, "Who is this king of Glory?" (Psalm 24:8). To which David answers: "I know the words of this cry, for I prophecied them by virtue of the Holy Ghost. And now I tell it as I did then: 'The Lord strong and mighty, the Lord mighty in battle, he is the King of glory'" (Psalm 24:8). "And the Lord beheld out of heaven into the earth to hear the groaning of them that were bound, to unbind the children of them that were slain" (Psalm 102:19–20). David's application of these verses to the harrowing of hell reflects a common view of certain psalms in medieval exegesis. There is a liturgical quality to the alternating question and answer sequence based on Psalm 24:7–10. Hell and his ministers acknowledge their defeat in a series of rhetorical questions, beginning "Who art thou?" And they end by affirming Christ's victory over them through his death on the cross. In his majesty Jesus then treads down death, binds Satan, and delivers him into the custody of Hell, who rebukes the prince of darkness for his failure to foresee the outcome of Jesus' redemptive act.

As Jesus leads the saints out of Hell, David recites for them the opening of that psalm which most clearly celebrates the new covenant: "Sing unto the Lord a new song" (Psalm 98:1). To this the saints respond appropriately, "Blessed be he that cometh in the name of the Lord" (Psalm 118:26), and recite additional prophecies from Habakkuk (3:13) and Micah (7:18–20). As the saints approach paradise, led by the archangel Michael, they encounter two very old men who come out to meet them. "Who be ye," ask the saints, "that are not dead nor with us in Hell, but be here in paradise in flesh and blood?" The first identifies himself as Enoch, whom God took (Gen. 5:24; Heb. 11:5), and the second as Elijah, who went up to heaven in a chariot of fire (2 Kings 2:11). Enoch explains that they have not tasted death but are being reserved for the coming of Antichrist, when they shall testify and be slain in Jerusalem, and after three and a half days be taken alive into the clouds (Rev. 11:3–12; cf. Mal. 4:5). They are then approached by a third man, who identifies himself as Dismas, the good thief on the cross to whom Jesus said, "Today shalt thou be with me in paradise" (Luke 23:43). Hearing this the saints rejoice and praise the Father of mercy who has granted the joys of paradise to sinful men.

The two sons of Simeon, Karinus and Leucius, having completed their report of the harrowing of hell, explain to the Jews how they personally were raised from death to life at the time of the crucifixion, and were sent by Michael the archangel to be baptized in the Jordan, where they and all those resurrected along with Christ were given white garments. Together they celebrated the first Easter, and after three days all the others who had been raised were ravished into the clouds and were not seen again. Karinus gave the book he had written to Annas, Caiaphas, and Gamaliel, while Leucius handed his book to Nicodemus and Joseph. Then suddenly the two men were transfigured in a white light and were seen no more. When the two reports they had written were compared, they were found to be identical. The Jews conclude that "all this was done by our Lord God, who is blessed forever, amen!" and they leave the synagogue in fear and trembling, each unto his own house.

Of all the New Testament apocrypha, the *Gospel of Nicodemus* came closest to acceptance in the sense that it was very popular in the Middle

Ages, and is even found in some Bible manuscripts, bound in a position following the four canonical gospels. Whether it was written in the hope that it would be accepted as scripture is difficult to decide, especially considering the uncertainty about its date of composition. If it was written before A.D. 400, when the New Testament canon was more or less firmly established, one might suppose the author to have been seeking canonical status for it; very long after that date, such an aim would seem to have been unrealistic. In any case, the biblical style of the work is unmistakable, whether it was intended to promote canonization or merely to provide a pious and persuasive vehicle for the narrative. If the aim was the more modest one of creating Christian literature, it must be admitted that the author was incredibly successful.

What I have been referring to as the *Gospel of Nicodemus* exists in at least four distinct forms to which have been assigned various titles, and on these there is no general agreement. The most recent scholar to grapple with the problem is O'Ceallaigh (1963), and I follow him in designating the original Greek version as the *Commentaries of Nicodemus*. The next form appears to be the early Latin version in two parts, part one a translation of the Greek *Commentaries*, and part two an addition apparently composed in Latin recounting the harrowing of hell. This early Latin version was then itself turned back into Greek, though the result is a paraphrase rather than a close translation. The nineteenth-century editor of these texts, Tischendorf (1853), believed this Greek paraphrase to have preceded the Latin, but O'Ceallaigh is convinced that the Greek text (surviving only in late medieval manuscripts) is derived from the early Latin version. This leaves a fourth form, the late Latin version, appearing first in the tenth-century manuscript Codex Einsidlensis, recently edited by H. C. Kim (1973). It was not until the thirteenth century that the title *Gospel of Nicodemus* was used, but since then this has been employed to designate all four versions. The only serious competitor is *Acts of Pilate*, applied to the late Latin form because it adds a letter of transmittal from Pilate to the Emperor Tiberius which turns the entire text into a supposedly official Roman document. Translations of all these texts survive in many vernacular languages.

The four versions of *Nicodemus* all belong to the first millennium of Christianity, but much uncertainty remains about the specific dates of composition. O'Ceallaigh is inclined to date the *Commentaries* no earlier than the latter part of the sixth century, whereas Scheidweiler in his contribution to the volume on the New Testament apocrypha by Hennecke (1963) allows the possibility of an origin as early as the second century. The sixth century date may well be correct for the text that we have in the earliest Greek manuscripts; but if we concede the hypothesis of an ur-form, then it remains possible that an earlier state of the text may have existed as far back as the time of Justin (martyred A.D. 165), or perhaps more reasonably in the period of Epiphanius (ca. 375), who speaks of those who try to date the crucifixion with the aid of the "Acts of Pilate."

A similar uncertainty necessarily plagues any effort to date the composition of the harrowing of hell narrative that shows up first in the early Latin version. The best clue would appear to be the clause of the Apostle's Creed "he descended into hell," which seems to have been the source of inspiration. But when was this formulated? It first appears in a creed known as the Fourth of Sirmium, dated A.D. 359, but was current in local Christian communities, especially in the East, well before that date. This might suggest some time in the third century as a *terminus a quo*, but provides no means of establishing a *terminus ad quem*, which at a guess I would place in the fifth or sixth century.

The late Latin recension of Nicodemus is customarily placed in the tenth century, the date of the earliest surviving manuscript, and it is this version that is the basis of Trevisa's translation into Middle English. The Trevisa text has been edited by Kim (1964) using the two manuscripts then known, Salisbury Cathedral MS 39 and British Library Additional MS 16165. Since then a third copy of Trevisa's translation has been identified by Power (1978) in the Fellows' Library of Winchester College (MS 33), and I have used this along with Kim's text in my study of the translation, and my comparison of it with the Latin of Codex Einsidlensis.

There are numerous manuscript copies of the late Latin recension of the *Gospel of Nicodemus* in the libraries of Great Britain, and it is perhaps useless to try to determine whether one of them might be the exemplar employed by Trevisa. After a preliminary search in London and Oxford, however, I hit upon the Oxford MS Bodley 556 as the closest of all to the Latin implied by Trevisa's translation. It is clearly not the exemplar, since it omits occasional material present in the Middle English, but its peculiar features are very often close to those of the Trevisa version. In the following discussion of the translation, therefore, I shall make use of the readings in Bodley 556 whenever these are closer to Trevisa's words than the Latin of Codex Einsidlensis as edited by Kim (1973). For ease of reading, I shall modernize the spelling of the Middle English unless understanding of textual matters requires citation in the original form.

Trevisa's version of the *Gospel of Nicodemus* has a unique passage near the beginning of the second chapter which I once thought might lead me to his Latin exemplar, but I have not discovered a single Latin manuscript that has it:

> Hereafter when it drew to the Eastertide, the princes of priests cast in what manner they might slay Jesus, and made covenant with Judas Iscariot that was one of the twelve and behight him money to betake them Jesus. Judas feng thirty pence of silver and took to them Jesus (cf. Luke 22:1–6). The tribune and a great company and ministers of the Jews took Jesus and bound him hard and fast, and brought him first to the bishop that areyned him of his lore (John 18:12, 13, 19). Then Pilate went out to them and said, What accusation put ye against this man? They answered and said, If this were not an evildoer, we would not have taken him to thee (John 18:29, 30). We found him overturning our law and forbidding the Emperor's tribute and saying that he is Christ and King. He hath turned away the people and began to teach in Galilee and hath taught in the jewry from Galilee into this place (Luke 23:2, 5).

As the inserted references indicate, this is a collage of passages from the gospels summarizing the events of Christ's betrayal, arrest, and the beginning of his trial. Unless a Latin text with this passage is found, I am inclined to the opinion that Trevisa himself inserted it. The opening chapter of *Nicodemus*, featuring the deferential treatment of Jesus by Pilate and the messenger, perhaps allows the inference that Jesus is not yet under arrest, in which case the unique passage in Trevisa's translation provides the circumstances of betrayal and arrest leading to the trial proper, which follows.

One of Trevisa's characteristics as a translator is his inclusion of occasional explanatory notes, and the *Gospel of Nicodemus* has two of these. The first comes near the beginning in the Prologue, which contains an elaborate dating of Christ's passion according to the regnal years of the emperor Tiberius and the ethnarch Herod, the consulates of Rufus and Rubellio, when Pilate was justice and Caiaphas high priest, on the eighth of the Kalends of April which is the 25th day of March, in the fourth year of the two hundred and second Olympiad. The identification by Olympiad prompts Trevisa to provide the following note of explanation:

Here have mind that sometime the Greeks made jousts and tournaments and other plays of mastery and of strength once in five year under the hill Mount Olympas and called the plays Olympiad. And for they had such plays but once in five year, the first five year in the which they hadde such plays they cleped the first Olympiad, and the second five year the second Olympiad, and so forth, so that Christ died in the fourth year of the Olympiad two hundred and two. Then it followeth in the book.

In order to signal an interruption of the translation, Trevisa generally puts his name at the head of each note. Here he seems not to have done so, although in British Library Additional MS 16165 (John Shirley's copy) the note begins: "Maistre Iohan Trevysa hathe here in mynde. . . ."

Chapter XXIV describes the release of the patriarchs and prophets from hell, during which David recites the opening of Psalm 98 and the saints respond with "Amen, alleluia." The other explanatory note then follows:

> Trevisa. *Amen* is to mean, so mot it be. *Alleluia* is to mean, Praise ye and herieth God all at once, and also, Lord save thou me. And it hath other meanings also as diverse authors telleth. Then it followeth in the book.

In such notes we see Trevisa learning in the course of translation, and sharing his new knowledge with the reader.

The most interesting insights into Trevisa as translator should come through a look at the body of the text itself in comparison with his Latin original, but such a comparison is not easy to make, for reasons already hinted. How are we to know certainly which form of the Latin text he had before him? Perhaps it will be best to examine a few problematical passages to illustrate the difficulty, after which we may more readily consider some probable examples of his technique.

A very common problem in the copying of medieval manuscripts was eye-skip, caused by the repetition of words or phrases in close proximity. The *Gospel of Nicodemus* is full of such repetitions because there is much dialogue involving the repeat of words like *dixit . . . dixit* (he said . . . he said) which can cause the eye to skip either in Latin or in English. The nature of translation being what it is, I doubt that Trevisa himself was often guilty of this error, but there are many examples of it in his texts, and they may come from a defective Latin exemplar or from faulty copying of the English translation. Which of these alternatives applies in any given case is almost impossible to determine, but the problem seems, for some reason, to be worse in English manuscripts than in Latin. My estimate is that the Winchester manuscript (much later than the other two) has lost more than 12 percent of its text, mainly through eye-skip.

A simple case occurs near the end of part one of the gospel, where the witnesses to Christ's ascension are being questioned (XVI.3):

> Tunc Annas et Cayfas sequestratos eos ab inuicem interrogantes singillatim, unanimiter ueritatem *dixerunt* uidisse se Iesum ascendentem in caelum. Tunc Annas et Cayfas *dixerunt*: 'Lex nostra continet, "In ore duorum uel trium testium omne uerbum stabit."

Compare this (noting the repetition of *dixerunt*) with its equivalent in Trevisa's translation:

> Then Annas and Caiaphas said, "Depart we them atwain and areyne we them each after other." And they said the sooth all by one heart. "And our law sayeth that in the mouth of two witnesses or three each's word shall stand."

This appears to be a very close translation, the only change being that Trevisa puts the action of questioning the witnesses separately in direct discourse. But it is clear that the statement of the witnesses, *vidisse se Iesum ascendentem in caelum* (that they saw Jesus ascending into heaven), and the identification of the next speakers, *Tunc Annas et Cayfas dixerunt* (Then Annas and Caiaphas said) have been omitted, precisely that portion of the Latin text that falls between the two occurrences of *dixerunt*, a classic example of eye-skip.

A more difficult case occurs in the dialogue between Jesus and Pilate in Chapter III (based on John 18:33–38). Pilate asks him if he is a king, and Jesus answers that his kingdom is not of this world; but when the justice again presses him for an answer, Jesus says that he came to bear witness to the truth, and it is this which prompts the question "What is truth?" In the gospel of John, Pilate does not stay for an answer, but in *Nicodemus* the conversation continues (III.2.15–18):

> Dicit ei Pilatus, 'Quid est ueritas?' *Dicit* Iesus, 'Ueritas de celo est.' Dicit ei Pilatus, 'In terris ueritas non est?' *Dicit* Iesus Pilato: 'Intende ueritatem dicentes in terra, quomodo iudicantur ab his qui habent potestatem in terris.'

Here is Trevisa's version of this:

> "What is soothness?" quoth Pilate. "Take heed of soothness that teacheth in earth," quoth Jesus, "how men be deemed by soothness of them that have power here in earth."

Because of the repetition of *dicit* (quoth), the passage has lost one exchange between Jesus and Pilate, and is no longer very clear. Jesus' first response to the question is: "Truth is from heaven." Then Pilate replies: "Is there no truth on earth?" which leads to Jesus' concluding statement. But what does Jesus mean? Here is how M. R. James (1924, p. 100) renders the original Greek:

> Thou seest how that they which speak the truth are judged of them that have authority upon earth.

Since Pilate will be forced to admit that he finds no fault in Jesus, and yet will sentence him to death, this is an apt reply. But it is not easy to extract this meaning from Trevisa's English, and I am inclined to think that the problem goes beyond the omission of part of the dialogue. The word "teacheth," for example, suggests that Trevisa's Latin at this point may have had *docentem* instead of *dicentes*. It is also possible that the final clause began *ab veritate*, or that Trevisa supplied "soothness" in an effort to clarify the passage. Because we cannot be sure of the reading of the exemplar, we are left in doubt about the exact origin of the flaw in the translation of this interesting passage. This uncertainty exists in a number of places where we suspect corruption in transmission of the Latin.

Pilate wishes to speak privately to the twelve witnesses, so he dismisses the multitude and "commanded Jesus to be set apart" (*et Iesum iussit segregari semotim*), a passage which Trevisa renders (II.6.1–4):

> Then Pilate bade that all the people should go out of the hall out-take these twelve men and Jesus, and hight the eldest men stand together. . . .

Evidently Trevisa's Latin read something like "et Iesum, et iussit segregari *seniores*," thus creating a group of elders who really do not belong in the story.

On orders from Pilate (John 19:19) a sign (*titulum*) is affixed to the cross reading "This is the King of the Jews." But Trevisa has an added detail which I have not found in any other version: the justice commands that the sign be prepared "in the presence of Seiymlus the writer." Here the Latin reads "Iussit autem preses pro sententia titulum scribi . . ." (X.1.16–17); that is, the justice ordered that the accusation against Jesus be written as a title. Bodley 556, however, reads "Iussit autem preses *in presentia sua titulum scribere*," the last word being abbreviated *scribe*. If the possibility of corruption of *sua titulum* to form the proper name *Seiymlus* is allowed, we are very close to Trevisa's version. The presence of this scribe at the crucifixion thus appears to have come about through corruption of the text, but his name bears an uncanny resemblance to Seleucus, the supposed author of numerous New Testament apocrypha, as pointed out by M. R. James (1924, p. 95).

When the story drifts from the canonical narrative, as in the arrest and imprisonment of Joseph of Arimathea, corrupt passages cannot of course be measured against the more stable biblical text. Joseph's captors explain to him that he will be locked up until after the Sabbath (XII.1.20–22):

> Agnosce quia hora inconpetit aliquid agere aduersam te, quia sabbatum inlucescit.

The point being emphasized is the unattractive combination of piety and vindictiveness in Joseph's enemies. They will avenge themselves on him, but not during the Sabbath. For *inconpetit* Bodley 556 has *non petit*. This perhaps explains Trevisa's "he shall ask no thing," but something even more serious seems to have gone wrong with *quia sabbatum inlucescit*:

> Know that from this time forward, he shall ask no thing to do against thee, for it shall be known.

The fact that the Sabbath is at hand is lost, and the text now seems to suggest that they are hesitating to harm Joseph for fear of discovery.

As we have noted, the style of *Nicodemus* is clearly modeled on that of the canonical gospels, while at the same time it occasionally seeks to depart from them in the interest of verisimilitude. Thus while Pilate in Matthew 27:24 is said to wash his hands "before the multitude," the author of Nicodemus has him do so "before the sun" (*coram sole*), perhaps suggestive of Pilate's pagan religion. Later Joseph in his reprise of the passion narrative uses the same phrase. But however felicitous this detail may have seemed to the author of *Nicodemus*, it inevitably collided with the beloved account of Matthew, and was bound to suffer in transmission at the hands of indignant scribes. Even the Codex Einsidlensis did not escape this sort of "correction": in one place it reads *coram populo* (IX.4.5) and in the other *coram sole* (XII.1.28). In both passages Trevisa has "before the people," thus completing the restoration of the biblical reading.

The three men who witnessed the ascension protest the truth of their testimony in words which vary in the different forms of the gospel. The original Greek is thus translated by James (1924, p. 108):

If these words which we have spoken [of what we have heard] and seen be sin, lo, we are before you: do unto us as seemeth good in your eyes. (For variants see Tischendorf, 244n.)

The same statement appears in the late Latin version of Codex Einsidlensis in a modified form (XIV.2.9–11):

Si verba qual avdivimus ab Iesu, et vidimus eum ascendentem in caelum, si tacemus peccatum habemus.

The submissiveness of the original has now vanished, and the witnesses are more assertive: it would be a sin *not* to tell what we have seen and heard. Trevisa translates as follows:

If these words be not sooth that we heard of God Jesus, and saw him sty up [ascend] into heaven, we have great sin.

Here the witnesses are more diffident, seeming to acknowledge the possibility that their words may not be true. But I suspect that the problem is again in Trevisa's Latin exemplar, which may have lost *si tacemus*. Bodley 556 omits *si*, leaving *tacemus* with very much the appearance of a superfluous verb.

Although the chief priests bribed the three witnesses to say nothing of Christ's ascension, the Jews themselves evidently sensed that their testimony was sincere, and they were uneasy about covering up what might be an act of God. Annas and Caiaphas try to reassure them by pointing out that the disciples paid the soldiers to say that Jesus was risen, just as the Jews paid them to say that his body was stolen by the disciples (Matt. 28:12–15). In other words, everyone has his price. This cynical observation concludes the discussion in some versions, but the original Greek includes a further response from the priests and the elders, who cannot forget the testimony of the three witnesses (p. 108):

Be it so, that his disciples did steal away his body; but how is his soul entered into his body, and how abideth he in Galilee? But they could not answer these things, and hardly in the end said: It is not lawful for us to believe the uncircumcised.

This must surely represent the original form of the narrative, since it provides the opening for Nicodemus who, immediately thereafter, begins his remarks with "You speak rightfully, children of Israel . . . ," referring to their instinctive trust in the word of three witnesses.

135

For whatever reason, this subtle depiction of a conflict of opinion within the Jewish community is lost in the later versions. Following the cynical statement of Annas and Caiaphas, the later Latin version has a single sentence (XIV.3.12–13):

Aut ex nobis habuerunt tenere fidem aut discipulis Iesu,

which Trevisa translates:

They should be true to us or to the disciples of Jesus.

Whether Trevisa thought this to be a part of the speech of Annas and Caiaphas, it is impossible to tell. It certainly seems irrelevant to their argument and unrelated to their concerns. The possibility of a change of speakers here is supported by the author of the English poetic version of the *Gospel of Nicodemus* (Hulme 1907, p. 80, lines 925–30):

> All þe iews þan þat þar ware
>   answerd and said þus:
> wheþer war oure knightes halden mare
>   vntill his men or till vs?"
> "sertainly ȝe say wele þare,"
>   þus said nichodemus. . . .

The thirteenth-century French version edited by Lindstrom (1974) indicates no change of speakers but does cast the sentence in the form of a question (version B, p 87):

As quels deveient il melz porter fei: as desciples Jesu, u a nus?

whereas the English prose version, which Lindstrom considers to be a translation of the French, expands the passage to make it a part of the argument of Annas and Caiaphas (version A, p. 87):

And now they have her feyth to vs and to the dyssyples of Jhesu; for y wene they have take goode bothe of hem and of vs for to folow the wylle of eythyr party. And therfor they ought not be beleued.

This is skillfully adapted to what precedes, but it leaves Nicodemus without an opening.

In view of all this, and giving Trevisa the benefit of the doubt, I would be inclined to punctuate his sentence as a question and as representing a change of speakers: "They should be trewe to us, or to the disciples of Jesus?" The Jews could thus be saying, in effect, though the soldiers can be bought, it is unlikely that both their reports are false; and given the testimony of the three witnesses from Galilee, the report of the soldiers concerning the resurrection could still be true. Thus interpreted, the cue for Nicodemus is left intact.

When Joseph receives the delegation from Jerusalem, and realizes that they no longer seek his life, he gives thanks to God (James, 1924, p. 109):

Blessed be the Lord God, which hath redeemed Israel from shedding innocent blood; and blessed be the Lord, which sent his angel and sheltered me under his wings.

The later Latin version reads (XV.3.5–8):

Benedictus Dominus Deus qui liberasti Israel ut non effunderet sanguinem meum. Benedictus Deus qui protexisti me sub alis tuis.

Here the angel is omitted, and Joseph is sheltered by the wings of God himself, but otherwise the text is well preserved. Trevisa, however, differs considerably from this:

Blessed be thou Lord God of Israel, that deliveredst me under thy wings.

The differences can be explained in part by recourse to Bodley 556, which begins, "Benedictus Dominus Deus *Israel qui liberavit me*," but it is also clear that repetitions in this passage have apparently caused eye-skip, with the consequent loss of Joseph's reference to the shedding of his blood. This is an especially interesting case because, although the two early manuscripts of Trevisa's version show this loss, the later Winchester MS 33 has the missing clause (fol. 84r):

Blissed be thou god of israel that delyueredest me *and sauedist me that y shed nat my blood; blissed be thou lorde that defendist me* vnder thy wyngis.

We note that this follows the Latin of Bodley 556 not only in the part found in the other two English manuscripts, but also in the unique italicized portion, where "y shed" is probably for "hy shed" (i.e., *they shed*), corresponding to Latin *effunderent* of the Bodley version. The evidence thus suggests that the corruption in this case resulted from copying of Trevisa's English rather than the Latin, and it is well to take note that authentic readings may sometimes be found in the Winchester manuscript, which in other respects is late and defective.

What is a translator to do when he suspects that his Latin is defective? We have seen that the anonymous translator in MS Harley 149

(Lindstrom's version A) attached the puzzling sentence at the end of Chapter XIV to the speech of Annas and Caiaphas with considerable ingenuity, but in doing so destroyed the link with the following speech of Nicodemus. Caution is often required in these circumstances, and it is worth noting that Trevisa rarely ventures onto thin ice when his Latin is uncertain. A case in point occurs in Chapter XXIV, at the end of the first section, where the saints are praising the victorious Christ (James, p. 139):

> Lord, set thou up the sign of the victory of thy cross in hell, that death may have no more dominion.

This is perfectly preserved in the late Latin version, *pone, Domine, in inferno signum victoriae crucis tuae, ne mors dominetur amplius,* which Trevisa translates as follows:

> Lord, set thou the token of thy victory of thy cross in hell,

omitting the final clause. It is possible, of course, that this is simply a careless omission, or that the whole clause was omitted from Trevisa's Latin; but it is significant, I believe, that at this point Bodley 556 has *ne dominentur amplius,* from which the single word *mors* (death) has been lost. Trevisa thus may have been faced with a text that seemed to say, "Lord, set thou in hell the token of the victory of thy cross, that they (who?) may have no more dominion." Rather than try to puzzle out a solution of his own, Trevisa apparently decided simply to omit the final clause, rather than provide a translation that makes no sense, or offer an emendation that might be wrong.

In citing these textual problems, I do not wish to suggest that they can account for every irregularity in Trevisa's translation, for it is certainly true that he occasionally fails to understand a word or phrase, or makes the wrong choice of two possible meanings. Thus in Chapter XX, Hell remarks to Satan that Jesus is perhaps the one who deprived them of Lazarus, "who was four days dead and stank and was corrupt" (*quodriduanum fetentem et dissolutum*). Trevisa translates the entire sentence as follows:

> In case this is he that by the word of his hest turned Lazarus to life and *unbound him* that I held dead when he had lain four days stinking in his grave.

It is evident that faced with the word *dissolutum,* which could mean either "rotten" or "unbound," Trevisa chose the figurative sense, rather than the very literal meaning implied by association with the word *fetentem* (stinking) from John 11:39. But even here it is possible that this was a sophisticated decision rather than a simple mistake, since a moment's reflection shows that an emphasis on Christ's power to release men from the bondage of death is relevant to the context.

Having completed our review of corruption in the Latin text of *Nicodemus*, we need to consider those cases where a simple variation in Trevisa's exemplar makes it appear that he has misunderstood or departed from his original, when in fact he is translating very literally. This is why it is important not to rely exclusively on Codex Einsidlensis in evaluating his translation, but to consider also the readings of Bodley 556. An example of the closeness of the latter manuscript to Trevisa's exemplar can be seen in the conversation between Pilate and Jesus, where Pilate uses the very words of John 18:35: "Thine own nation and the chief priests have delivered thee unto me" (*Gens tua et principes sacerdotum tradiderunt te mihi*). For this Trevisa has "Thine own people and the *bishops* have taken thee to me," suggesting at first glance that Trevisa himself introduced the word *bishops*, perhaps aiming for some special effect. But in fact Bodley 556 reads "Gens tua et *pontifices* et sacerdotes tui . . . ," which supports the conclusion that this was the reading of Trevisa's Latin original. But the validity of such a conclusion is contingent on the presence of numerous other instances, which I shall present in compact form in order to save space. In the following additional examples, I cite first the Latin of Codex Einsidlensis as edited by Kim (1973), second the English of Trevisa, and third the Latin of Bodley 556, with each example separated by a slash.

VI.2.1 Caecus natus sum: *Lo*, I was born blind: *Ecce*, natus sum cecus / IX.2.3 qui pro uobis fuerunt contrarii eis fuistis: contrary to them that *fighteth* for you: contrarii eis fuistis qui pro vobis *pugnabant* / X.1.8 diuiserunt sibi uestimenta eius: they departed his clothes *and threw lot thereupon*: diuiserunt uestimenta eius *mittentes sortem* / XV.6.4–5 uidi Iesum sicut fulgorem: I saw Jesus as it were bright blazing *of light*: uidi iesum sicut fulgorem *lucis* / XIX.1.20–22 qui faciet resurgere corpus Adae et conresuscitare corpora mortuorum *ac sanare omnem infirmitatem*: (he shall) arear Adam's body and he shall arear the bodies of dead men: resuscitare corpus ade et cum resuscitauerit corpora mortuorum / XXII.1.16–18 Quis es tu qui illos qui originali peccato asstricti detinentur absoluis captiuos et in libertatem pristinam revocas? [*Trevisa and Bodley 556 omit*] / XXIII.1.3–4 derisio angelorum *Dei*, sputio iustorum: scorn of angels, and *disputation* of rightful men: derisio angelorum, *disputatio* iustorum / XXIII.1.25 nunc per lignum crucis perdidisti: by the tree of the cross thou hast lost *the orchard of paradise*: nunc per lignum crucis *paradisi ortum* perdidisti / XXVIII.2 Claudio: *Tyberius: tiberio* / XXVIII.11–12 paralyticos curasse: healed men of the palsy *and cast out fiends out of men that they had in their mastery*: paraliticos curasse, *demones ab hominibus fugasse*.

One final example of the correspondence of Trevisa's translation with the Latin text of Bodley 556 deserves separate comment. It has often been noticed that Longinus, the soldier who pierced the side of Christ (19:34), is represented in the *Gospel of Nicodemus* as doing this before the death takes place (X.1.15–16), despite the fact that he does so after the death in the canonical gospel. Because this is such a glaring discrepancy, we must allow the likelihood that in the course of copying it was "corrected" independently by numerous scribes. Thus the scribe of MS Harley 149 edited by Lindstrom (1974, pp. 72, 74) first had it before the death, then canceled it and placed it following the words of the centurion (Matt. 27:54), even though the French version he consulted had it in the former position. Most versions, however, including the poetic translation edited by Hulme (1907), place the episode before Christ's death, as it occurs in the Codex Einsidlensis. Hence it is worth noting that in both Trevisa and Bodley 556 it is moved precisely to a position following Christ's last words and preceding the speech of the centurion.

Having assessed the corruption of Trevisa's Latin exemplar, and the extent of its deviation from the norm of the late Latin recension, we are at last in a position to identify and perhaps to interpret some of the individual features of his translation. Trevisa is famous for his tendency to use two English words for one Latin word, and these doublets are quite frequently employed in *Nicodemus*. In the following examples I give the Latin word or phrase from Kim's text followed by Trevisa's translation:

II.4.6 non est verus: is neither true ne sooth / VI.2.6 curvus: crooked and lame / VI.2.8 mundavit: healed and cleansed / IX.1.3 seditio: strife and conspiracy / IX.1.4 Ipsi uideant: Advise them and busy them / IX.1.6 consuetudo: custom and usage / X.2.6 mali: evil, wrong ne misdeed / XII.1.5 opera: deeds and works / XIII.2.12 uiuit: he liveth and is alive / XIV.1.6 monte Oliueti: the hill and mount of Olivet / XIV.2.3 gloriam: bliss and joy / XV.6.11 sepelisti: thou buriedest and laidest in a grave / XX.3.15–16 conturbata sunt: were astonied and afraid full sore / XXII.1.12 occisum: dead and slain / XXII.1.29 intrepidus: boldly without any dread / XXIII.1.3

dux: duk and leader / XXIII.1.11 insultant: rebuke and despise / XXIV.1.20
redemisti: ransomed and saved / XXV.5 uetusti dierum: of great age and ful
olde of days / XXV.7 corpore: in flesh and blood / XXVII.4.6 sollicitudine:
busyness and thought.

In such a list it is difficult to assess the function of these doublets, but
suffice it to say that they are not merely decorative. Some add emphasis,
others clarify, and still others provide a fix on the meaning of the Latin
where a single English word is simply inadequate. A few examples in
context should illustrate the point and conclude our examination of
Trevisa's technique as translator.

When Joseph's captors lock him in the cell, they announce that they
intend to kill him when the Sabbath is past (XII.1.22–24):

> We know that thou shalt not be worthy to be *buried ne brought in earth*
> (sepultura), but we shall *throw and give* (dabimus) *thy body and thy flesh* (carnes
> tuas) to beasts of the earth and fowls of the loft.

It is readily apparent that the three doublets in this single sentence
underscore and magnify the malice of the speakers, especially when
it is compared with the same text in MS Harley 149 (pp. 79–80):

> . . . they said that they knew right well that he was not worthy to have no
> sepulture . . . and then we shall give thee to the birds of the air and to the
> beasts of the earth for to be devoured.

The contrast between the careful burial that Joseph arranged for Christ
and the nonburial threatened by Joseph's adversaries is underscored in
the poetic version (p. 72, lines 777–80):

> "for he gan ihesu graue,"
> þai sai, "fer in þe felde
> his beriele sall he haue,
> wilde bestes his banes to welde."

This is skillfully done, but again very different from what we find in
Trevisa's translation. The use of doublets is especially noticeable in
Trevisa's *Gospel of Nicodemus*, and sometimes reminiscent of biblical
poetic parallelism, suggesting perhaps that as a translator he may have
been influenced by the style of the Bible, particularly the Old Testament.
The extent of Trevisa's knowledge of the Bible is not known, but should
have been considerable, if the hypothesis to be discussed in the next
chapter has any foundation in fact.

When the Jews accuse Pilate's guards of dipping their standards in adoration of Jesus, the guards protest that they are pagans, and have no reason to worship him (I.5.14–15):

> Etenim tenentes nos signa curuauerunt se et adorauerunt.

Trevisa translates:

> We held the banners and they bent down and worshipped him, *not by our doing.*

This is a common type of addition in which Trevisa emphasizes or makes explicit something that is implicit in the text but might be missed in a first reading. Here are a few other examples quoted from the translation, with Trevisa's addition in italics:

> IV.2.4–7 By the emperor's heal, quoth the Jews, who that dispiseth God, he is worthy to die. This man dispiseth God, *therefore he is worthy to die.*

> XIII.2.1–3 The Jews cleped together all knights that kept the sepulchre of Jesus and spake to them and said: What were the women that the angel spake to *as ye telleth?*

> XXV.8–9 I am Enoch, quoth that one, that was translated hither by God's word, *and am here in Paradise.*

> XXVI.6–7 I was a thief and did many other evil deeds upon earth *while I was alive.*

The explanatory function of these additions is self-evident, but the second one (XIII.2.1–3) is especially noteworthy in its expression of the skepticism of the questioners.

We have observed that the Latin text is subject to harmonization with the canonical gospels, but there is some evidence that Trevisa himself engaged in this kind of "correction," even including details from the Old Testament, as in the first of the following instances:

> V.1.12–14 And there were *witches* (curantes medici), Iamnes and Mambres, and they did wonders as Moses did, but not all . . . (Exod. 7:11).

> VI.2.6–7 I was crooked and lame, and he healed me with a word, *and made me go upright* (John 5:8–9).

> VII.2–3 I touched the hem of his clothes, and the stream stint of my blood, *and I was whole anon* (Mark 5:28).

XXVIII.27–29 . . . they gave my knights much money and said: Tell ye that his disciples came by night and stole away his body *while ye were asleep* (Matt. 28:13).

A final and most interesting category consists of glosses on individual words that go beyond an explanatory function to express and enhance the emotion inherent in the passage:

II.1.7–8 Ecce *somnium* misit ipse ad uxorem tuam: Lo how he hath made thy wife have *a wonder dredful sweven and a grisly.*

IV.3.13 qui uero in Deum blasphemauerit *lapidari*: and he that despiseth God *to be stoned to the death with stones.*

XII.1.16–18 non recogitastis ne eum crucifigeretis sed et *lanceastis eum*: ye bethought you not that you should not have nailed him to the cross, and also *ye sticked him with a spear into the heart.*

XXVII.3.6–7 Et subito *transfigurati* sunt [*candidi*] nimis, et non sunt uisi amplius: And were suddenly *transfigured and changed into a glorious likeness and shape* and worth wonder *bright and white*, and were seen no more.

In summary, it seems from our review of Trevisa's *Gospel of Nicodemus* that his translation is not only literal and accurate, but also at times almost lyrical in its underscoring of the emotional effects of the original. Earlier we considered the question why Trevisa undertook this particular project; perhaps it is enough to say that the text interested him, and he wished to share it with those who knew no Latin. But I noticed a single phrase that could be the clue to a more substantial, theological reason for Trevisa's interest in this gospel.

The Lord took Adam by the right hand to lead him out of hell and said to him (XXIV.1.8):

Pax tibi cum omnibus filiis tuis, iustis meis.

Translators generally have treated this statement by Christ as a simple benediction. The poetic version has merely:

'pese be to þe,' he sayd,
'and to þi childer all.

The prose version in MS Harley 149 reads (p. 117): "Peace be to thee and all my true children"; and the two parallel French versions are similarly innocuous: "Pais a tei, e a toz tes feeilz, e as miens" (B); "Ma pes soit o toi, et o tes filz, et o mes sainz" (C). It is therefore of some interest to find in Trevisa:

> Peace be to thee and to all thy children *that be rightful.*

Christ's blessing is now qualified to show that only the righteous among the children of Adam will be freed from hell. There is a limit to what the sacrifice of Christ can accomplish: only the just shall be saved.

We are indebted to Turner (1966) for a valuable discussion of medieval attitudes toward the descent into hell in relation to the salvation of the righteous who lived before the Redemption. Why did Christ descend into hell? The simplest answer was to bind Satan and release all souls. But were all these souls to be saved, regardless of their life here on earth, simply because they had the misfortune of living before salvation through Christ became available? To meet this objection there were those who argued that he descended to preach to the saints in prison (1 Pet. 3:19), that all men might have the same free choice granted to those who live after Christ. But the most widely accepted solution became that of Augustine, who believed that Christ descended into hell to free Adam, the patriarchs, the prophets, and all the just who had been held there because of original sin. Those who were not righteous were not liberated when Christ descended, and therefore remained in hell. For this reason Augustine concluded that there must be two regions in hell: one where the damned were tortured, and another where the souls of the righteous were at rest.

I do not find that these concerns rise to the surface in Trevisa's *Gospel of Nicodemus* except in the single slim instance cited above. But they need not show themselves thus in order to be a factor in Trevisa's motivation for making the translation. Some ten years later, as we shall see, he expressed his opinions more openly in a translation of Ranulph Higden's *Polychronicon*, and in one of his notes there we find a discussion of hell that reveals an interest very close to that which I have suggested in connection with *Nicodemus*. Higden tells us that when King Edwin died, his soul was delivered out of hell by the prayers of St. Dunstan, to which Trevisa appends the following note (*Poly.* vi, 461):

> *Trevisa.* Here take heed, Christian men, of the meaning, for the words be perilously set. Therefore have mind now of two manner hells. In one was Adam, Abraham, Isaac, and Jacob, and other holy fathers that died to-fore Christ. Into that hell Christ alighted after his passion, and brought with him

thence the holy fathers that were there. The other hell is a place for them that be and shall be damned forever more; who that cometh in that hell shall never after be saved nor come out of pain. But as men say in common speech that a thief is delivered from hanging and from the gallows though he come not there, if he is delivered out of their power that would lead him to the gallows and hang him thereupon, so in some manner meaning he that is delivered out of the fiend's power that would bring him in hell, is delivered out of hell, though he come not there. So meaneth the prophet in the psalter, and sayeth: "Thou hast delivered my soul out of the lower hell" [Psalm 85:13, Vulgate: *eruisti animam meam ex inferno inferiori*].

We have devoted more space to *Nicodemus* than will be possible for the other translations, but there are reasons which I hope justify this lengthy excursus. First, it is probably the least known of Trevisa's texts, and deserves more attention than it has received; second, it may well be his earliest effort, and thus shows him in the process of learning his craft; and third, as we have seen, its Latin original is beset with many knots that must be untangled, a problem that nearly every medieval translator had to face. It is possible that there was no satisfactory Latin text of *Nicodemus* available to Trevisa; on the other hand, the somewhat aberrant text that he used may reflect his lack of experience in choosing a good exemplar, or perhaps his lack of the financial resources necessary to obtain one. Whatever the case, the resulting text is a remarkably good one, cautious in its handling of defects in the Latin, and skilled in its modest underscoring of the literary effects of the original work. I have no hesitation in pronouncing it the best of the medieval English translations of the *Gospel of Nicodemus*.

Dialogus inter Militem et Clericum

From an apocryphal gospel of the first millennium Trevisa next turns his attention to a controversial tract which at the time of translation was perhaps eighty years old but still very much in the news. The English manuscripts regularly call it *Dialogus*, while the Latin texts designate it *Disputatio inter Clericum et Militem* (the participants are often reversed). For convenience in discussion we may speak of the *Disputatio* when referring to the Latin text, and the *Dialogus* in reference to Trevisa's translation.

In the broadest sense the subject of this treatise is the relationship of church and state, a topic hotly debated at Oxford, where we may suppose Trevisa to have been working on this translation in the early 1370s. The author of the *Disputatio* is unknown, though a note in the Vatican MS Borghese 29 mentions two candidates, Marsilius of Padua and William of Ockham. The latter became the popular choice in the early Latin printed editions, as well as in the sixteenth-century edition of Trevisa's *Dialogus* (1531), where the original is confidently attributed to "Gulielmus de Occam." In modern times a more plausible candidate, Pierre DuBois, has been proposed, but the problem is unresolved, and the *Disputatio* remains for our purposes anonymous.

Despite the elusiveness of its author, the *Disputatio* is clearly one of those tracts of the late thirteenth century defending the policies of the French king Philip IV, known as "the Fair" (Philippe le Bel), in his conflict with Boniface VIII (1294–1303). The pope wanted to organize a crusade while Philip was more concerned with consolidating his position as a power in western Europe. In the phase of the conflict with which we are concerned (ca. 1297) a burning issue was the right of the king to tax the clergy "for defense of the realm." Of course those projects, which Philip classified as national defense (such as war with England), were looked upon by Boniface as the usual sort of political and military adventures in which secular rulers were often recklessly engaged. As the conflict between king and pope heated up, people began taking sides. The king's beloved tutor, Aegidius Romanus (whose *De Regimine Principum* Trevisa will later translate), turned against Philip and wrote a powerful defense of papal authority. But there were many clerics, particularly those with legal training whom we would call civil servants, who took up the royal cause and wrote skillfully and effectively in its defense. The author of the *Disputatio* was undoubtedly one of these lawyers (*legistes*) of Philip the Fair, writing perhaps in 1297, the year in which Boniface was forced to back down from the extreme position against taxation represented by his bull *Clericis Laicos* (1296).

The *Dialogues* opens with an exclamation from the clerk, who represents the papal point of view (spelling modernized):

> I wonder, sir noble knight, that in few days times be changed, right is buried, laws be overturned, and statutes be trodden under foot.

He goes on to claim (thinking no doubt of the tax policies of Philip the Fair) that Holy Church is no longer held in honor, and her goods are taken from her by force and against the law. When asked by the knight

146

to explain what he means by "law," the clerk specifies "the statutes and ordinances of bishops of Rome and decrees of holy fathers." This triggers an attack by the knight on the pope's presumption in supposing that he can, simply by issuing a decree, make himself lord of temporal wealth. The argument draws on a concept of dominion which must have appealed to Wyclif and his colleagues at Oxford. "No man," says the knight, "hath power to ordain statutes of things over the which he hath no lordship (*dominium*)." Thus princes can make no laws respecting religion (*de vestris spiritualibus*), and priests can make no laws respecting temporal things (3.5–9):

> Therefore I laughed well fast when I heard tell that pope Boniface had made a new statute, that he himself should be above all secular lords, princes, kings and emperors, and above all kingdoms.

The knight's language is exaggerated, but he does seem to refer here to the bull *Clericis Laicos*, which so enraged the king in 1296.

The clerk replies by using biblical authority to prove that Christ was lord of all things, including the temporal, and that his appointed vicar, the pope, has the same power. To this the knight responds by distinguishing between two times or phases of Christ's life. The first was that of his humility, that is, his life on earth until his death on the cross; the second was and is the time of his power and majesty (*potestatis*), after his resurrection, when he said (Matt. 28:18): "All power is given unto me in heaven and earth." The power granted to Christ's vicar relates only to the time of his humility, and not to that of his power and majesty, for as Jesus himself said (John 18:36), "My kingdom is not of this world." To this text the knight subjoins many other verses supporting the same point.

The extremism of this complete separation of the spiritual and temporal realms is of course intolerable to the clerk, because it would paralyze the church's ministry in the world. A most obvious example is the hearing of confession, where the loss of power to assign penance in specific, material terms would destroy the effectiveness of this sacrament. The clerk seizes on this point (11.4–5):

> Denyest thou that Holy Church shall know and correct men of sins?

When the knight concedes that the church has the power of the confessional, the clerk then argues that this is a case where the pope has authority over temporalities. But this counterattack merely prompts the knight to launch an extended reductio ad absurdum, showing what would happen if church and state entered into a competitive enforcement of secular laws. Then, he says, we would have that state of affairs envisioned by Habakkuk (1:4): "Therefore the law is slacked, and judgment doth never go forth." But in fact the scriptures require obedience to secular rulers both in the Old Testament (Deut. 17:12) and the New (Rom. 13:1, Titus 3:1). As a clincher to his case, the knight aggressively argues that the church should not, because of its concern with the institution of marriage, seek to extend its jurisdiction in matters of inheritance in the secular realm, since Jesus said (Luke 12:14), "Man, who made me a judge or a divider over you?"

In the face of this tour de force, the clerk shifts his ground in order to make the general claim that the function of the temporal realm is to serve the spiritual realm: therefore "the temporal is subject to the spiritual, and the spiritual power shall govern and rule the temporal power." Implicit in this position is the soul-body analogy and the view that man does not live by bread alone: temporal rulers are thus in a clearly subordinate position, looking for direction to those in spiritual authority. But the knight of course will allow nothing of the kind. He concedes only that every nation has naturally chosen to provide material support for its priesthood. Even the pagan pharaoh did as much (Gen. 47:22), and both Moses and Paul agree that "Thou shalt not muzzle the ox when he treadeth out the corn" (Deut. 25:4, 1 Cor. 9:9). But while the pope may rule in spiritual matters, it is absurd to argue that he is ruler over the temporalities of secular kingdoms. The Old Testament shows that "kings corrected priests and undertook them and blamed them when they erred in governance of temporality" (1 Kings 1 and 4, and 2 Kings 12). This remark sparks an amusing exchange (19.8–14):

> *Clericus.* Me wondereth that ye say that the king undertook the bishop in governance of temporality.
>
> *Miles.* Ye stirreth me and waketh me as it were of my sleep, and maketh me speak otherwise than I thought.
>
> *Clericus.* Let the hound wake and bark.
>
> *Miles.* For ye cannot use manhood sufferance and patience of princes, I trow ye shall feel barking and biting.

The clerk seizes this momentary tactical advantage and presses his point: since kings and princes have their own possessions, why can't they let us have ours? But the knight, as always, has his reply ready. The essence of it is that secular lords, who traditionally granted temporalities to the church for spiritual purposes, have a solemn responsibility to see that the church uses this wealth for the purposes intended by the donors: prayers for the souls of the departed, and alms deeds for poor and needy men. Shall not he who will not do the deeds of knighthood be deprived of his wages? The same applies to priests who spend their income in folly and self-indulgence. The clerk is here lashed with his own ideal: clerical literature of this period is filled with variations on the theme of the priest as one of God's knights, a practitioner of celestial chivalry. Even more than the earthly knight, the priest should be held strictly accountable for his actions. This is then reinforced from scripture by the example of King Joash, who rebuked the priests for their neglect, and diverted money from their treasury to provide for the repair of the temple (2 Kings 12:7–12). "I know well it liketh you not to hear these words," says the knight gleefully, "and natheless I speak naught but words of Holy Writ." And he concludes this argument by assuring the clerk that if the church does not use its wealth for pious purposes, princes are responsible for doing something about it.

The knight has of course represented the secular power in the best possible light, and this is clearly the view of the author. But at this point recognition is given to the different view of the church, and in particular Boniface, toward the behavior and objectives of the secular arm, in the following objection raised by the clerk to the knight's use of the example of Joash (quoting here from the more literal translation of the printed edition of the *Dialogus*, 23.26–33):

> This king Joash took not the goods and chattels to his own use, but he bestowed them on Holy Church's use. But nowadays ye take our goods, which ye spend not to the use of holy church, but on your busy and unruly soldiers, and on ships and on engines of war. And therefore the ensaumple that ye bring forth is not against us, nor against our works and deeds, but ye would thereby color your violence and wrong.

It takes a bold polemicist to put such powerful words in the mouth of his opponent, and it is interesting that here Trevisa seems reluctant to acquiesce in this confident strategy. Where the Latin says that nowadays kings spend the church's substance "on your busy and unruly soldiers, and on ships and on engines of war" (*militares tumultus et bellicosas classes*), Trevisa has merely "in chivalry" (23:10).

That Trevisa deliberately tones down the clerk's condemnation of royal policy seems borne out by his intensification of the knight's retaliatory reference to clerical abuses. In the *Disputatio* the knight merely asks (23.15–24.1):

> Is it not grievous to you that your cousins and your kinsmen take to them of Holy Church's goods and chattels, and sometimes other persons that be not honest?

But to this simple question Trevisa adds a full-scale denunciation for which there is no basis in the Latin (24.1–6):

> in great slander to you and to all the people that is under you, and be full venimous by your own evil example in living? This ye suffer that may be cause of God's wrath upon the king and upon all the realm, that recklessly suffereth you so frowardly work against God Almighty.

There is considerable heat in this passage, and it seems to indicate that Trevisa, though he does not agree with everything the knight says (as we shall see), here shows himself to be a militant member of the church reform party. The knight then concludes (and here Trevisa follows the Latin) that while churchmen appear not at all disturbed by ecclesiastical abuses, it seems to them terribly wrong when the king gently asks for a subsidy, not for himself, but for their salvation and the defense of the church and its possessions (24:11–13):

> *Clericus.* Alas! woe is me wretched man, ye tear and hale and take away my flesh and my skin, and that ye clepeth salvation!

In response to this riposte, the knight paints a grim picture of what would happen to society if the control of the king were removed. The have-nots would turn against the haves, and chaos would result. Or an enemy would invade, and leave churchmen stripped of all their possessions. But if despite your ingratitude kings and princes put themselves in peril to defend you at their own expense, while you eat and drink and are at ease without giving them any aid, then it would surely seem that you churchmen are the only lords, and kings and princes mere bondmen and slaves. Is it so hard a thing that while you rest yourselves, your riches take the place of personal service? You say that this is cruel, but scripture shows that it is necessary, as when King Joash stripped the gold from the temple to buy peace with Hazael king of Syria (2 Kings 12:18), and when Hezekiah did the same to mollify the king of Assyria (2 Kings

18:16). If you fail to understand the teaching of scripture, how is this an argument against kings and princes? Therefore when Christian men are imperiled, the wealth of the church must be used in their defense. But because the king seeks to follow the law of Almighty God and do it with your assent and good will, you are not ashamed to exasperate him who deals graciously with you. But beware what Solomon says (Prov. 16:14): "The wrath of a king is as messengers of death."

The fullness of the royalist position is here finally revealed. Is it love that holds the cosmos together, as Troilus sings? On the contrary, it is the tight control of secular kings over their peoples. The church is more of an onlooker, tolerated and protected, and so required to pay for this privileged position. We have come a long way from the early years of the church of Christ, when the prophecy that kings shall shut their mouths because of him (Isa. 52:15) was being literally fulfilled. The European nations are now beginning to make their move, and in England, at least, it was to be a king whose command inaugurated the Reformation. One can perceive these momentous developments between the lines of the *Dialogus*, but the poor clerk is allowed to see only the clear and present danger to the church represented by the royal policy (29.14–15):

> *Clericus.* May what is once given be withcleped and withdrawn? Then may every vow be destroyed and foredone.

To which the knight responds by saying that there is no intention on the part of kings and princes to withdraw gifts offered to God, but rather to see that those gifts are properly used for his service. And what more appropriate use can there be than the withstanding of enemies and criminals, and the purchase of peace for Christian men?

The clerk now tries to employ scripture in his own defense, interpreting Jesus' saying on the payment of tribute (Matt. 17:24–27) to mean that the clergy should be free, that is, exempt from taxation. The knight counters that this saying applies only to Christ himself, for, as Paul says (Rom. 13:7), "Render therefore to all their dues: tribute to whom tribute is due." The most that the knight will concede is that clerks in their persons are free, but even here he does not allow this grace to those who are obviously in orders simply to make a living: only those who truly serve God at the altar are exempt. This concession does not extend to property: if the church buys a field, that field does not thereby become exempt from paying rent. Here the clerk interjects: "We speak not of rent and tribute, but of exactions." To this the knight replies that if possessions may be subject to rent, it is even more proper that they be taxed for their defense. And if the church has long-standing exemptions from such taxation, clerks should be the more ready to accept it when circumstances make it necessary, lest their burdens be increased and they end by being stripped of all their power and wealth.

Bereft of arguments, the clerk makes one final effort to withstand the knight by recurring to his conviction that the sacred vows of previous donors should be respected: may the king take away from the church what his noble predecessors had given to her? To this the knight responds that all such generous kings had made their bequests for the common good, and when present circumstances require that these gifts be appropriated for that same purpose, churchmen should not object. It is for this reason that every statute must be considered subject to revocation in cases of dire necessity. Thus Solomon changed God's law for the punishing of theft. The knight leaves little doubt in his concluding statement about the ultimate authority of the king to change and even create law (36:35–37:18):

> And therefore, sir clerk, refrain your tongue, and acknowledge the king by his royal power to be above your laws, customs, privileges and liberties, and he may add or diminish whatsoever he think according with equity and reason or by the advice of his nobles.

I have used the form of the printed edition here (in part) to show the sense of the original Latin, which is uncompromising in its statement of complete royal authority. With this we may compare Trevisa's version of the same passage (36:9–37.2):

> And therefore, sir clerk chasteneth your tongue and acknowledge that the king may be above customs, privileges, and freedoms while he is rightful king with full power, and that he may put to privileges and laws, and withdraw and change and redress every (one) that erreth, by counsel of reason and assent of lords as it seemeth that reason asketh.

Notice that Trevisa does not allow the king to be above the *laws*, and further qualifies his supremacy by alluding to the possibility that under certain circumstances it may be determined that he is *not* "rightful king with full power." This hint of a check on royal authority seems confirmed in the slight change from the Latin to the English which appears to *require* the advice of the lords rather than leaving such consultation optional.

Thus while Trevisa finds much to applaud in the knight's denunciation of corruption in the church, he does not hesitate to disagree with him, as here in the argument for royal supremacy. Textual problems preclude certainty in our conclusions: did Trevisa deliberately refrain from saying that the king was above the laws, was his Latin exemplar defective, or did the phrase drop out of the English manuscripts? Interestingly it is restored in the printed edition, published during the reign of Henry VIII: "acknowledge the king by his royal power to be above your laws." My own view is that Trevisa's omission was deliberate, not only because he might be expected to share his patron's conviction on the limitations of royal power, but also because of his own belief in the prerogatives of Holy Church. But to come to a better sense of the reliability of our text we must now review the facts concerning its transmission and then examine some of its peculiarities for such evidence as may be found of Trevisa's views and attitudes.

Although the *Disputatio* was written about 1297, the surviving Latin manuscripts belong to the early fifteenth century, which means that we have no direct evidence of the state of the Latin text during the first hundred years of its transmission. Yet we have indications of a strong interest in it during the fourteenth century, not only through Trevisa, but also because it was adapted to a new setting in the *Somnium Viridarii* (ca. 1378), an anonymous and lengthy treatise on the relations of church and state, and made the subject of a commentary by Bernard Alamand (ca. 1342–1401). The commentary survives in a single manuscript, but the *Somnium* was popular and often recopied, thus bringing the *Disputatio* imbedded in its text to a new and wider audience. A list of the manuscripts and printed editions of the *Disputatio* may be found in Perry (1925), and a more complete list with a critical edition and translation have been provided in the dissertation of Erickson (1966), which was subsequently published in a more compact form (1967). To the list of eleven Latin manuscripts in Erickson may be added the Oxford MS Rawlinson G40 (fols. 32–38) in the Bodleian Library, specifically the B portion of that manuscript which is dated 15th century (*Summary Catalogue* no. 14771, pp. 348–49). A preliminary check of the Rawlinson MS (R) suggests that it has the characteristics of the five manuscripts of

English provenance classified by Erickson, but more study is needed to see exactly where it fits into that scheme.

Trevisa's translation, the *Dialogus*, is of course edited by Perry (1925) and based on the British Library MS Harleian 1900, with variants from the other known copies. Perry was unable to have access to the Burleigh House manuscript, an important copy now accessible to scholars as Huntington Library HM 28561. Perry also includes, on the lower half of the page, the sixteenth-century printed edition of Trevisa's translation to which I have already referred. This text has obviously been revised with a view to making it a closer, more literal translation of the Latin, although some of Trevisa's unique contributions remain. These then are the texts needed in any consideration of Trevisa as translator of the *Disputatio*, a subject to which we may now turn.

Textual corruptions are sometimes disguised, and there is always the danger, as we have noted in the case of *Nicodemus*, of interpreting them as changes introduced by the translator. Every omission, for example, should be scrutinized carefully for indications that it may have a textual origin. When the knight makes his argument for the separation of spiritual and temporal powers, he makes this flat statement (3.19–21):

> Wherefore it is a thing in vain, whatever ye ordain of temporal things, over which ye have of God received no power.

Trevisa omits this sentence completely (it is quoted here from the text of the printed edition), and one might suppose that he is here resisting the knight's extremism. The Latin is clear, and has no repetitions that might cause eye-skip. But when we notice Trevisa's translation of the preceding sentence, the possibility of scribal error behind the omission is revealed (3.4–5):

> Also ye may ordain no statutes of temporality, over the which ye have no *power nother authority*.

The italicized phrase translates *auctoritatem*, while the corresponding word in the omitted sentence is *potestatem*. Hence it looks as if Trevisa formed a doublet from these two Latin words, and thus the missing sentence may have ended with that same doublet, *power nother authority*, a repetition which may have caused scribal eye-skip, and thus the omission of the sentence. Other explanations for the loss are possible, but it is best not to base any conclusions about Trevisa as translator on any problematic passage where a scribal explanation is an evident alternative.

A clearer case of omission due to eye-skip occurs in the knight's account of the pious King Joash (22.26–30):

> ... the king's writer and the bishop went up into the treasury, and poured out and told the money that was found in *God's house*. And they gave it after the number and weight into their hands, that were surveyors of the masonry of *God's house*.

Trevisa's text omits the second of these two sentences, almost certainly because of the repetition italicized above, although the corresponding repetition in the Latin (*domo domini . . . domus domini*) means that we must allow the possibility of omission from Trevisa's Latin exemplar.

Despite the valuable assistance of Erickson's critical edition of the Latin *Disputatio*, it is sometimes difficult to be sure whether Trevisa's departure from the established text is a deliberate change or a faithful translation of an errant Latin manuscript. I shall first list examples of this kind of problem that I have noticed, and then comment on some of them. Each example is, as usual, located by page and line number in Perry, followed in order by the accepted Latin reading, the English translation, and Latin variants, the latter identified mainly by sigla from Erickson.

> 3.12 Nihil alius ergo erit ius habere quam velle: T *om*, BOR *om* (*repetition of* velle?) / 17.2 magnum est? hit is nouȝt þe moste, non est magnum R / 17.4 L *om*: þat sowiþ spiritualte, vestrum spirituale BO / 20.7–8 vestris necessitatibus: in youre synnes & ȝoure vanite, BO *add* quinymo voluptatibus / 21.8 delere (C): ȝe auȝt be sory, dolore DFGR debere BO / 30.5–6 preciosius domino: licher to þe doom of God, (domino *mg*) iudicio similius R / 31.11 principaliter: in his presence, presenter (?) R / 32.2–3 Tales enim inquam plane sunt liberi non per evangelium: We graunteþ atte fulle þat þei beþ fre, but y say nouȝt playnlich by þe gospel, Concedimus inquit plane de hijs quod sunt liberi non dico plane per euangelium R / 33.1 censum: silver oþer gold, agrum (*sic*) R /

Most of these cases are self-explanatory, but it is worth observing that 21.8 suggests either that Trevisa used more than one Latin text or, equally conjectural, that his exemplar had been corrected from a continental manuscript, the tradition represented by MSS BO. The final instance (33.1) could show Trevisa coping with a nonsensical reading: Sicut ego super certos agros habeo certum *agrum* (R) "Just as from certain fields I have a certain *field*." Knowing that this was wrong, but not knowing for certain what word belonged in place of *agrum*, Trevisa perhaps supplied "silver or gold" (if *aurum* was the intended word), a perfectly satisfactory alternative to *censum* ("rent"). Alternatively, as Hanna has suggested to me, "silver oþer gold" could be accepted as a legitimate (if free) translation of *censum* ("property, wealth"), leaving *agrum* in MS R a simple error by attraction from preceding *agros*. It is well to keep in mind the fallibility of Trevisa's exemplar in the case of all his translations. Comparison of his works with corresponding modern editions often conveys a false impression of ineptness, when the real reason for apparent aberrations may be a problem in the exemplar that was beyond the translator's control. As the Wycliffite translators found, it was very difficult in those days to find a Latin Bible "somedeal true," and the problem would naturally be even greater for copies of secular works.

There are of course doubtful cases, where it is difficult to say whether the problem is in the Latin, in Trevisa, or in the eye of the beholder:

> 21.8–9 fortissimum et apertissimum: wiþ ioye & wiþ gode wille / 26.7–8 sub umbra: vnder her wynges / 31.15 sicut patet ad oculum tonsorati: as hit is y-seye alday / 32.13 quia Christi officio estis applicati: by priuylege of princes / 32.17–18 sed de exaccionibus: but of doyng & dedes / 36.8 qui est summus: in his owne lond /

Certainly we must allow for aberrations in Trevisa's Latin exemplar that do not appear in the surviving manuscripts (21.8–9, 31.15, 32.17–18), but some of the above appear to be calculated changes, whether for (32.13) or against (36.8) the rights of kings it is difficult to decide.

Did the Latin ever leave Trevisa completely baffled? This is not easy to prove, but one passage seems to point in that direction. The knight is arguing that justice can be maintained only by the enforcement of secular laws under a single authority, the king:

> Nulli dubium est quin iustum et iniustum secundum humanas leges, que de talibus sanxerunt, sit de temporalibus iudicandis, secundum quas et sub quibus subiectis omnibus est vivendum.

This is translated by Erickson as follows:

> No one can doubt that, concerning temporal things, justice and injustice should be judged according to secular laws, which are established for such matters, and according to which and under which laws all subjects must live.

Here is Trevisa's translation of the same passage (12.4–7):

> For hit is no doute þat riȝtful & unriȝtful in temporalte schal be demed by
> lawes þat men haue made of temporalte, *but me mot take hede al aboute what
> longeþ to þe cause þat schal be demed.*

The concluding clause, indicated by italics, seems to depart recklessly
from the original, but why? Trevisa does not hesitate to change the
meaning of his text when he feels strongly about something, yet here
there seems at first glance to be no ideological reason for the change. The
Latin manuscripts are in general agreement (for "sit de temporalibus" R
has "etiam de temporalibus"), yet in this case the editor of the printed
edition of Trevisa's translation (12.21–23), who rarely hesitates to revise
his text if it is not in agreement with the Latin, lets the reading of this
sentence stand. Being reluctant to charge Trevisa with negligence or
ignorance, I offer the following explanation. Trevisa does not accept the
knight's argument for complete secularization of the laws, because he
believes firmly in the medieval system of secular *and* ecclesiastical courts
which protects the rights of the clergy. Therefore, he simply replaces the
knight's argument with his own: in the administration of justice, each
case must be examined individually in order to decide whether it should
be tried in an ecclesiastical or in a secular court. If my interpretation of
this difficult passage is correct, then I may more confidently assert my
conviction that Trevisa almost always knows what he is doing.

Biblical arguments abound in the *Dialogus*: does Trevisa evince any
particular interest in these? In general the answer must be in the negative,
although the biblical references do contain much that is of interest. We
may note, in passing, for example, a culturally significant difference in
the rendering of the phrase *verbum dei* (9.5), first by Trevisa as "the *law*
of God" (which must be obeyed), and then by his sixteenth-century
editor as "the *word* of God" (that must be proclaimed). At times Trevisa
seems to fill out biblical verses that are incompletely quoted in the
Latin. Thus Psalm 2:8, cited in full in its first occurrence (4.12–14), is
abbreviated in Latin the second time but there given in full by Trevisa
(9.10–11), seemingly in a translation independent of the earlier one. Yet
he sometimes garbles the text (unless his exemplar was at fault), as in
the following quotation from Habakkuk 1:3–4:

> fiet quod dicit Abacuc propheta in principio, "factum est iudicium, et contra-
> dictio potentior. Propter hoc lacerata est lex, et non pervenit usque ad finem
> iudicium." Quia vere non erit hoc iusticiam et iudicium in terra facere sed
> iusticiam et iudicium in terra lacerare.

Trevisa translates this as follows (13.1–5):

þanne is fulfild þe prophecie of Abacuc: "In þe bygynnyng was made riȝtful doom, & wiþsigginge of the prophete is stronge. þe lawe is y-tore & to-rent, þe dome com nouȝt to þe ende." For þat schal nouȝt be to-rent riȝtwisnesse in erþe.

Clearly the repetition in the final sentence has caused eye-skip, whether in the Latin or English is not certain, but it is also evident that Trevisa has mistakenly made the locating phrase *in principio* (meaning "at the beginning" of the first chapter of Habakkuk) a part of the quotation, and has understood the *contradictio* to be that of the prophet himself. All of this, together with the corruption of the final sentence, makes this passage in Trevisa's translation well-nigh impenetrable. Even the printed edition fails to correct the final sentence, so I quote for comparison the translation of Erickson:

there will come about what the prophet Habakkuk said: "Strife and contention arise. Therefore the law is torn in pieces and judgment cometh not to the end," Hab. 1:3–4. For, truly, this will not make justice and righteousness on earth, but will tear them to pieces.

Having shown by the quotation from Habakkuk that competition between the ecclesiastical and secular authorities in the administration of justice would result in a rending of the law, the knight now wishes to point out precisely where he believes the role of the church does come into play. In brief, his argument is that priests should be the enforcers of conscience, and leave the enforcement of law to the secular arm. But in seeking support for this in the Bible, the knight seizes on a verse that does not easily serve his purpose (Deut. 17:12):

Qui autem superbierit, nolens obedire *sacerdotis imperio*, qui eo tempore ministrat Domino Deo tuo, et decreto iudicis, morietur homo ille.

(And the man that will do presumptuously, and will not hearken unto the priest that standeth to minister there before the Lord thy God, or unto the judge, even that man shall die.)

This legislation enforces the command of the priest (*sacerdotis imperio*), and only as an afterthought the decree of the judge (whether ecclesiastical or secular is not specified, even if such a distinction had any place in ancient Israel). But the knight solves this problem by changing the wording of this verse, and adding a commentary on it that is difficult to distinguish from the verse itself if one does not have the Bible at hand. Here I must quote from the text as preserved in the *Somnium Viridarii* (ca. 1378), which seems closer to Trevisa's exemplar than Erickson's critical text:

> Principes de suo iure de iusto et iniusto cognoscunt et eius finem; un- usquisque sicut tenetur attendet, et ei obediet, sicut praecipitur Deut. 17c: "Si quis autem tumens superbia non obediverit *ejus imperio*," nec principes, cujus officium fuerit judicandi, habet potestatem resistendi et cohercendi: tunc incipit vestra cognitio, quia tunc attendere (accedere R) debet vestra monitio.

Here is Trevisa's translation (13.6–13):

> þe princes by her lawes schal knowe & deme riȝtful & vnriȝtful, & þe ende þerof; euereche man schal take hede as he is y-holde & be obedient to hym, as hit is yhote Deuteronomy 17o: " 'Si quis autem tumens,' if eny man is prout & wole nouȝt be obedient to þe princes hestes," & þe princes office haþ no power to deme & to chastee siche mysdoers, þanne bigynne ȝoure knowleche & ȝoure dome, for ȝoure monicioun schal refreyne & chastee.

Notice first that the knight has altered the Vulgate phrase *sacerdotis imperio* to *ejus imperio*, intending that we understand it to refer to the prince, and, second, that Trevisa, as he often does, supplies the antecedent intended in "þe *princes* hestes," thus becoming an (unwitting?) accessory to the knight's misuse of Deuteronomy 17:12. The sixteenth-century editor, interestingly, though he usually inserts biblical references on the slight- est provocation, here *deletes* the reference to Deuteronomy 17, while allowing the argument to stand. There are other cases where one might have expected Trevisa to check for biblical accuracy. In one case, where the knight refers correctly to "Josaphat et Joram et Ochozias, patres eius reges Juda" (2 Kings 12:18), it is evident that Trevisa's exemplar had "josaphat et *aaron* et occasias *pater* eius *rex* iuda" (MS R), which Trevisa obediently translates "Josophath, Aaron & his fader Ocosias kyng of Juda" (27.4), apparently without a glance at the biblical passage cited in his exemplar. But corrections of this kind would be merely pedantic. The case that really surprises is Deuteronomy 17:12, where the knight clearly misuses a text, and does so with impunity.

There is some evidence that Trevisa wanted to compress the argument of the *Dialogus*, even though it could not be called especially wordy, and we find that as a rule his editor conscientiously restored the full text in his revision. In the following instances I quote first Trevisa's version, followed by its equivalent in the printed edition, so that the extent of Trevisa's abbreviations can be readily appreciated.

> *Miles.* I am a lewed man and may not understand subtle and dark speech; therefore thou must take more plain manner of speaking. (1.4–6)

> *Miles.* These words pass my capacity. I am a lewed man, and though I went to school in my childhood, yet got I not so profound learning that those your words can of me be understand. And therefore worshipful clerk, if ye desire to have communication with me, ye must use a more homely and plainer fashion of speaking.

★

> These be God's own words; but what Christian man doubteth whether God be true of his words? (4.15–5.2)

> These be not ours, but God's own words; nor we wrote them not, but God sent them, and the Holy Ghost spake them; and who doubteth whether he may ordain and make statutes, whom he knoweth to be Lord of all things?

★

> Also to Timothy: (8.13)

> That the bishop is made ruler in those things that long to God, thou mayest perceive by the words of St. Paul writing to Timothy, the 2nd epistle and 2nd chapter where he saith:

★

> Joas did that by mildness and by good intent, and not by covetousness. (22.4–5)

> The said king, in his so doing, did not offend, for so much as he did it not for any covetousness, but of Godly zeal, not of ambition, but of devout religion.

These condensations seem harmless enough and perhaps in some cases add to the effectiveness of the arguments. Other instances could be cited where the motives may be different: for example, where he may wish to tone down the harshness of the knight's description of social anarchy (26.3–5), or where he may simply be in a hurry to finish (35.8–9). Simple omissions are more difficult to interpret, especially where there is no evidence of textual corruption. Of many examples that could be cited, I subjoin a single passage containing no less than four omissions, which I indicate here by supplying the missing translation in italics (7.9–17):

> Peter was ordained Christ's vicar for the state of his manhood and not for the state of his bliss and majesty. He was not made Christ's vicar in doing that Christ doth now in bliss, *for those things are unknown to us*; but for to follow

him in his doing that he did here on earth, *for those things are necessary to us.*
Then he gave his vicar that power that he used here in earth deathly, *not
that which he adopted when glorified.* And for to prove this by Holy Writ I take
witness of Christ and of Holy Writ as thou dost. Lo! Christ said to Pilate:
"My kingdom is not of this world." Also he saith that "he came not to be
served but to serve other men." *This witness is so manifest that it can confound
the man who resists it and break the stiffest of necks.*

Passages like this, however, are the exception; for the most part it can be
said that Trevisa provides a full rendering of the Latin, and very seldom
cuts corners.

In keeping with the evidence of compactness that we have noted,
however, it is worth mentioning that the incidence of doublets, which
were quite numerous in the *Nicodemus* translation, are comparatively
uncommon in the *Dialogus*. The following are representative examples:

2.4 infringuntur: despised and withsaid / 3.8 principatus: secular lords,
princes, kings and emperors / 4.3–4 versute: slily and wilily enough / 4.6
potestatem vel dominium: lordship, power and authority / 9.2 negotiis: needs
and business / 11.8 cognoscere: know and deem (*twice*) / 11.10 iudicare:
deme and rule / 14.7 sententiam: sentence and doom / 14.8 evidentiam:
open evidence and knowledge / 15.14–15 in cognitione: in doom and in
knowledge / 16.3 homo mortalis: man shaped for to die / 16.6 regere:
govern and rule / 23.12–13 vestram violentiam: your violence and your
wrong / 23.16 de bonis ecclesiae: of holy church goods and chattels / 26.2
querulosi: plaineth and grudgeth / 28.14 salus: help and salvation / 30.2
applicare: putting and turning / 30.11 libertates nostras: our privileges and
our freedom / 34.6 rebellionem: unkindness and rebelness /

What remain to be considered are those passages in which Trevisa
seems deliberately to have departed from or added to the Latin. When
all corruptions and other textual problems have been eliminated, I note
the following cases:

5.4 quia christianus sum et esse volo: for he may be withsaid in no manner
wise / 8.8–10 Et ut scias Christi vicarium ad spirituale regimen, non ad
temporale regnum seu dominium, assumptum: But for to know that Peter
was Christ's vicar in ghostly kingdom *of souls,* and not in temporal lordship
of castles and of lands / 14.14–15.1 Artare autem vos volo et urgere una nova
questione, utrum est vestrum de causa matrimonii cognoscere: It longeth to
you to know and to deem in cause of matrimony and of wedlock; *I pray
you, will ye therefore say that it followeth that ye shall know and deem of all that
longeth thereto, for the knitting of the deed?* / 17.9–11 Ecce quibus vos comparant

Christus et Paulus apostolus, utique operariis et stipendariis: Lo! how Christ likeneth you to workmen, to hired men, *to oxen and not to kings* / 24.11 me miserum: Alas! woe is me, wretched man / 24.14 ne perstrepite: I pray you, let be your noise and your grudging / 25.3 converterentur ad vestra: turn to your own *and destroy all that ye have* / 25.14–15 quando omnia bona vestra dispensanda saluatis: and save your own goods and chattels, *that should be destroyed with your own neighbors and with men of strange lands, ne were the king's help and his succor* / 28.15 And so it followeth that it longeth to the ghostly of holy church (*not in Latin*) / 31.10 Et sic illa responsio proprie videtur esse pro Christo: and so that answer was given for Christ, *and not for you* /

Apart from these, there is one passage I noticed which particularly illustrates Trevisa's indignation in regard to corrupt churchmen that we noted earlier. The knight is condemning ecclesiastics who use for their own purposes gifts that were intended to be used in prayers for the souls of the departed and charitable gifts to the poor and hungry. Trevisa follows the Latin closely except for the additions which are italicized (20.9–21.4):

Were it not needful that they that be dead were yholpe, and they that be alive be saved by deeds of mercy, *for the which our forefathers have given you great lordships and huge?* Spend ye not such lordships amiss and so wrongfully, that ye grieve both quick and dead and do them wrong against the will of them that gave you so great lordship and riches? *While ye recketh not of honesty of your own law, and of deeds of mercy and of charity, masses ye say not nother singeth in church; but in folly, in bobance, and in liking of this world, ye spend all that was given you with holy entent.*

In an earlier chapter we had occasion to notice the deterioration of the abbey of St. Augustine's, Bristol, and how the corrupt state of those canons may have been related to the circumstances of Trevisa's appointment as vicar of Berkeley. In any case, it seems unlikely that Trevisa would have been unaware of the sad state of the Bristol community so closely associated with the Berkeley family, and it is tempting to see in the above expansion of the knight's remarks an expression of the translator's own indignation on this subject.

An example of the translator's sharp disagreement with the argument of the knight is found in the one note that he allows himself in the *Dialogus*. It is near the beginning, and comes in response to the knight's distinction between the two different "times" of Christ. The first he calls the time of his humility (*humilitatis*) and the other the time of his power (*potestatis*). It is interesting that Trevisa translates the former not as "humility" but as "manhood." Later, in other contexts, he continues to avoid a straight use of "humility" in reference to Christ. One is where the knight refers to the power that Christ used and taught *in sua humilitate*, which Trevisa translates "in his deathly living." In another passage, which does not refer to Christ but to the clerk, the knight criticizes the latter for not responding appropriately to the *humilitate et paciencia* of princes, a doublet which Trevisa renders as "manhood, sufferance and patience," where "manhood" is clearly inappropriate to the context. Having first employed "manhood" to translate *humilitas* in a theologically important passage, it would seem that Trevisa continues to employ that word in order to be consistent even at the expense of accuracy in this case.

What Trevisa means by this emphasis on Christ's manhood rather than his humility is well expressed in the note which he inserts immediately following the knight's distinction between his humility and his power. And with this note, an eloquent expression of Trevisa's sense of the significance of the life of Christ both on earth and in eternity, we may conclude our review of his translation of the *Dialogus* (6.7–7.8):

> *Trevisa.* Here take heed of the knight's meaning and of the clerk's meaning also, for the words be not fully chambered. For all the time of Christ's manhood, that was tofore his passion, was time of his might, power, and majesty. For before his passion he turned water into wine; and healed blind, and lame, and many manner sick men; and had the sea, and wind, and weather, and fiends attendant to his hests; and fed five thousand of men with five loaves of bread and left twelve cups of relief; and reared men from death to life; and gave his disciples might and power over all the devils and fiends; and showed of his bliss to Peter, James, and John; and yede upon the sea in great tempest of weather and of the sea. Also when he sent his disciples to fetch him the ass to ride on into Jerusalem, he said: "If any man saith ought to you, saith that the Lord hath to do therewith"; and in his riding he was worshiped as a king, and some spread clothes in his way and some boughs; and then was the prophecy fulfilled [that] saith: "Daughters of Zion, lo! thy king cometh to thee, meek and mild, sitting upon an ass." Also in a time he drove beggars and sellers out of the temple as lord and king. Also his lore was in might and power, and he did all this and many other great deeds before his passion; then before his passion was time of his power and of his might and after his passion was and is time of his manhood. For after his passion St. Stephen saw him in his manhood stand in the father's right side [Acts 7:55–56].

FitzRalph's Defensio Curatorum

The famous sermon against the friars, *Defensio Curatorum*, was delivered in 1357, less than five years before Trevisa began his studies in Exeter College. Even if his translation was made in the late 1370s, his Latin exemplar represented a text that was then scarcely twenty years old. This stands in contrast to the age of *Nicodemus* (centuries) and the *Disputatio* (seventy years), and may explain why the textual problems of the sermon are comparatively insignificant. Unfortunately, T. P. Dolan's critical edition of the sermon is not yet available, but the text that we do have for comparison with Trevisa's translation is in reasonably stable form. Of the seventy-six manuscripts listed by Aubrey Gwynn (1937) and Katherine Walsh (1981), I have chosen the text in the Sermon Diary (MS Bodley 144, fols. 255r–271r) as a check against the printed editions of Melchior Goldast (1612–14, II, 1392–1410) and Edward Brown (1690, II, 466–86). When the Latin appears with no accompanying identification, it may be assumed that these authorities are in general agreement. When individual readings are given, I use the following sigla for MS Bodley 144 (B), Goldast (G), and Brown's *Fasciculus* (F).

Having already reviewed FitzRalph's career in an earlier chapter, we may now focus on events leading to his clash with the friars at Avignon in 1357, a conflict that lasted until his death in 1360. The archbishop had crossed over from Ireland to England in the summer of 1356, and released his dialogue, *De Pauperie Salvatoris* ("On the Poverty of the Savior"), at Oxford, where there already was controversy between the friars and the secular faculty of arts. In this dialogue FitzRalph argues that mendicancy is not biblical, and that the fraternal orders should be abolished. Invitations to speak soon came flowing in, and FitzRalph proceeded to develop ideas from the *De Pauperie Salvatoris* in his sermons, mainly in London, from June 1356 through March 1357. Perhaps the most powerful of these was the sermon preached at St. Paul's Cross on 12 March 1357 (Bodley 144, fols. 112v–127r) in reply to the *Appellacio* against him issued by the friars two days before. From this point there was no turning back: FitzRalph and the friars were at war. The latter obtained an order from King Edward III forbidding FitzRalph to leave the country, but the archbishop was able to elude the authorities and arrived in the papal court at Avignon during August 1357.

By November of the same year representatives of the friars had reached Avignon, notably the Augustinian John of Arderne. Aware of dark clouds on the horizon, Pope Innocent VI made the by now customary gesture of ordering the enforcement of *Super Cathedram*, a bull originally issued by Boniface VIII in 1300 to reduce resentment of the secular clergy against the friars. The reissuance of this bull one more time by Innocent VI in 1357 proved about as effective as a garden hose against a forest fire. The controversy was inaugurated by FitzRalph's sermon on 8 November 1357 delivered before the pope and cardinals in consistory by the archbishop himself. We may now consider the nature and content of this sermon as preserved in Trevisa's translation and edited by Perry (1925, pp. 39–93). Where necessary I have revised Perry's edition, both in punctuation and in choice of manuscript variants, to fit my understanding of Trevisa's intention based on comparison with the Latin.

FitzRalph begins by seeming to back down from the extreme position of his *De Pauperie Salvatoris*, which advocated the dissolution of the orders, by assuring the pope that his only intention is "that these orders should be brought to the cleanness of their first ordinance" (39.8–9). He then tells how he became involved in this dispute with the friars, preaching seven or eight sermons in the vernacular in London, and summarizes the nine conclusions which, he says, caused the friars to appeal to the papal court *licet frivole*, "though it turn them to a jape" (39.18). These nine conclusions are as follows (cp. Walsh 1981, p. 423):

I. Christ was always poor during his life on earth, but not because he wanted or loved poverty for its own sake.
II. He never begged voluntarily.
III. He never taught voluntary mendicancy.
IV. He actually taught that nobody should beg voluntarily.
V. Nobody can prudently assume a vow of mendicant poverty for perpetual observance.
VI. The Franciscan rule does not impose the obligation of mendicant poverty.
VII. The bull of Alexander IV condemning the *Libellus* of Guillaume of St. Amour did not contradict any of the preceding conclusions.
VIII. The parish church is a more suitable place for the confessions of the parishioners than the churches of the friars.
IX. Parishioners should confess to a single parson, and for this purpose the ordinary parson is more suitable than a parson of the friars.

FitzRalph begins his attack by focusing on the last two conclusions, VIII and IX, which deal with the matter of privileges granted to the friars, and actually devotes most of his sermon to these, adding little more than a bare summary of conclusions I–VII at the end.

That the parish church is a more suitable place for confession of parishioners (VIII) is supported in three ways: (1) it is more lawful, (2) it is safer, and (3) it is more beneficial to the parishioners. The first point is proved by recourse to scripture, quoting Deuteronomy 12:5–6, 13–14 and Leviticus 4 to show how the law of Moses stressed the role of the priest and the singular location specified by God for worship. In contrast to the papal legislation permitting the activities of friars, "the place which the Lord shall choose" is understood to refer to the parish church, and the words "take heed to thyself that thou offer not thy burnt offerings in every place that thou seest" is taken as a warning to parishioners not to turn from their own places of worship to the churches of the friars. We thus see right in the beginning the importance of biblical proofs in the arguments of FitzRalph.

The parish church is safer in that it is less likely to have come under threat of interdiction. Under this head FitzRalph is able to enumerate abuses of the friars in the context of concern for the spiritual safety of parishioners. There was, for example, a prohibition in one of the decretals warning members of religious orders not to advise or cause anyone to commit himself to burial in their church, and violations of this were to be punished by interdiction of the church and its burial ground. But since it was common knowledge that friars frequently engaged in this kind of "recruiting," parishioners should realize that their churches are under threat of interdiction, and hence may not be lawful places of worship or burial.

The third argument of the VIIIth conclusion was that it was more profitable for parishioners to seek shrift (confession) and burial in their own parish church, and this for three reasons. The first is that, as is evident from the scripture already quoted, the parish church was chosen by God and is therefore more pleasing to him. Second, the parishioner by remaining true to his home church has the reward of double obedience: not only does he confess his sins in accordance with God's law, but he does so in the place which the Lord has chosen, namely the parish church; whereas those who go to the friars for confession lose the reward of this second obedience. A third point is that in the parish church there is more prayer power (43.12–16):

> Also in the parish church over all, or nigh over all, by law of God and of holy church, is or should be more beadmen than in any church of friars, yea such ten! Then every parishioner may trow that he is more yholpe by prayers of more beadmen than in any church of friars.

FitzRalph now turns to the IXth conclusion, namely that the parish priest is more worthy to hear confession than is a parson of the friars, and his discussion of this matter constitutes the central topic of the sermon (43.23–79.27). We cannot consider all of his arguments in detail; hence it will be well, before looking at some of them, to have before us a list of his main points. He begins with arguments similar to those used for the VIIIth conclusion: the parish priest as one's confessor is more lawful, he is more trustworthy, and he is safer (because of the danger of interdiction in the case of the friars). The friars are self-serving, and there is a clear and present spiritual danger to those confessed by them. FitzRalph then launches new arguments, beginning with what might be called the practical advantages of loyalty to the parish priest. But the greatest space is devoted to what he calls the "damages" that result when parishioners go to the friars: despising of the parish priest, slacking of devotion, shamelessness in confession (to a stranger), and the withholding of confessional offerings and tithes. Moreover, friars illegally siphon off all the income due to parish priests, and skillfully avoid legal retribution. At the university they ruthlessly recruit children and hold them captive, causing a reduction in enrollment, and with their wealthy resources buy up all the books or at least force prices beyond the reach of the average student. To conclude this section FitzRalph points to the "damage" of unlimited numbers: the size of the fraternal orders needs to be brought under control. The final category is the sins of the friars: injury and wrong, disobedience (especially of their own rule), covetousness, and pride. Furthermore these sins are deadly, because they are committed willfully. The sermon then closes with a brief review of the first seven conclusions (listed above).

In arguing that the friars are self-serving, FitzRalph presents this interesting portrait of a suspicious parishioner (47.10–21):

> Then may the parishioner skillfully argue in his heart: "Why would this beggar sit and hear (*sedendo* B, *audiendo* G) my shrift and leave his begging

and getting (*acquirendis*) of his livelihood, but he hope to have of me such manner help? And need driveth to sin, by the which sin the need might be relieved, as (Proverbs 30:8–9) Solomon saith and prayeth: "Give me neither beggery nother riches, but give me only what is needful to my livelihood, lest I be excited to deny and say, Who is our Lord? and compelled by need for to steal, and forswear the name of my God." Then it followeth that for all manner sins he will enjoin me almsdeeds for to relieve his own beggery, and so I shall not be clearly bequit of my sins.

Obviously this is an exceptional layman, one who is able to use scripture skillfully in his own defense. Indeed he proceeds to quote and interpret a passage from the gospel to discredit further the efficacy of confession to the friars (47:21–29):

> Therefore when his disciples asked of our Lord, "Why might we not cast him out?" and spake of a fiend, our Lord answered and said, "These manner fiends be not cast out but with beads and fasting" (Matt. 17:19–21). Of this word it is taken that as for every diverse sickness of body diverse medicines help, so for every ghostly sickness must be ordained his proper medicine. And this beggar that is so busy about his beggary will not without suspicion ordain me such medicines for my sins.

FitzRalph finds confirmation of the friars' self-interest as confessors in the fact that only after they obtained the privilege of hearing confession did they begin to build such magnificent churches: *monasteria pulcherrima et regula palatia*, which Trevisa translates "fair minsters and royal palaces (as) though it were for kings" (48.1).

Among the damages that result from granting the friars the privilege of hearing confession is the enticing of children into the order. This comes about, says FitzRalph, because friars ingratiate themselves in the homes of those to whom they are assigned, enticing the children with trinkets to join their order, since they cannot so easily attract adults. Once they have the children, the latter are not free to come and go, but are held virtually as prisoners, unable to speak to their parents except under the watchful eye of the friars. One is reminded of certain twentieth-century practices among religious cults, and the resulting custody battles. FitzRalph illustrates his point with a current example of overzealous recruiting at Oxford, communicated to him by a distraught father who has come to the papal court appealing for the return of his child (56.10–13):

> In evidence hereof this day, as I came out of my inn, came to me a good man of England that is come to this court for socour and remedy. And he told me

that anon after Easter that last was, at Oxford friars benom (deprived) him
his son that was not thirteen year old, and he came thither to speak with his
son and might not speak with his son but under ward and keeping of friars.

He goes on to point out that the Mosaic law prescribes the death penalty
for anyone who steals a man and sells him into slavery (Exod. 21:16),
and adds that if one can be punished for stealing an ox or a sheep, then
surely an even greater punishment should be reserved for anyone stealing
a child from its parents. Moreover if the friars claim that what they are
doing is for the benefit of the child and his devotion to God, they should
remember Paul's denial that the end justifies the means (Rom. 3:8). As
we noted, the recruiting of children by the friars was a controversial
subject at Oxford in the 1350s, and still hotly debated when Trevisa
arrived in 1362.

FitzRalph firmly believed that a basic cause of the problem represented
by the friars was the failure of the ecclesiastical authorities to limit their
numbers. If they are as learned as they claim, he says, they should realize
that both philosophy and scripture require that their numbers should
be limited. To illustrate the point from philosophy, he cites Aristotle,
De Anima (II, 4): "In the case of all complex wholes formed in the
course of nature, there is a limit or ratio (*logos*) which determines their
size and increase," or in FitzRalph's Latin, *omnium natura constantium
determinata est ratio magnitudinis et augmenti*, which Trevisa turns into an
emphatic negative (59.26–27): "the worst that is in kind (=nature) is
passing reason of greatness and of increasing." The scriptural authority
is that favorite verse from the Book of Wisdom (11:21) to the effect that
"God made and ordained all in measure, number and weight" (59.30–
31). Against these principles of philosophy and scripture the orders of
friars multiply themselves *per hoc clerum et populum importune velut effrontes
ubilibet onerantes*, or as Trevisa has it (60.11–12), "and benim (=snatch)
thereby the fleece of the people and of the clergy, and charge (=burden)
them in every place." This is followed by a vivid description of the
aggressive begging technique of the friars (60.12–21):

> For now unnethe (=scarcely) may any great men or small, lewed (=layman)
> or lered (=cleric), take a morsel of meat, but such beggars come unbid, and
> beg not as pore men should at the gate or at the door, asking alms meekly as
> Francis taught and hote (=commanded) in his testament, but they come into
> houses and courts (*curias sive domos sine verecundia penetrantes*: cf. 2 Tim. 3:6)
> and be harbored and eat and drink what they there find unbid and unprayed

(*nullatenus invitati*). And natheless they bear with them corn, or meal-bread (*similam panes* B), flesh or cheese: though there be but twain in the house they bear away that one. And no man may warn them but he put off all kindly shame (*nisi verecundiam naturalem abjiciat*).

The argument is rounded off with a trenchant quotation from Pope Gregory (the IX?) and further verses from scripture (Luke 10:6 and Ecclus. 29:24).

The sins of the friars are presented in a relentless indictment (61.12–79.27). Of the sins treated, disobedience receives the most attention. FitzRalph points out that in their *Appellacio* against him, the friars claim that their orders are based on begging and poverty, and yet they also have been granted the privilege of preaching. Surely, he argues, these two things are not compatible (62.19–26):

> It seemeth that having right to preach to Christian men may not stand with such a foundment of beggary, if power of asking and of challenging of livelihood longeth to this privilege, as it doth to rightful law, so that friars might challenge their livelihood of them that they preach to the gospel, as Christ's disciples had when Christ them sent to preach the gospel and said: "In what house ye go in, there abide, the workman is worthy his meed" (Luke 10:7).

In other words, receiving subsistence for responsibilities duly carried out is not begging (62.27–29):

> How should he be cleped very beggar (I say not begging) that hath free right to challenge (=demand) his livelihood? I see not how it should stand.

To this instance FitzRalph adds the less innocent example of inquisitors, who use their power to threaten people into contributing to their income. This sharply worded passage is preserved defectively in Trevisa's translation, whether because of a fault in his exemplar or corruption in transmission of the English it is difficult to say (62.29–63.3):

> Unde nec inquisitores pravitatis haereticae [mendici dici possunt], qui dicuntur abuti saepissime poetestate eis concessa, vexantes saepe diversas personas literatas et laicas, volentes remedium quaerere de injuriis illatis per eosdem inquisitores aut ordinis sui fratris, ita ut timore verecundiae seu notationis super causa haeresis et finalis injusti judicii, quale dicuntur saepius execere, pecuniae summas graves ab eis extorquent.

For this Trevisa has:

> Nother inquisitors nother friars of their order that have office by the which they may certainly challenge their livelihood should be cleped beggars for

shame of the name, when they should know in cause of heresy and of the last rightful doom. Men saith that they use such office full oft and take masterfully great sums of money.

What fails to emerge from this is the focus of attention on heresy hunters, who should not be called "beggars" for several reasons. They often abuse the power given to them, injuring various persons of all ranks who want to seek remedy for injuries inflicted by those same inquisitors or friars of their order, so that for fear of shame or notoriety over the charge of heresy and the final unjust decision, men say that these inquisitors use their office very often to extort from their victims great sums of money. Clearly, this goes beyond merely establishing that these inquisitors have an income and are not beggars! This being a point with which Trevisa would surely agree, I suspect that the blurring of the passage is likely due to a defect in his Latin exemplar. Fortunately, deficiencies of this kind are not common in the *Defensio Curatorum*.

For the most part FitzRalph speaks generally of the orders of friars, without specifying any one in particular. But under the rubric of disobedience he speaks at length on the rule of St. Francis and the violations of that rule by members of the Franciscan Order. In the broadest sense, they violate the rule of their founder when they seek the privileges that have been discussed, since these privileges assure them an easier and more worldly life. More specifically, they have abandoned the strictness of the rule in their recruiting practices, their unlicensed preaching, and their persistence in seeking additional privileges. Friars were not supposed to preach in any diocese without the permission of the bishop, but St. Francis went further (65.18–22):

> Though I had as great cunning as ever had Solomon, an I find poor priests of this world in parish there they wone (=dwell), I will not preach against their will, and them all I will dread and love and worship as my Lord's; and they be my Lord's.

Contrast this attitude, says FitzRalph, with what we find today (65.22–25):

> But what worship friars do now to pore priests it may not be hid while it is none (*cum sit nulla*); but unreverence in every place may be found done in stead of reverence.

In seeking privileges that will enable them to evade the wishes of their founder, the friars act "contrary to their rule and to their profession *and to their perfectness also*" (66.10), the third point not in the Latin and presumably added by Trevisa. FitzRalph completes his review of disobedience by arguing at length that the rule of St. Francis is still in force.

Before continuing his list of sins, FitzRalph pauses to explain why he has given so much attention to the Franciscans, and to provide a brief critique of the concept of poverty in the rule. It was the Franciscans, he says, who particularly emphasized during the debates in London that the perfection of the gospel is embodied in voluntary begging. One of their number, preaching on All Hallows Day (perhaps Roger Conway, as Walsh suggests, p. 410), described four degrees of poverty, and declared that the highest of these was the life of the beggar who followed Christ, leaving the rest of us in the lower ranks. Who can reconcile this wretched view of the Church with that holy city prepared as a bride adorned for her husband (Rev. 21:2)? And who can endure the assertion that Francis, who was but a novice in the faith, ordained the way of perfection for mankind better than God himself? For God decreed that man should earn his bread by the sweat of his brow, and elsewhere says that "man is born to labor as the fowl to flight" (Job 5:7 V). Thus we see that the archbishop does not hesitate to launch a frontal assault on the Franciscan ideal of poverty itself.

The self-interest of the friars comes in for further treatment under the heading of covetousness. Why are the friars vitally interested in confession, but do not show concern for baptism and other responsibilities with which the secular clergy are burdened? Their extraordinary interest in confession, a heavy responsibility when properly administered, is certainly not shared by the monastic orders, who find it enough to look out for their own spiritual health. Clearly the implication is that the friars do not treat confession responsibly, but engage in such work for the financial rewards they are able to obtain. The same reasoning will account for their interest in burial rights, and their particular interest in hearing the confessions of women.

The roll call of sins concludes with pride, evident in the friars' desire for primacy in the Church. But the final emphasis of FitzRalph is on the point that in all cases the sins of the friars are compounded because it is evident that they are incurred willfully, notably in their assent to the wicked procuring of the many privileges that the preacher has listed. If the friars are to be cleansed, repentance and restitution are necessary.

It is no use alleging that everything they have done is legal, because the sin of desiring privileges in violation of their own rule cannot be so excused, as is illustrated in St. Bernard's letter to Adam the monk (77.13–20):

> The case is that this monk, after his profession that he made (in his monastery) to dwell there alway to his live's end, as men say went with his abbot to another abbey and dwelled there by hest and leave of his abbot, and thereto he asked and had leave of the pope; but St. Bernard reproveth him and fondeth to prove by many manner reason that without sin he might not so do by hest of his abbot nother by leave of the pope, whose leave he should not ask.

St. Bernard draws support for this view from Aristotle's *Ethics* and adds his own principle that if two superiors issue contrary orders, you should obey the command of him who is higher in rank. In this case the vow of obedience was made to God, who should be obeyed rather than the abbot. Concerning the pope who gave the monk leave, he says (78.26–28):

> Who denieth that it is evil to assent to evil? That would I not trow that the pope did, but he were beguiled with lesing (=lying) or overcome with greediness.

From this example FitzRalph concludes concerning the friars that the sin of desiring privileges that result in disobedience to their own rule will bring them an evil reward.

After summarizing what he has said concerning the willful sins of the mendicants, FitzRalph calls upon the pope and cardinals to suspend all privileges of the friars. He then spends the remainder of his time on the first seven conclusions that were enumerated at the beginning of his sermon, and of these seven the one receiving the most detailed treatment is the second: Christ never begged voluntarily. And it is here that we find the most extensive use of scripture to refute the friars' teaching concerning mendicancy.

If Christ had taught willful begging, he would have violated the commandment against coveting your neighbor's possessions (Exod. 20:17), and the legislation on the year of release, especially that which says "In all wise a needy man and beggar shall not be among you" (Deut. 15:4). FitzRalph's argument here is not easy to follow, but my understanding of it is that he is invoking social legislation against beggary to show that it is a problem to be eliminated, rather than a way of life to be admired. His analogy at this point is a bit distracting (81:8–16):

For he that suffereth other men to be unarmed, while he might help them of armor, breaketh the king's law that hoteth that in the city should be no man unarmed; and not only he breaketh that law, but also he that might abide armed and throweth his armor into a deep river. Also this priest that maketh himself willfully unmighty and unable to offer gifts and sacrifices for sins breaketh the law of holy church that hoteth that he should offer gifts and sacrifice for sins.

This analogy seems to relate to the legislation for the year of release (Deut. 15), because FitzRalph goes on to defend its relevance to Christians (81.18–21):

And no man may feign that the foresaid hest is ceremonial *to be used among the Jews alone*, for it is very moral, *longing to good thews*, and harder charged in the new than in the old law.

Trevisa here adds glosses (italicized) by way of explaining what FitzRalph means by *ceremoniale* and *morale* (i.e., tropological), but we are left in some uncertainty about the application of the Mosaic legislation to the argument. Could it be simply that the year of release is designed to eliminate beggary, and that Christians should observe it? In any case, the proof that the law is not ceremonial comes in the citation of passages from the New Testament. Thus Christ teaches us to "give alms of such things as ye have" (Luke 11:41) in order that "no beggar should be among the people" (Deut. 15:4). The punishment for disobedience in this matter is given in Christ's teaching on the corporal works of mercy, where those who failed to do them are told, "Depart from me, ye cursed, into everlasting fire, prepared for the devil and his angels" (Matt. 25:41).

FitzRalph also takes pains to show that Christ lived under and in obedience to the secular laws of the empire, natural laws which had similar legislation for the prevention or elimination of beggary. This he proves by citing Christ's instructions to Peter regarding the payment of tribute (Matt. 17:24–27) and his remarks to the Pharisees concerning the image of Caesar on the coin (Matt. 22:15–22). Since it appears that Christ lived in conformity to secular laws, we should not suppose that he would violate the emperor's law prohibiting beggars. Even more to the point, Christ would never disobey fundamental spiritual laws that he taught, such as love thy neighbor, and he would never incur the opprobrium mentioned in Proverbs 14:20, "The poor is hated even of his own neighbor." Nor would he who fed five thousand with loaves and fishes be dependent on begging for his food and thus slander his own gospel. Not only would such a way of life lead to distrust of his motives, but it would be in violation of the golden rule (Matt. 7:12), and the teaching of Paul (1 Tim. 6:5, 10–11), who derives his authority from Christ (Gal. 1:1).

But Christ did not contradict his own teaching, and was not a hypocrite; therefore he did not beg willfully or guilefully, nor did any of his disciples, or St. Clement, who was Peter's successor. Also, if begging were the highest way of life, laws of the Church stipulating that no man should be ordained without assurance of income must be judged erroneous, and the same would have to be said of similar requirements concerning subsidy of the priesthood, both in the old law and the natural law of secular societies. Certainly we would have to question the endowment of churches, which it seems unlawful to say. If beggary is such perfection, it is a wonder that neither Christ himself nor the Holy Ghost, whom he promised to send (John 16:13), said anything to the disciples about it. Nor does it seem at all likely that Melchisedec, king of Salem, whom Paul praises above Abraham (Heb. 7), could be ranked so high without engaging in willful begging. Moreover, since the prophet says in the Psalter, "yet have I not seen the righteous forsaken, nor his seed begging bread" (Psalm 37:25), it is not reasonable to suppose that Christ, who was certainly righteous, would beg bread against the prophet's word. For he instructed his disciples in such a way as to show his opposition to beggary (Luke 10:7), and he himself labored as a carpenter (Mark 6:3).

The citation of scripture continues apace in the remainder of the sermon, particularly in the discussion of the fourth conclusion, but I wish to call attention to only a single instance, and that for a particular reason. The arguments we have traced are for the most part presented with an intensity and seriousness that seem to preclude the use of humor. Can we point to any passage that may have penetrated the decorum of the consistory, forced at least a smile from the pope and cardinals? If there is such a moment, I would suspect it to be in FitzRalph's discussion of the parable of the great feast (88.5–18):

> "when thou makest a feast clepe thou thereto poor men, halt and blind, and thou shalt be blessed, for they have not whereof they may quite it to thee" (Luke 14:13–14). Then poor men that be stalwart and strong should not be cleped to the feast of beggars, for they may quite it with their travail. Nother rich feeble men, nother rich halt men, nother rich blind men should

be cleped to the feast of beggars, for they may quite it with their chattels. And for Christ rekeneth not deaf, nother dumb, nother lame that be not halt (*manchos* BF) among them that should be cleped to the feast of beggars, I see not that such men should be cleped to such a feast; for if they be nother feeble, ne blind, ne halt, they may go about and beg from place to place, and so may not the feeble, blind, and halt. But friars set this exposition among errors.

From this parable, I take it, FitzRalph draws the conclusion that only the helpless are invited to the Lord's feast, which would exclude even those unfortunates possessing the minimum ability to beg. Presumably then the friars are excluded, reason enough for them to declare FitzRalph's "exposition" erroneous. But as my paraphrase indicates, I doubt that the archbishop was offering this to his distinguished audience as a serious exposition of the parable. Near the end of his hard-hitting sermon, he seems to have provided his listeners with a bit of comic relief, which must surely have been appreciated. But behind all this was a serious point: alms should be given only to the poor *and* infirm, not to those who were (because of idleness) simply poor (Scase 1989, p. 63). Then FitzRalph closes his sermon with these words (93.22–27):

> I would say much more and argue against myself and resolve the arguments for to confirm that I have said; but I have travailed your Holiness enough and the reverence of my lords the Cardinals. Therefore I conclude and pray meekly and devoutly as I prayed in the first that I touched: "Deemeth not by the face, but rightful doom ye deem" (John 7:24).

We have seen that Trevisa occasionally inserts glosses to clarify or emphasize the archbishop's arguments, but there are no notes in this sermon signed by Trevisa, such as we have seen in *Nicodemus* and the *Dialogus*, and the translation is very straightforward and, yes, professional. It would seem that Trevisa has reached a point of confidence and assurance in his career as a translator which will stand him in good stead as he turns now to his first large-scale project, the translation of Ranulph Higden's universal history, the *Polychronicon*, working now with the guidance and support of his patron, Thomas IV, Lord Berkeley.

Higden's Polychronicon

Ranulph Higden was a Benedictine monk who entered the abbey of St. Werberg, Chester, in 1299 and remained there until his death in 1363. When he began writing his history, the most popular work of that kind was the *Brut* chronicle, derived from Geoffrey of Monmouth's *History of the Kings of Britain*. This was a national history that began with Aeneas and the Troy story, but followed especially the fortunes of Brutus who founded Britain, to which were attached continuations extending through the fourteenth century. Higden, however, in writing the *Polychronicon*, chose to emulate the traditional pattern of universal history represented by Orosius in his *History against the Pagans* (early fifth century), and hence begins his account with the creation on the biblical model, dividing history into the seven ages of the world. Soon his history had matched and even surpassed the popularity of the *Brut* chronicles. By the end of the fourteenth century more than a dozen continuations had been added to Higden's *Polychronicon*, and it remained a standard authority as late as the seventeenth century.

In *The Bible in Early English Literature* (1976), I have discussed the *Polychronicon* at some length (pp. 207–46), and hence will confine my remarks here to a more concise recapitulation of its contents which draws on my earlier work. Higden divides the *Polychronicon* into seven books because, he says, the Lord created the world in six days and rested on the seventh. These books, however, do not correspond to the seven ages of the world; thus they are a valuable index to the emphasis that Higden gives to the different periods of history. The first book is entirely devoted to a geography of the world, climaxed by a description of the British Isles. Book II covers the first four ages of the world, from the Creation to the fall of Jerusalem (586 B.C.). Book III treats the fifth age, which extends from the Babylonian captivity to the coming of Christ. All the rest of history is contained in the sixth age, which will last until Doomsday. In Higden this is divided as follows: Book IV, from the coming of Christ to the fall of Britain (A.D. 449); Book V, from the Anglo-Saxon settlement to the Danish occupation (A.D. 871); Book VI, from King Alfred to the Norman Conquest (A.D. 1066); and finally Book VII, from the Norman Conquest to Higden's own time (A.D. 1352).

Some two decades after Higden's death, Trevisa translated the *Polychronicon* into English (ca. 1385–87), while a second (anonymous) translation was made in the fifteenth century, which the *Middle English Dictionary* (Ann Arbor) dates circa 1425. Caxton printed a modernized form of Trevisa's translation in 1482, and added a continuation of his own extending down to the year 1460. Subsequent reprintings of this translation meant that Higden's *Polychronicon* was available to a growing body of readers in the Renaissance, thus keeping alive the medieval view of universal history as an expression of the divine purpose being worked out in the course of human events. The Latin text, with the two medieval English translations on facing pages, was published in the nineteenth century in the Rolls Series in nine volumes (1865–86), and it is from this edition that I quote, though in modernized form. It is to be hoped that a new edition of the *Polychronicon* may soon be published. A text based on the Huntington Library manuscript HM 28561 (formerly Burleigh House) has been prepared by Richard Seeger (1974), and a critical edition based on British Library MS Cotton Tiberius D. vii, but with consideration given to all the known manuscripts, is being planned by Ronald Waldron.

Trevisa's translation of the *Polychronicon* differs dramatically from all his other translations in the number and magnitude of the notes that he has inserted by way of comment on or explanation of Higden's text. These notes contain personal observations, epigrammatic remarks on various topics, definitions of terms, biblical exegesis, and sometimes extended theological argument. Taken together these notes provide almost a running commentary on the *Polychronicon*, or what might be called a translator's diary. The fact that Trevisa had just lived through perhaps the most exciting and stimulating period of his life—his expulsion from Queen's, the Peasants' Revolt, and Courtenay's inquisition of 1382— makes these notes the liveliest and most informative of his career. Since it is not possible to treat his major works in detail in this chapter, our consideration of his translation of the *Polychronicon* will be limited to the following review of some of his notes to that text.

In light of the possibility that Trevisa had been working on a translation of the Bible before turning to the *Polychronicon* (a matter to be discussed in the next chapter), it is well to observe first those notes reflecting a biblical interest on his part. These range from simple identification of names, or explanation of terms, to a rather full discussion of Noah's ark. It is the sort of information that today would be found in a bible dictionary. Thus Trevisa identifies Ham as Noah's son, who "had his father's curse, for he laughed his father to scorn, for he saw his privy harness all bare and unheeled (=uncovered) while he lay asleep" (I, 121). Later he explains that the group known as the three-score and ten, or the seventy, were those translators who turned Holy Writ

from Hebrew into Greek (II, 221, 245), the version today known as the
Septuagint. Considerable space is devoted to explaining the division of
the chosen people into two nations, Israel and Judah, as a result of the
civil war following the death of Solomon (III, 19), and briefer notes
explain what is meant by the "high places," and the Babylonian exile
(III, 85, 93). The calculation of Olympiads, and so forth, is explained in
a note reminiscent of the one provided at the beginning of the *Gospel
of Nicodemus* (IV, 253–55), and the term *apocrypha* is defined as writing
of which the author is unknown (V, 105). Extrabiblical sources seem to
have been used by Trevisa in his notes regarding Lazarus and the seamless
robe of Christ (IV, 389–91; V, 419–21). Concerning the former he
remarks: "Lazarus died once and was reared from death to life, and lived
afterward four and twenty years, and was Bishop of Cyprus, and died
eft; and so Lazarus had four and twenty years between his two deaths."
Higden reports the discovery of our Lord's seamless robe in the Vale of
Jehoshaphat; it was found by Gregory, bishop of Antioch, and brought
to Jerusalem. But he also points out that this account disagrees with
the story of the death of Pilate, who is said to have been immune to
condemnation as long as he was wearing the seamless robe. If Pilate had
this robe with him at Rome, Higden argues, it seems that it was not
afterward taken hence and brought again to the Vale of Jehoshaphat; or
if it *was* found in the Vale of Jehoshaphat, then Pilate did not have it
with him at Rome. To which Trevisa replies (V, 419–21):

> It was no more mastery to bring that curtel out of Rome into the Vale of
> Jehoshaphat, than it was to bring that curtel out of Jerusalem into Rome,
> and so it may well stand that Pilate had on that curtel at Rome, and that the
> curtel was afterward found in the Vale of Jehoshaphat.

It is interesting to find Trevisa here defending the veracity of apocryphal
legend in something of a fundamentalist spirit, making his view of history
seem even more conservative than Higden's.

Following the monk's description of Noah's ark, Trevisa adds this
note (II, 235):

> Here men may wonder how the window was made beneath in the side of
> the ship, for coming in of water. Doctor de Lyra moveth this doubt, and
> saith that where we have *fenestra*, that is, a *fenetre*, a *window*, the letter of the
> Hebrew hath *lucerna*, that is, a *lantern*; and some men say that that lantern
> was a carbuncle or some other precious stone, that shone and gave light clear
> enough where it was set. But some others say that that window was a whole

crystal stone which took in light and held out water. Many other windows were in the ship, as was needed, for the ship was full great and huge, and had in it full many beasts.

It is this kind of explanatory note, introduced for its own sake without any particular prompting by Higden's text, that seems to me a consequence of an already existing interest in the biblical text on Trevisa's part. Nicholas of Lyra, to whom Trevisa refers here, was one of the most influential exegetes of the later Middle Ages, and he is frequently cited by the Wycliffite translators.

Among the wonders of Rome is a monument depicting two great horses, carved from marble, said to have been erected by Tiberius in memory of two philosophers, Praxitellus and Fibia. According to tradition, the two young philosophers came to Rome and walked naked. And when the emperor asked them why they went naked, they replied that it was because they had forsaken all things. This story seems to have reminded Trevisa of his exasperating opponents at Oxford, the friars, who claimed by their vows to have forsaken all things. Here is his comment on Higden's narrative (I, 227–29):

> The first point of this doing and answer teacheth that who forsaketh all thing forsaketh all his clothes; and so it followeth that they that be well clothed and go about and beg and gather money and corn and chattels of other men forsaketh not all thing.

One of the most puzzling of Trevisa's epigrammatic additions to the *Polychronicon* occurs in the description of Ireland, where Higden speaks of Irishmen as "given to idleness" (*otio deditorum*), which Trevisa renders as "Irishmen that were alway idle as Paul's knights" (I, 349). On the strength of this single (and admittedly colorful) reference, "idle as Paul's knights" finds its way into Whiting's *Proverbs* (1968, p. 449, no. P62), but the meaning remains obscure. It seems unlikely that Trevisa would be referring to the old soldiers of later days known as Paul's Men or Paul's Walkers. On the strength of the common characterization of the priesthood as "holy chivalry" (e.g., the *Dialogus*, 23.1), with which Trevisa was certainly familiar, I venture to suggest that "Paul's knights" is here used ironically, and refers to those priests who have abandoned their parishes in order to pursue a more lucrative career as chantry priests in London at St. Paul's cathedral. Their "idleness" results from the fact that a chantry assignment means few responsibilities (compared to those

of a parish priest) along with perhaps a larger income and much more
free time. The phrase "idle as Paul's knights" may have been proverbial,
but it may equally well be Trevisa's invention.

Definitions of unusual words occur frequently in Trevisa's translation,
some extended and some brief and compact. His definition of *laborinth*
is a good example of the former (I, 311–13):

> For to bring their hearts out of thought that hear speak of *laborintus*, here
> I tell what laborinth is to meaning. Laborinth is an house wonderly built
> with halks and herns, with turnings and wendings and wonderful ways so
> diversely and so wrinklingly wrought, that who that is within that house and
> will out wend, though he wend well fast one way and another, hitherward and
> thitherward, eastward and westward, northward and southward, whitherever
> they draw, and of all the ways choose the fairest; though he travail never so
> sore, al is for nought. For out he goeth never, but he have a craft that needeth
> therefor.

The definitions are usually very businesslike, but it is gratifying now and
then to come upon a felicitous choice of words such as "wrinklingly"
unexpectedly applied to the layout of a *laborinth*. The following are more
prosaic: a *bastard* is one who is "begotten of a worthy father and born
of an unworthy mother" (II, 269); a *eunuch* is "he that is gelded, and
such were sometime made wardens of ladies in Egypt" (II, 305); and
a *cokedrille* (crocodile) is "a four-footed beast that liveth both in water
and on land, and is commonly twenty cubit long, with claws and teeth
strongly armed; his skin is so hard that he recketh not of strokes of hard
stones; he resteth by day in water and by night on land; the cokedrille
alone among beasts moveth the overjaw, so saith Isidore" (III, 109).

It is not always easy to anticipate which terms Trevisa will choose
to define. The word *problem* seems to us a common word, but Trevisa
deemed it worthy of this explanation: "A problem is a question that is
hard to assoil (=solve), and also a hard riddle is also cleped a problem"
(III, 365). In this same passage Trevisa provides a definition of *perspective*,
a concept usually associated with the Renaissance: "Perspective is a
science that specially longeth to the sight; that science teacheth how
a thing is seen, and is less or more than it seemeth, or even as much
as it seemeth, even or crooked and right as it is, or otherwise shaped
than it seemeth." Scientific definitions are perhaps the most common
type, some long and involved, as in Trevisa's careful explanation of the
solstices and equinoxes in connection with Higden's instructions for the

calculation of Easter (VI, 107), and some brief and to the point, as in his definition of the *comet* as "a star with a light blasing crest above, and ever bodeth pestilence, death, and war, or some hard haps" (VI, 135). It should be noted, finally, that when the term involves people, Trevisa's own views are often not far from the surface, as in this definition of *questor*: "he that gathereth tribute to Rome, and the doomsman was sometime cleped *questor*. Also the wardens of the treasury were cleped *questores*. But now churls and pardoners be cleped *questores*" (IV, 49).

Trevisa's notes include much that reflects personal observation, and actually contain information about his travels that we have from no other source. Thus in a note appended to Higden's description of the town of Bath, Trevisa remarks (II, 61):

> Though men might by craft make hot baths for to endure long enough, this accordeth well to reason and to philosophy that treateth of hot wells and baths that be in diverse lands, though the water of this Bath be more troubly and heavier of smell and of savor than other hot baths that I have seen at Aachen in Allemagne, and at Aix in Savoie. The baths in Aix be as fair and as clear as any cold well-stream. I have assayed, and bathed therein.

It is evident from this that Trevisa's travels in Europe were rather extensive, and may have included a trip to Rome (via Aix in Savoie).

Higden remarks that Charlemagne founded as many abbeys as there are letters in the alphabet, and in each of these abbeys he set a letter of gold weighing a hundred pounds Turoneis. Trevisa comments (VI, 259):

> God wot what weight that should be; but by a statute of the University of Oxford, when any man is permitted there to commence in any faculty, he shall swear that he shall not spend at his commencement passing three thousand of groats Turoneis. The groat Turoney is somewhat less worthy than an English groat, for at Breisach upon the Rhine I have yfonge in change eleven groats Turoneis for a ducat, that is worth half an English noble.

Although specific place names are not mentioned, we may infer from another note that Trevisa probably traveled a good deal in France as well. Higden expresses wonder that English is so diverse of sound in its native land, while French, imported from Normandy, has a single correct form wherever it is spoken in England. Trevisa feels compelled to correct Higden's provincial view (II, 161):

> Nevertheless there is as many diverse manner French in the realm of France as is diverse manner English in the realm of England.

Though this could be hearsay, when taken with the other evidence of Trevisa's travels it suggests that he had been an observant pilgrim in France.

Places too remote to travel to in person were visited by Trevisa in his reading and recorded in his notes, such as this one derived from Mandeville's *Travels* (1953, pp. 136, 339), on India (II, 377):

I read among the wonders of India that snails be there so great and so huge that a man may be harbored in a snail's house.

At the other extremity of the world, in the British Isles, Trevisa is on the alert for wonders to match those of India. Thus he reports hearing of a man in Ireland who "hath one bone all whole in one side instead of all his ribs," and in his own parish of Berkeley he tells of Thomas Hayward, who "hath in the mold of his head, poll and forhead, but one bone all whole; therefore he may well suffer great strokes above on his head, and bush against men and horse-heads, and break strong doors with his head, and it grieveth him not" (II, 191). Another marvel was a very old man named Roger Bagge, who lived at Wotton-under-Edge and apparently enjoyed very good health: "he spat never, he coughed never" (II, 195). Trevisa also includes a report from one of his parishioners (II, 209):

William Wayte of Berkeley saw a child with two heads and two necks born and yfulled (=baptised) at Metz in Lorraine, the year of our Lord a thousand three hundred and six and fifty, that year the king of France was taken at the battle of Poitiers. This child had two arms and two legs, as other children have, and he had the third leg growing out above the buttocks behind, and the third arm between the two shoulders.

Undoubtedly the most frequently quoted passage in all of Trevisa's writings is the note that follows Higden's reference to the practice of teaching children French rather than English (II, 159–61):

Trevisa. This manner was much used before the first Death, and is since somedeal changed. For John Cornwall, a master of grammar, changed the lore in grammar school and construction of French into English; and Richard Pencrich learned this manner of teaching of him, and other men of Pencrich; so that now, the year of our Lord 1385, in all the grammar schools of England, children leave French and construe and learn in English; and they have thereby advantage in one side and disadvantage in another side; their advantage is that they learn their grammar in less time than children were wont to do; the disadvantage is that now children of grammar school know no more French than their left heel, and that is harm for them if they should pass the sea and travel in strange lands and in many other places. Also gentlemen have now much left off teaching their children French.

That the Berkeley family had been fluent in French is suggested by the choice of French for the biblical inscriptions on the walls and roof of the family chapel. But it may be that before Trevisa's tenure as vicar of Berkeley there had been a decline in the use of French for the education of younger members of the family.

Our final (and largest) category of notes is those in which an argumentative translator takes issue with his author. Some differences of opinion might well be anticipated, of course, since Higden was a monk and Trevisa a secular priest. At one point, for example, Higden mentions that when Odo was made archbishop of Canterbury, he became a monk in order to conform to tradition and to receive the honor of this high office in a worthy manner. Our priestly translator takes a different view (VII, 5): "Odo was lewedly moved therefor to make him a monk, for Christ nor none of his apostles was never monk nor friar." But there is also a great variety of topics in these notes, as we may see in the following examples.

One of the marvels of Ireland was Saint Patrick's Purgatory, a cavern where men were supposed to be able to witness the pains of the wicked and the joys of the blessed. They say that whoever endures the pains of Patrick's purgatory shall never suffer the pains of hell, unless he die finally without repentance of sin. At this point the translator cannot resist a comment of his own (I, 363):

> Though this saw might be sooth, it is but a jape. For no man that doth deadly sin shall be saved, but he be very repentant, whatsoever penance he do; and every man that is truly repentant at his life's end of all his misdeeds, he shall be certainly saved and have the bliss of heaven, though he never hear speak of Patrick's purgatory.

It is a curious fact that Higden, who elsewhere uses Latin prose, composes his chapter on Wales in rhyming couplets, and Trevisa does likewise in the English translation, including those passages added by way of commentary. In speaking of Merlin, for example, Higden remarks (following Geoffrey of Monmouth) that he was begotten by a goblin. Trevisa interrupts at this point to make a distinction. While it may be true that a devil (incubus) can make women pregnant, he says, in no case does the child himself have characteristics of the devil. If that were so, the child would be immortal (I, 419–21):

> Learned men deny
> That devils ever die;
> But death slew Merlin,
> *Ergo*, Merlin was no goblin!

It was in Caerleon, says Higden, citing Gerald of Wales, that the messengers of Rome came to the great Arthur's court, adding "if it is lawful to believe it." Trevisa comments (II, 77):

> If Gerald was in doubt whether it were lawful for to trow this or no, it was not full great readiness to write it in his books, as some men will ween. For it is a strange dream indeed for to write a long story to have evermore in mind, and ever have doubt if it be amiss to believe it. If all his books were such, what lore were therein, and especially while it maketh no evidence for either side, nor telleth what him moveth for to say so?

In a section devoted to the history of Greek philosophy, Higden alludes in passing to the belief of Zeno that "man's soul shall die with the body" (III, 217):

> *Trevisa.* I would a wise man had yseie his water (=tested his urine) and yheeled (poured) it in his throat though it were a gallon!

The freedom that the translator allows himself in these sharp responses is found almost exclusively in his notes to the *Polychronicon*.

The Oxford background is evident in a number of notes that touch on theological issues and other topics naturally associated with the university. When someone told Diogenes that a friend had spoken ill of him, the philosopher replied: "I doubt if my friend hath said such words by me; but it is openly known that thou hast that thing said" (III, 317–19):

> *Trevisa.* It is wonder that Diogenes used so lewed sophistry, for here he maketh no difference between the liar and him that accuseth the liar and warneth men of his leasings (=lies), and rehearseth the leasings; it is not one (thing) to speak evil by a man and warn him that men speak evil by him and rehearse what men saith. St. John, in his gospel, saith not that the devil was in Christ; but St. John saith that the Jews said that the devil was in Christ: and Christ himself despised not God; but he rehearseth how men bear him in hand that he despised God.

It is interesting that Trevisa seems not to recognize Diogenes' implied rebuke to rumor-mongering; but perhaps, as Alastair Minnis has suggested (1975), he is passing on to his readers a distinction picked up from his logical training at Oxford, or perhaps even from Wyclif himself, who uses the same example.

Higden includes an unflattering story of the death of Aristotle. Gregory Nazianzenus tells how the great philosopher drowns himself when he is unable to solve the problem of the ebbing and flowing of the waters at Black Bridge (III, 371):

> *Trevisa.* It is wonder that Gregory telleth so mad a maggle tale of so worthy a prince of philosophers as Aristotle was. Why telleth he not how Aristotle declareth the matter of the ebbing and flowing of the sea? Why telleth he not how it is written in the book of the Apple how Aristotle died and held an apple in his hand and had comfort of the smell, and taught his scholars how they should live and come to God, and be with God without end. And at the last his hand began to quake, and the apple fell down of his hand, and his face wax all wan, and so Aristotle yielded up the ghost and died.

Obviously Trevisa prefers the version of Aristotle's death that places him, by implication, among the saints, a holy philosopher who has mastered the art of dying.

As we have noted, a major issue at Oxford in Trevisa's time was that of predestination and free will. A comment on this topic is elicited by the statement of Nectanabus: "No man may flee his own destiny" (III, 401–3):

> *Trevisa.* Nectanabus said this saw, and was a witch, and therefore it is never the better to trowing (=believing): but it were a vile shame for a Christian man to trow this false saw of this witch; for from every mishap that man is shaped in this world to fall in, God may him save if it is his will.

One of Higden's favorite Romans was the emperor Trajan, and he gives several anecdotes illustrating his justice and generosity. "For such great righteousness," he concludes, "it seemeth that St. Gregory won his soul out of hell." The theological basis of Trajan's salvation, however, was a matter often in dispute (V, 7):

> *Trevisa.* So it might seem to a man that were worse than wood (=mad), and out of right belief.

This criticism of Higden calls for an alternative explanation of Trajan's status, but Trevisa does not give us his opinion.

It is interesting to observe that the arguments used for the veracity of sacred scripture are sometimes used by Trevisa to defend the authenticity of secular literature. Such is the case in his defense of Geoffrey of

Monmouth against all comers. The issue arises in Higden's account
of the reign of King Arthur, in which he quotes the famous *dictum*
of William of Malmesbury that Arthur, of whom the Britons tell idle
tales, is worthy to be praised in true histories, and recounts also the
"discovery" of his body in Glastonbury in the time of Henry II. But
if Arthur had conquered thirty kingdoms as Geoffrey says (wonders
Higden), why is this not related in other histories? And why are not other
men also mentioned? Who is Frollo, and what about the emperor Lucius,
overcome by Arthur? It is a wonder that Geoffrey of Monmouth praises
so many people who are not even mentioned elsewhere. In response
to these searching questions, our Celtic translator appends one of his
longest notes (V, 337–39):

> *Trevisa.* Here William telleth a maggle tale without evidence; and Ranulph's
> reasons, that he moveth against Geoffrey and Arthur, should move no clerk
> that can known an argument, for it followeth not. St. John in his gospel
> telleth many things and doings that Mark, Luke, and Matthew speaketh not
> of in their gospels, *ergo*, John is not to be believed in his gospel. He were of
> false belief that trowed that that argument were worth a bean. For John in
> his gospel telleth that our Lord's mother and her sister stood by our Lord's
> cross, and many other things that no other gospeller maketh of mind, and yet
> John's gospel is as true as any of them all that they make. So though Geoffrey
> speak of Arthur's deeds, that other writers of stories speak of dark, or make
> of no mind, that disproveth not Geoffrey's story and his saw, and specially if
> some writers of stories were Arthur's enemies. It is wonder that Higden saith
> that no Frollo was King of France, nor Lucius procurator of the community,
> nor Leo emperor in Arthur's time, since often an officer, king or emperor
> hath many diverse names, and is diversely named in many diverse lands; and
> in the third book, chapter nine, he saith himself that it is no wonder though
> William Malmesbury were deceived, for he had not read the British book;
> and even if Geoffrey had never spoken of Arthur, many noble nations speak
> of Arthur and his noble deeds. It may well be that Arthur is oft overpraised,
> but so be many other. Sooth saws be never the worse though mad men tell
> maggle tales—and some mad men will mean that Arthur shall come again,
> and be afterward king here of Britain, but that is a full maggle tale, and so
> be many other that be told of him and of others.

Much personal feeling has gone into the writing of this note, in which
the armor of scriptural inerrancy is employed in the defense of Arthurian
tradition.

Do we find anything in these notes at all reminiscent of Trevisa's life
at Berkeley beyond the references already mentioned? In his chapter

on Charlemagne, Higden tells the story of Aygolandus, pagan prince of Spain, who came to Charles to be christened. The prince noticed that all at the royal table were finely clothed and pleasingly fed, while nearby there were thirteen poor men on the ground being given poor and simple food without any table; so he asked who these were. "These thirteen be God's messengers," was the reply, "who pray for us and remind us of the number of Christ's disciples." "Your law is not right," quoth the prince, "that suffereth God's messengers to be thus poorly treated; he serveth badly his Lord that thus receiveth his servants." And so, taking offense at this, he despised baptism and went home again. But Charles afterward honored poor men the more. This story displeased Trevisa (VI, 253):

> Aygolandus was a lewed ghost (=stupid fellow), and lewedly moved as the devil taught, and blinded him, so that he did not know that men should be served as their estate asketh (=according to social rank).

We may conclude our survey by noting some representative examples of the clash of opinion between the monastic author and the secular translator. Higden says that when Aldhelm, abbot of Malmesbury, was tempted by the flesh, he would overcome it by holding a fair maid in his bed while he recited the Psalter from beginning to end. This feat of ascetic derring-do seems to have appealed to the imagination of medieval man, for it reappears in the lives of other saints, notably St. Bernard, and indeed is found in secular Arthurian literature among the adventures of Lancelot. But Trevisa will have none of it (VI, 179):

> Save reverence of St. Aldhelm, this seemeth no holiness or wisdom but pure very folly, both for himself and for peril and dread of temptation of the woman, as it may be proved both by authority and by reason.

The specter of ecclesiastical corruption is raised by Higden when he describes the reforms brought about during the reign of King Edgar (960–75) through the leadership of Archbishop Dunstan. The king punished the wicked and cherished the good, repaired churches, and in many places he put away clerks that lived in outrage, and put monks in their place. This last point is too much for Trevisa, who comments (VI, 463):

> In that, saving the reverence of Edgar, he was lewedly moved, while there were other clerks who lived well enough.

A little further on, Higden lists the numerous monasteries founded by King Edgar, among which was the new abbey at Winchester. Here we are told that the clerks lived in luxury, neglecting divine services, spending the church's money on themselves, and hiring vicars for a mere pittance to discharge their responsibilities for them. After repeated warnings, the king threw out these clerks and assigned their income to the starving vicars. When the vicars became even more corrupt than their predecessors, the king finally had to throw them out and put monks in their place. No doubt for Higden, this seemed a fitting and final solution to the problem. But Trevisa is scarcely able to finish the story without intruding his own angry comment on the status of the monasteries in his own time (VI, 465–67):

> And now for the most part monks be worst of all, for they be too rich, and that maketh them to take more heed about secular business than ghostly devotion. Therefore, as it is said before in the fourth book, 26th chapter, by Jerome: since holy church increased in possessions it has decreased in virtues. Therefore secular lords should take away the superfluity of their possessions, and give it to them that need it; or else when they know that, they be cause and maintainers of their evil deeds, since they help not to amend it while it is in their power, whatever covetous priests say. For it were alms to take away the superfluity of their possessions now, more than it was at the first foundation to give them what they needed.

The conviction of these words is unmistakable. Not only did Trevisa encounter these opinions at Oxford but he carried them with him to Berkeley, where, as we have seen, he found a ready listener in his patron, Thomas IV, whose bequests at the end of his life failed to include a single foundation such as his predecessors had established in numerous churches and monasteries between Gloucester and Bristol. Examples such as this one show that more than any other of the translations, the English *Polychronicon* of Trevisa preserves for us the translator's most cherished opinions and beliefs.

Aegidius Romanus, De Regimine Principum

In light of the controversial tone of some of the notes to the *Polychronicon* translation, Trevisa would appear to have sailed into calmer waters in choosing for his next project the "Rule of Princes" by Aegidius Romanus (also known as Giles of Rome or Egidius Colonna). Indeed this treatise on the education of princes has nothing to say about ecclesiastical issues, nor does the English version contain opinionated notes by our translator. But when we consider that the project was probably undertaken during a critical period of the reign of Richard II (1388–92), it is not difficult to see that the distinction Aegidius makes, for example, between a king and a tyrant (e.g., 1.3.3) would have been a matter of concern in baronial circles during the time of the "loyal conspiracy" of the lords appellant (Goodman, 1971). As we have seen, Thomas Lord Berkeley avoided taking a stand against the king until the last minute, but it would appear from Trevisa's choice of this treatise that, during the decade preceding his involvement in Richard's deposition, Thomas was doing his homework. Moreover, the choice of this particular text seems fair and unbiased. Indeed a French translation of the same work was in the library of Simon Burley, tutor of Richard II himself (M. V. Clarke 1937, p. 120, n. 2). But before looking at this text, it is necessary to consider briefly the Latin original, and the state of the English translation.

Aegidius Romanus (ca. 1247–1316) joined the order of the Hermits of St. Augustine and studied theology at Paris, where he came under the influence of Thomas Aquinas. During the reign of Philip III of France (1270–85) he wrote the *De Regimine Principum* for the king's son Philip, who in 1285 succeeded his father as Philip IV the Fair (1285–1314). In this treatise Aegidius advocates a strong role for the ideal king, who is principally restrained by his own commitment to moral law. The reign of Philip the Fair gave his tutor a rare opportunity to see the consequences of his teachings in action. Unfortunately, the conflict between Philip and Pope Boniface VIII (1294–1303) over the relationship of church and state (specifically the king's right to tax the clergy without the pope's approval) raised issues not covered in *De Regimine Principum*, and it would appear that Aegidius was stung into a realization that in a fallen world the power of the king must be restrained by the authority and power of the head of Holy Church. Hence in 1301 he wrote the *De Ecclesiastica Potestate* in defense of Boniface and in defiance of his former pupil, now Europe's most powerful monarch. It speaks well for Philip that he seems not to have harbored a grudge against his tutor for siding with his adversary in the crisis of 1301–2. I see no evidence that Trevisa was aware of the *De Ecclesiastica Potestate*, but there are occasionally some hints in his translation of *De Regimine Principum* and the *Dialogus* (discussed above) that he sees the importance of restraints on the royal power.

Trevisa's translation of *De Regimine Principum* is uniquely preserved in MS Digby 233 in the Bodleian Library, Oxford, and is usually dated early fifteenth century, although the translation itself has no colophon or other indication of date or place of completion. As mentioned at the beginning of this chapter, my estimate is that the work was done in the period 1388–92 at Berkeley. The *De Regimine Principum* translation occupies folios 1–182 of the Digby MS, and is followed by a translation of the treatise on warfare by Vegetius, *De Re Militari*, folios 183–227. This second work is dated 1408 (six years after Trevisa's death), and is attributed somewhat cryptically to "worschepful ⬚ toun" in an elaborate colophon on folio 227 (printed by Perry, 1925, p. xcvi). At the moment I see no clear solution to this puzzle: the two most likely candidates are John Walton, who translated Boethius for Thomas Berkeley's daughter Elizabeth in 1410, and William Clifton, master of Berkeley's grammar school at Wotton in 1416.

A good case has been made by Hanna (1989, pp. 897–901) for identifying Digby 233 as a "Berkeley book," in the style of Thomas's Psalter (Bodley 953). This accords well with my sense of the text itself as a Berkeley project of the late 1380s and early 1390s; and Hanna's comments on the provenance, dialect, illustrations, and other features of the manuscript all support the conclusion that the Digby manuscript may be a product of a Berkeley scriptorium.

The only major defect of Digby 233 is the absence of a leaf following folio 116, with the consequent loss of most of the last chapter of Book 2, Part 3 (2.3.20), and all of the twenty chapter headings that should have preceded the first chapter of Book 3. Since the only two illustrations now in the manuscript occur at the beginnings of Book 1 and Book 2 (fols. 1r and 62r), it seems likely that there was a third illustration at the beginning of Book 3 on the missing leaf, and that its loss was occasioned by the theft of the picture. The absence of this one leaf may not have been noticed because the numbering of the manuscript was done after the theft occurred, and is consecutive, showing no gap after folio 116. A minor slip occurs on folio 153r, column 2, where a chapter number is omitted just before the sentence beginning "As it is declared" (3.2.27), so that numbering of the last nine chapters of this part are off by one.

Lacking a modern critical edition of the Latin text of *De Regimine Principum*, we have no study or classification of manuscripts and early printed texts to help us identify the version of this treatise that Trevisa might have used. But at an early stage of my investigations I was fortunate enough to attract the interest of the late Neil R. Ker, then bibliographer of the Bodleian, in this problem, and he ventured the opinion that Trevisa's exemplar may have been close to the text found in Bodley manuscript Hatton 15. Subsequently I have found, while editing Trevisa's translation on the computer, that the occasional disagreements between the English and Latin texts (I use a printed edition of the Latin published in Rome, 1556) could often be resolved by recourse to the Latin readings of the Hatton manuscript. Thus, according to the Rome edition, Trevisa omitted nearly five lines of Latin preceding the last sentence of Chapter 4 (Book 1, Part 1); but a glance at Hatton 15 (6v, col. 2, top) shows that it lacks those same lines, agreeing exactly with Trevisa's translation.

Although I am inclined to agree with Hanna that the Digby manuscript may be located in Berkeley within Thomas's lifetime, I think it would be an exaggeration to say that the text "was not written consecutively" (Hanna 1989, p. 897, n. 47). The crucial case is folio 55 (Book 1, Part 4, Chapters 1 and 2), especially 55v, column 2, where the text continues for eight lines below the margin. But an examination of the text at this point, comparing it with the Latin, shows that the irregularities on this folio are the result of scribal error. Chapter 1 describes six good manners of children and applies them to kings and princes, while Chapter 2 describes six bad manners of children and explains why kings and princes should avoid them. While in the process of copying the first half of Chapter 1 (on the six good traits of children), the scribe made a serious error when he reached point six: he skipped about 140 lines of text and copied point six in the middle of Chapter 2. Hence instead of the good trait (modesty), point six treats a bad trait (impetuosity), and then continues with a listing of the bad traits of children from Chapter 2 until we reach number six, at which point the scribe seems to have noticed his error and tried to correct it. Rather than erase the fifty lines he has copied by mistake, he now goes back to point six in the original series of good traits (modesty), and proceeds to copy the 140 lines that had been omitted: the last of the good traits (modesty), the application of all these traits to kings and princes, and, in Chapter 2, the enumeration of the bad traits of children through number five (number six, impetuosity, had already been included above by mistake). Finally, in place of point six (impetuosity), the scribe inserts the conclusion of Chapter 2, which is the application of this sixth bad trait to the lives of kings and princes (they should avoid it). He has now copied everything in these two chapters, but in the wrong order:

Chapter 1: good traits of children
  1. liberal
  2. hopeful
  3. magnanimous
  4. innocent
  5. merciful

---

  6. impetuous (Chapter 2: bad traits)
Why kings and princes should avoid these bad traits:
  1. passionate
  2. unstable
  3. credulous
  4. contentious
  5. mendacious

---

  6. modest (Chapter 1: good traits)
How these good traits apply to the lives of kings and princes:
  1. liberal
  2. hopeful
  3. magnanimous
  4. innocent
  5. merciful
  6. modest
Chapter 2: bad traits of children
  1. passionate
  2. unstable
  3. credulous
  4. contentious
  5. mendacious

---

  6. impetuous (why kings and princes should avoid this)

It is still something of a puzzle that there is crowding on 55v, since the disorder in these chapters does not involve the addition of anything new, and the preceding and following leaves exhibit no crowding whatever. I can only suppose that the stages of error in cases like this are never fully recoverable.

A somewhat more compact example of copying error occurs in Book 2, Part 1, Chapter 15 (MS fol. 77v, col. 2), where the manuscript reads:

for among suche barbares ben kyndelich straunge and seruant he is barbarus
þat is strange to a man is no kyndelich prince but swiche laborers and it is not
vnderstonde of hym for a man is barbarus to anoþer for þe oþer vnderstondeþ
hym not.

The Latin helps clear up this jumble:

quia inter barbaros nullus est naturalis principans. Sed idem est esse naturaliter
barbarum ab aliquo, hoc est esse estraneum ab eo et non intelligi ab illo potest
enim quis esse barbarus huic vel illi, quia non intelligitur ab hoc vel ab illo
vel ab alio.

Now we can see that repetition of the word "barbares" has caused
the scribe's eye to skip, resulting in the omission of "is no kyndelich
prince but swiche barbares." Before noticing this, the scribe copied one
more line ("ben kyndelich straunge and seruant he is"), after which
he attempted to repair the damage in the next few lines (possibly over
erasure). A caret in the manuscript at the point of omission is our only
tangible clue to the scribe's intention. By recourse to the Latin we may
restore the original translation with only two changes: "laborers" should
read "barbares," and the pronoun "it" should be omitted:

for amonge suche barbares is no kyndelich prince; but swiche barbares ben
kyndelich straunge and seruant, for he is barbarus þat is strange to a man
and is not vnderstonde of hym, for a man is barbarus to anoþer for þe oþer
vnderstondeþ hym not.

In other instances there occurs a gap in the English text that is not
repaired, either because the scribe failed to detect it, or perhaps because
the gap was in the Latin exemplar. In Book 2, Part 1, Chapter 3, for example, Aegidius makes a distinction (near the beginning of the chapter)
between the use of the word "house" to designate a physical building,
and its use to designate the people who live there, the household. The
job of the moral philosopher, he points out, is to treat "house" in the
second sense:

But it longeth not to hym to trete principalliche of hous þat is bulde of
walles, stoon, and fundament but he schulde trete of hous þat is ibuld and
hath order to þe hous þat is comynte of persones of oon hous, *sicut spectat ad
politicum determinare de ordine domorum, et de constructione vici, et de fabrica civitatis,
vt ordinantur ad communitatem, et ad politiam ciuium. Intendimus ergo ostendere de
domo, quae est communitas personarum domesticarum* of oon hous, and how suche
an hous is þe firste comynte.

Because of the repetition of the Latin phrase *communitas personarum* ("comynte of persones"), causing the scribe's eye to leap from the first to the second occurrence, we here lost (in English) the end of the first sentence and the beginning of the second (here supplied in Latin). Lapses of this kind are not as common as one might expect (considering the length and repetitive style of the treatise), but they do occur. Nevertheless the text is a reasonably accurate piece of work, and is carefully corrected.

In his introduction to Trevisa's minor works (1925), Perry briefly discusses the *De Regimine* translation, and calls attention to the fact that it contains two signed notes by Trevisa in Book 3, Part 2, Chapters 16 and 17 (fols. 143v, col. 2, and 144v, col. 1). He then adds that "a careful reading and comparison with a Latin MS may reveal others" (p. xcix, n. 1). There is, in fact, one other signed note in Book 3, Part 2, Chapter 7 (near the top of the first column of folio 136v):

Treuysa: whanne fewe men ben lordes and ben not good and vertuous but riche and myȝty and louen not þe comune profit but desireþ here owne profite and ouersetteþ oþer men, such principate is icleped eliga[r]chia. And here tirandise is icleped þe worst eligarchia, for it is most greuous to sogettes.

Without any claim of completeness, I can offer the following unsigned notes that go beyond the Latin original and therefore appear to be the work of Trevisa:

45v, col. 1	And here it is to wetyng þat þe obiecte of siȝt is þyng þat is iseie as colour o[r] liȝt, and þe ob[i]ecte of heryng is þyng þat is herd as voys and soun; and so þe obiecte of loue is þyng þat is iloued as good þyng. (1.3.3)
54, col. 2	Touching þe passions of þe concupiscible, þat þei mowe loue and desire and haue abhominacioun and be sory as þei scholde and do in alle þese as ordre and reule of resoun axeth of passions, be þis inow at þis tyme. (1.3.11 end)
95, col. 1	[concupiscence:] that is for to say corrupcioun of vile stenkyng caryoun or elles vilþe and concupiscible þat is coueitous þat is likyng. (2.2.12 end)
96v, col. 1	It is to wetynge þat þes twey wordes, mollis and ductilis, ben here itak in anoþer manere þanne in þe comyn speche. For in þe comyne speche mollis is nesche and ductilis is a thing þat streccheth in le[n]gþe oþer in brede with betyng of hamers.

195

And as we speken heere he þat wiþstondeþ no temptacioun is icleped mollis, nesche; an[d] he þat folweþ sone oþere menne maneres oþer is ilad by oþere is icleped ductilis. (2.2.14 mid)

117v, col. 1   habitus electiuus is a sad vertue with fre choys. (3.1.2)

136v, col. 1   Magnificus is he þat makeþ grete workes. (3.2.7 end)

137, col. 2   And a childe þat is ifonge in þat wise is icleped filius adoptiuus, a wel-welled sone. (3.2.8 mid)

137v, col. 1   And heere he is icleped fortis þat wol fiȝte whanne it nedeþ and whare it nedeþ and for what cause it nedeþ and aȝenst wham it nedeþ and as it nedeþ. (3.2.8 end)

Having touched on the problem of scribal error, and the identification of the translator's notes and definitions, we need now to consider the possibility that Trevisa might occasionally put a spin on his translation in order to point up the relevance of a particular passage to the behavior of Richard II. Even Chaucer, who was quite reticent as a political commentator, held forth on the duty of kings in a way that suggests he had the young king in mind (Prologue to *The Legend of Good Women*, F 373–411, G 353–97), and invokes the same "philosopher" (Aristotle) cited often by Aegidius in the *De Regimine*. In Chaucer's poem, his sovereign lady, Alceste, offers the god of love this advice (F 373–77):

This shoolde a ryghtwis lord have in his thoght,
And nat be lyk tirauntz of Lumbardye,
That han no reward but at tyrannye.
For he that kynge or lord ys naturel,
Hym oghte nat be tiraunt ne crewel. . . .

Aegidius makes a formal distinction between king and tyrant in his instructions to the future king Philip, which Trevisa translates as follows (1.3.3):

46, col. 1   þe friste wey is declared in þis wise for, as it is iseid tofore and as þe philosofer preueth in Politicis, a kyng and a tyrand ben diuerse. For a kyng loueth principalliche þe comune profit, and in louynge þe comune profit he loueth his owne profit; for ȝif þe regne is saaf, þe kyng is saaf. But a tyraund doþ þe contrarie and loueth principaliche his owne profit, and, by þe consequent folwynge and by hap, he loueþ þe comune profit wherof cometh his owne profit. þanne for a kyng and a tyrant hauen contrarious maners, for þe manere of loue of a tyraunt

setteþ his awne profit tofore þe comyne profit and þe manere
loue of a kyng scholde sette þe comyn profit tofore his owne
profite; also for eche kyng and prince is in special manere
Goddes seruant and a comyn persone: in a special manere it
is semelich to kynges and princes to sette God and þe comyn
profit tofore singuler profit.

The paragraph just quoted is typical of the work as a whole: Trevisa
is following the Latin original very closely, neither adding to nor subtracting from what he sees before him. But is there an instance where he
appears to be adding something of his own—an addition going beyond
the explanatory function that we have noted in the definitions cited
above? I have found only two instances, both on the same page (fol.
48), occupying the final four lines of each column. An alert reader has
drawn a line through them, no doubt to indicate that they do not reflect
anything in the Latin original. Without these extra lines both passages
(from 1.3.5) make perfect sense. I quote the Latin, followed by the
English, in each case:

Possumus autem duplici via investigare, que non decet reges
et principes aliquid aggredi ultra vires, et sperare vltra quam sit
sperandum.

48, col.1   And by twey weyes we may preue þat kynges and / princes
scholde not auentre in doyng þat passeth here owne myȝt and
strengþe noþer hath more hope þan he scholde.

★

Si ergo inconueniens est totam gentem et totum regnum
periculis exponere, diuturno consilio et magna diligentia ex-
cogitare debent reges et principes quid aggrediantur, ne as-
sumant arduum aliquod vltra vires, et ne sperent aliquid non
sperandum.

48, col. 2   ȝif it is inconuenient to putte al þe men and al þe regne /
to peril, kynges and princes schulde wiþ longe counseille and
with greet besinesse and auysement bythenke in what doyng
he schulde auenture leste he take uppoun hym sum doynge þat
passeth here owne myȝt and strengthe, and lest þei hopede to
haue sum what þat is not to hopynge.

Column 1 of folio 48 originally ended as follows (with canceled material
in italics):

> And by twey weyes we may preue þat kynges and *princes schulde auenture hemself as in goodnesse schewyng to alle oþer sogettes, for foly hardynesse of hem myȝt destrue manye. And kynges and*

Likewise column 2 originally ended as follows:

> ȝif it is inconuenient to putte al þe men and al þe regne *in subiectioun and peril and þerfore it is semelich þat euery astat take hede þerof for it is nedfol þat kynges and princes put hem in strengþe.*

The italicized sentiments clearly interrupt the flow of thought, and do not correspond to anything in the Latin original. Since they occupy the last four lines of each column, we might at first suppose that they were added to the text by someone; but not only do they seem to be in the original hand and ink, they also fit into columns of a standard length for this manuscript: 43 lines. Without these lines, the columns would be too short.

What these additions signify is not entirely clear. The context is a warning to rulers against foolhardy behavior, and the italicized statements seem to offer refinements or qualifications of this warning. The first suggests that kings and princes should be bold in doing good, while the second seems to concede that since it is necessary for them to strengthen themselves, people in all ranks of society should exercise caution and restraint ("take hede"). It sounds as if, at the time these lines were written, English society was beginning to feel like an armed camp.

There is, finally, an addition that may tell us something a bit more specific than the preceding ones. This occurs on folio 34 of the manuscript *in the margin*, so that there can be no doubt: it was written there after the text had been copied, presumably by a reader. The translation at this point is of Book 1, Part 2, Chapter 23, setting forth the properties of a magnanimous man, and explaining why it is incumbent on kings and princes to be magnanimous. The relevant sentence in the Latin original occurs near the end of Chapter 23:

> Decet etiam eos esse manifestos oditores et amatores, vt manifeste odiant vitia, persequantur malos, et non permittant maleficos viueres.

The translation reads (with marginal addition in italics):

> 34, col. 2   Also þei schulde be oponliche iknowe wheþer þey loue oþer hate, *and rese opon no man vnwarned nor sodaynly nor with feyned sembland of luf,* so þat þei hate opunlich vices and pursewe euel doers and suffre not passyng euel doers alyue.

The context calls for rulers to be open in their dealings, while the marginal addition provides a negative example: they should not rush upon a man without warning or suddenly or with feigned countenance of love. Here we may believe with some confidence that Richard II is the target, and that the reference is to the arrest of his uncle, Thomas of Woodstock, the duke of Gloucester, in July 1397. Thomas was perhaps the most notable of the lords appellant who were seized at the same time, and the duke in particular was arrested by the king himself at Pleshey (the duke's residence). According to one report, when the arrest took place Richard said to the duke, "By St John the Baptist, fair uncle, all this will turn out for the best for both of us" (Gervase Mathew, *The Court of Richard II*, p. 151). But, in fact, the duke was then removed secretly to Calais, where he seems to have been executed (despite attempts at a cover-up).

If the marginal addition on folio 34 is in fact a reference to the duke's arrest, we may ask: for what length of time after July 1397 would it be likely that a reader would be prompted to think of this incident and record it thus? There is of course no certain answer to a question of this kind. But I suspect that the anger which prompted the entry, if not the memory of the event itself, would have subsided soon after the death of Richard himself in 1399. I leave it to paleographers to judge whether the hand of the annotator can be early enough to fall in the period 1397–99.

As mentioned above, present opinion would place the copying of Digby 233 no earlier than 1408 (date of completion of the *De Re Militari*), but there remains the possibility that Trevisa's translation of the *De Regimine Principum* was copied earlier (in the mid-1390s?), and the Vegetius tract added later. An important factor in this equation will be Kathleen Scott's opinion of the date of Digby's illustrations in the forthcoming *Survey of Manuscripts Illuminated in the British Isles* (vol. 6, *Later Gothic Manuscripts*), under the general editorship of J. J. G. Alexander. In any case, this unique marginal entry provides us with the striking reaction of an early reader of Trevisa's text, apparently seeking to apply the doctrine of Aegidius to the behavior of Richard II.

Trevisa's work on Aegidius was his third largest project, exceeded only by the *Polychronicon* and the *De Proprietatibus Rerum* of Bartholomaeus Anglicus. There is as yet no accessible modern edition of the *De Regimine Principum* translation; I have prepared one in diskette form which, in its printout version, runs to 512 pages, without apparatus. Dr. C. F. Briggs of the Department of History, Georgia Southern University, who has made a careful study of the Latin manuscripts, will collaborate with me on an edition of Trevisa's text to be published in the Garland Medieval Texts series. Meanwhile, there is room in the present chapter for nothing more than a brief description of the aim and scope of this major treatise on the education of kings and princes.

The work is divided by Aegidius into three books: Book 1 devoted to the prince's rule of himself; Book 2 to the rule of his household; and Book 3 to the rule of the kingdom. The four parts of Book 1 treat respectively: (1) introductory matters (thirteen chapters), (2) the virtues (thirty-four chapters), (3) the passions (eleven chapters), and (4) manners (seven chapters), for a total of sixty-five chapters in Book 1, although the numbering of chapters begins anew in each part. The three parts of Book 2 treat: (1) mainly marriage (twenty-four chapters), (2) children (twenty-one chapters), and (3) the household including property, wealth, and servants (twenty chapters), for a total of sixty-five chapters in Book 2. The three parts of Book 3 treat: (1) rule of the city (twenty chapters), (2) rule of the kingdom (thirty-six chapters), and (3) rule in time of war (twenty-three chapters), for a total of seventy-nine chapters in Book 3. Books 1 and 3 are about the same length, while Book 2 (on the rule of the household) is somewhat shorter.

Since this text is not yet available to the reading public, it seems best to offer here an example of its argument in concise form. I have chosen for this the Introduction and first seven chapters of Book 1, Part 1. What follows is not simply a modernization, but also a condensation of the text without, I hope, any substantial loss of content. I have chosen this particular section because it includes an interesting discussion of the distinction the author makes between moral and scientific discourse, and how this affects the strategy of the writer.

Of the Rule of Princes

BOOK 1, PART 1

Aegidius's dedication to Philip the Fair:

> Not all governments are equally enduring, for some last but a year, some a lifetime, and some are judged perpetual by succession in children. Now since nothing violent in nature lasts forever, the ruler who wishes his government

to be perpetual should take care to imitate nature and avoid violence in his governance. This means that he must not be a slave to passion but must rule like a true lord by reason and law.

You have required me to compose a book on governance, and in this you were stirred by God, who has inclined you to follow in the footsteps of your forefathers who loved the faith, which calls for government by laws, and not by self-will. In response to your noble request, and for the benefit of all good men, I gladly undertake this work with the help of God.

1

Since the language used should accord with the subject, we must first decide what kind of speech to use in discussing the governance of princes. Now the treatment of all moral matters is figural, and this in three ways: first, in the matter that is treated; second, in the purpose that is intended; and third, in the scholar that is taught by this art.

First, moral matter cannot be subjected to subtle investigation, since in-dividual deeds are ambiguous, their nature being dependent on intention, or inward meaning, which is unique and can only be expressed figuratively. Hence the quest for certainty must be tempered by the nature of the subject. The nature of morality, for example, is contrary to mathematics: in the latter science demonstrations can attain certainty, which is not possible in the case of morality. That is why demonstrations are appropriate to mathematics, but not to morality; and persuasion is appropriate to morality, but not to mathematics.

Second, the purpose of studying morality is to learn to be good. Hence we do not want subtle reasons that dazzle the intelligence, but those that incline the will toward goodness, and for this we need similes and figures of speech, that will promote a love of the truth.

Third, consideration must be given to the audience intended for the book. Though it is called the Lore of Princes, this book is intended for all in the sense that every man should want to make himself worthy to be a prince, even though this is not possible for everyone. Hence the treatment should be simple and straightforward, and subtleties should be avoided.

In this book princes are told how to conduct themselves, and how to command their subjects. And since subjects should also learn from it how to obey their prince, the treatment should be general and figurative.

2

This treatise will be divided into three books. The first will show how the king, as well as every man, is to rule himself; the second, how he is to rule his household; the third, how he shall rule a city and a kingdom. Hence the first book is concerned with ethics; the second with economics; and the third with politics.

The above order is reasonable, since just as our friendship with another derives from something within ourselves, so it is in the case of governance. For he that would rule others must first learn to rule himself. Hence we must speak of self-governance before turning to the governance of households or of kingdoms.

It is also natural that we proceed from the imperfect to the perfect, as from child to man, and from imperfect knowledge to wisdom. For the amount of knowledge needed increases as we progress from the king's knowledge of himself, to the rule of his household, and finally to the rule of cities and kingdoms.

In the treatment of self-rule there are four points to be considered. First, what shall be the king's ultimate end, concern or felicity; second, what virtues he should have; third, what passions he should follow; and fourth, what manners he should use. In all this the purpose is to teach the king to rule himself in order to give himself to good works and deeds.

Now our deeds are prompted by four things: by ends, habits, passions, and manners, and these four things are interrelated, and will be treated in the first book. But first we shall discuss the end, for this comes before all others as the prompter of deeds.

3

Having gained the attention and good will of the king's majesty by the choice of a straightforward method of treatment, and having aided the understanding by setting forth the organization of this work, we now explain the benefits to be gained from the study of it.

The king who understands and observes the precepts that shall be given will have four benefits: first, he shall win the best good; second, he shall win himself; third, he shall win other men; and fourth, he shall win and have God himself and eternal happiness.

For the first, an important distinction must be made, for there are three degrees of what is good: one is outward good, which is good; another is inward good, which is better, and may be possessed by both good men and evil men, as wisdom, cunning, and common sense; but the best good is inward, and evil men have no part in it: these are the moral virtues, which cannot be misused. Elsewhere the philospher classifies these three degrees as pleasing, profitable, and honest good. And the purpose of this book is to show how the king may be made honest and virtuous and thus instill these virtues in his subjects.

The second benefit is that the king wins not only the highest good, but he wins also himself. For an evil man is said not to possess himself when his appetite is contrary to reason. If, as the philosopher says, reason is not master, then man is not lord of himself, for he wills one thing by reason and another by passion. But the good man possesses himself.

The third benefit is that he wins other men, for only the man who rules himself is worthy to govern others. If he lacks this ability, even though he may rule by temporal strength, he is more worthy to be a subject than a lord.

The fourth benefit of observing the teachings of this book is that we shall have God and eternal bliss. For the more a man approaches to goodness, the more he is in accord with the first principle, that is God; and a perfect man has God. Unlike the evil man, in whom reason and appetite are at war, the good man, who is abundant in virtues and the highest good, shall win the good, himself, and others, and shall have God and bliss eternal, God willing.

4

Since the end is principal cause of deeds, we shall begin this treatise with a consideration of the diverse ways of life that influence the ends chosen, and show how felicity in them shall be attained. Philosophers distinguish three ways of life: voluptuous, politic, and contemplative, corresponding to the three main categories of life, that is beasts, man, and the angels. We will consider man first as he relates to the other animals; second, as he is in himself; and third, as he relates to the angels. Thus every man lives in one or the other of these three ways: the voluptuous life of an animal, the civil life of a man, or the contemplative life of an angel.

Though there are three ways of life, philosophers allow only two forms of happiness, for they deny that happiness is to be found in a voluptuous life. Hence there is a dual happiness, one for the civil or political life, the other for the contemplative life. He who lives and acts in accordance with reason has felicity not only as a man, but to some extent also shares the felicity that belongs to God and the angels in his knowledge of the truth.

Every man is either worse than a man, and therefore a beast, or he is better than a man, and therefore godly or semidivine. And what else is a man but a companionable beast, living a politic life ruled by readiness and reason? When he sinks lower than a man, then he is ruled by passion and leads a willful or voluptuous life; but if he is godly and better than man, then he has the intelligence and wisdom of the contemplative life.

Those who live a politic life and are engaged in worldly deeds are often disturbed by passions, whereas the contemplative man is somewhat detached from these and communes with angels. Hence the latter should be held in honor as set somewhat higher than a man. But though the philosophers made valid distinctions, they came somewhat short of the full truth, since they thought that man could avoid sin by purely natural action, and could thus achieve a perfect life, whether active or contemplative. But that is false, since all that would live rightfully are in need of God's grace, especially kings and rulers of other men. They were also wrong to define the contemplative life as one of pure speculation, since such a man will fall short of perfection, unless he have in him the love of God. But they are in agreement with theologians and the faith of Holy Church when they place the contemplative life above the active or political life.

Hence it becomes a king to flee the voluptuous life of beasts, and adopt both active and contemplative life, the former for ruling his subjects, and the latter for inward devotion to the highest judge.

5

To achieve his end and his felicity, a man must know what it is, so that his actions will bring him to it, and so that he will be able to rule other men. To achieve his end through his actions a man must do three things: he must do well, do it by free choice, and do it with pleasure. However good his intentions, if he does not actually do well, he will not attain felicity, just as in battle it is not the strong who win the crown, but those who actually perform courageous deeds. Further, good deeds must come from free choice, not willfulness, for there is no merit in deeds done by chance. Finally these deeds should be done with pleasure, for thereby they will be done well, and also will become habitual.

But even when we do good by choice and with pleasure, in order to attain our end, it is important to know what that end is, since it is this end or felicity that ultimately moves the will. Without this objective, the deeds of all mankind would cease. But it must be a good end, for no deed is good if it is done for an evil purpose. And of course knowledge of this end is necessary in order to make possible both a free choice, and the pleasure in action that comes from consideration of the benefits to be derived from it. This is especially true for a king, who seeks benefits not just for himself, but for the community as a whole, and performs deeds that are in some sense God's deeds. And this brings us to the final point, namely that the king must know his end because he must rule others. Just as the archer controls the flight of the arrow on its way to the target, so the king must know his end more than his subjects.

6

As used in this work, happiness may be defined in three ways: first, it is that which is good and sufficient in itself; second, which follows from the first, it is in accord with right reason; and third, it is good for the soul rather than the body. Therefore felicity is not to be sought in the bodily appetites, which can never be satisfied, whereas those things that are good for the soul bring true felicity. Also bodily pleasures, if they are strong, impede the reason and make it blind, whereas the body is ordained to serve the soul, and not the reverse. Therefore a man should devote himself to virtuous deeds for the good of his soul, even though it may be conceded that there are some pleasures permissible to a good man, who understands that no bodily delectations are conducive to true felicity.

If it is detestable for any man to put his felicity in bodily pleasures, it is especially so for a king, for three reasons: first, they make him sink low; second, they cause him to be despised; and third, they make him unworthy to be a prince. For the higher the rank, the farther he will fall, and it is not right that a prince should choose the life of unreasoning beasts, for to do so would make him unworthy to rule. Hence the philosopher says that he should have pleasure with moderation, lest he become like drunken or sleeping men, who lose the use of reason and are soon despised. Princes should also avoid childish behavior, regardless of their age; and to show themselves at all times wise and ready, and worthy to rule, they should despise immoderate and voluptuous living.

7

There are two kinds of riches: natural and artificial. Natural riches are products of the earth or of animals: anything that serves as food, drink, or clothing for man. Artificial riches are produced by the ingenuity of men such as gold and silver or money that can be exchanged for natural riches, but do not in themselves relieve bodily needs. Felicity should not be set in either of these riches.

Our trust should not be placed in artificial riches for three reasons: first, because they are merely a means of obtaining natural riches; second, because they exist only by the ordinance of man, and have no value in themselves; and third, not only do artificial riches not fulfill the soul, they do not even relieve bodily needs, since it is possible that a rich man may die of hunger, like Midas.

That felicity should not be set in natural riches—things that relieve bodily needs—is easily demonstrated. For since the soul is better than the body, felicity should be sought not in the good of the body, but in virtuous deeds that are the good of the soul. And if it is detestable for any man to set his felicity in riches, it is even more so for a king, and this for three reasons: first, because the kingly virtue of magnanimity would be inhibited; second, by encouraging the king to consider his own rather than the common profit, this love of riches would turn him into a tyrant; and third, it would encourage him to despoil and injure his own subjects. Therefore if it is detestable for a king to lose the best good and become a tyrant and a thief, it is detestable and horrible for him to set his felicity in riches.

By way of conclusion let me point out one possible use for this text not previously mentioned. We have already touched on its relevance to the reign and the deposition of Richard II; apart from this, it is likely that we will think of it as a book to be read in private. But there is one possible social function that the modern reader might not think of: the *De Regimine* as a book to be read aloud to a group. Aegidius himself suggests this near the end of Book 2 on the rule of a household. Unfortunately, the passage has been lost from the Digby manuscript (as mentioned above), so it is given here in modern English translation (2.3.20):

> In fact, if at the tables of kings and princes some useful things were read, so that at the same time as the throats of the recliners take food their ears might receive learning, this would be altogether fitting and proper. Therefore kings and princes ought to ordain that praiseworthy customs of the kingdom, if such have been reduced to writing, be read at the table; or also praiseworthy deeds of their predecessors, and especially of those who have comported themselves in a sacred manner and religiously with respect to divine things, and who have ruled the kingdom justly and in due fashion; or that there be read at the table this book *Of the Rule of Princes*, so that even princes themselves might be instructed in how they should rule and others might be taught how to be obedient to princes. These things then or other useful things, reported in the common idiom so that all could be instructed through them, would be the things to be read at the tables of kings and princes.

Whether Trevisa's version of this treatise was ever read at the table of Thomas, Lord Berkeley, must unfortunately remain a matter of conjecture.

Bartholomaeus Anglicus, De Proprietatibus Rerum

Bartholomew the Englishman was a Franciscan who was educated at Paris and completed his great encyclopedia, *On the Properties of Things*, about the year 1245. Soon thereafter a Dominican, Thomas of Cantimpre, produced a rival compilation, *On the Nature of Things*. In comparing these two works Traugott Lawler has this to say (*DMA*, 4:448):

> Of the two books Bartholomaeus' was the more complete and influential. It was translated into six languages and was printed several times, the last edition in 1601; it was the most widely read and quoted of all late-medieval encyclopedias.

Here at last was an encyclopedia to rival the *Etymologies* of Isidore of Seville (d. 636), drawing as it does on a much more sophisticated body of knowledge than had been available to Isidore. As Lawler remarks (pp. 448–49):

Bartholomaeus' conception of the properties of things includes the operation of cause and effect: he shares Isidore's interest in origins and a notable interest of his own in results. His nineteen books are far better organized, better informed, and more thorough than those of his predecessors or Thomas of Cantimpre, whose book is more than half zoology. Bartholomaeus quotes extensively from Aristotle and the Arab savants and is particularly good on medicine and geography.

Trevisa's decision to translate the *De Proprietatibus Rerum* thus appears to have been a sound one. The work is organized according to the great chain of being, beginning with God and his angels and extending downward to man and the physical universe, as can be seen in the following list of contents of its nineteen books:

I.   On God and the divine names.
II.   On the properties of angels, both good and evil.
III. On the properties of the reasonable soul, the simplicity of its nature, its various powers, and its function in relation to the body, to which it gives form and perfection.
IV.   On the properties of bodily substance, including the elements and things that are made thereof, the qualities of which all bodies are made, and the four humors from which are made the bodies of men and beasts.
V.   On the parts of the human body.
VI.   On the properties of mankind (mortality, children, the two sexes, motherhood, servants, lordship, food and drink, sleep, dreams, exercise, and rest).
VII. On sickness and poisons.
VIII. On the world and the heavenly bodies.
IX.   On time and the motions of the heavens: seasons, months, days, new moon, sabbath, and the calendar.
X.   On matter and form and the properties thereof, and the elements, beginning with fire.
XI.   On the air, and the passions and properties thereof.
XII. On birds, the ornaments of the air.
XIII. On water and its various forms.
XIV. On the earth and its features (mountains, valleys, fields, deserts, caverns).
XV.   On provinces and regions (geography).
XVI. On precious stones and metals.

XVII.   On herbs and plants.
XVIII. On animals.
XIX.   On accidents: colors, odors, tastes, liquids, and eggs; numbers, measures, weights; music.

Indeed the above organization is something of a compromise between the order of the chain of being and the order of creation described in the beginning of Genesis. Bartholomaeus is at pains to point out, more than once, that his encyclopedia does not include everything, and in so saying he often invokes the biblical relevance of his work in order to set limits. Thus in defining the limits of his treatment of birds at the beginning of Book XII he says that he does not include mention of "all things, but only of birds and fowls of which special mention is made in the text of the bible or in the gloss."

There was no modern edition of Trevisa's translation until 1975, when the text was published in two volumes, under the general editorship of Michael Seymour assisted by a team of scholars assigned to individual books. Volume 3 appeared in 1988 containing an introduction, textual commentary, glossary, and indexes. A fourth volume appearing separately, *Bartholomaeus Anglicus and His Encyclopedia*, was published by Variorum Press in 1992. Thanks are due to Seymour and his colleagues that this major work by Trevisa is at long last available to the modern reader, with scholarly apparatus.

For an assessment of Trevisa's translation of Bartholomaeus we are indebted to Traugott Lawler (1983). His study begins with a consideration of some of Trevisa's practices as a translator in the *Polychronicon*, and then presents a detailed analysis of his work on the *De Proprietatibus Rerum*, of which Lawler was one of the editors. He concedes that Trevisa did not always understand fully the scientific text that he was translating, but decides that "the overall competence, the broad command of the vocabulary of so many different fields of knowledge, is impressive" (p. 280). He compares our translator with other writers of the late Middle Ages (including Chaucer and Nicholas Loue), and concludes (p. 288):

> What ultimately transcends all these comparisons in Trevisa is the scope of the books he translated. The task he undertook, and the breadth and sophistication of linguistic resources it required, are incomparable. He stands apart from his contemporaries because of the magnitude of his accomplishment, and especially because in translating *De Proprietatibus Rerum* he helped to

make English a capable instrument for conveying technical information to the average educated man. And he did so in an English that, even for the most technical medical, botanical, or physical material, is surprisingly fluent and competent—or, by his own criteria, accurate, intelligible, and idiomatic.

By way of illustrating Lawler's point I have chosen a pair of chapters from one of the books on medicine (Book VI, On the properties of mankind) with which to conclude this chapter on Trevisa's translations. Readers of Middle English will of course want to consult the original in Seymour's edition (1:331–34); the text provided below is modernized (as usual) and also contains Latin words and phrases in parentheses from Bartholomaeus's original where there may be some uncertainty in the text of Trevisa's translation or in Trevisa's choice of words. Thus "limb" may seem strange as a translation of "organum," and so forth. The subject of these two chapters is Sleep, and it sets forth compactly the late medieval understanding of what sleep is, based on both traditional authority and on the latest knowledge acquired from the rediscovery of Greek medicine through translations into Arabic and thence into Latin, as represented in the work of Constantinus Africanus, who is mentioned by name in the following discussion.

VI, 24

Aristotle says that sleep is a resting of the animal powers along with a strengthening of the natural powers (*quies animalium virtutum cum intentione naturalium*). For the power of feeling and motion is bound in sleep, whereas it is the opposite with the natural powers, such as the power of digestion, which then works most effectively, and is in sleep both comforted and strengthened. In his book *On the Greatness of the Soul* Augustine says otherwise, maintaining that sleep is a natural lack of feeling common to the body and the soul; hence sleep is common to both. For he says that sleep is a natural immobility and a help to the senses, and that natural lack of feeling is caused by a diversity of things that are contrary to nature. He goes on to say that sleep is not privation of waking in the way that blindness is privation of sight. For privation destroys powers and other things of nature, but sleep helps and comforts nature, and is just as natural as waking. Moreover the soul takes no pleasure in privation, yet it enjoys sleep; and so sleep is not privation but a natural disposition.

Sleep is otherwise described in this way. It is a pleasing passion that blocks the way to the brain and the senses, comforts the natural powers, and summons natural bodily heat from its extremities to its inner parts. In sleep the inner parts heat up and the extremities cool, so that when the heat is deep inside, the limb of the common wit (*organum sensus communis*) is bound, which is at the center in relation to all the particular senses (*omnium sensuum particularium*); and all of the individual senses spring out from there and stretch like lines drawn from the center of a circle to its circumference. So if that limb is blocked, the particular powers may not extend to the extremities of the limbs of wit and feeling (*ad organorum sensuum extremitates*). Nature makes this happen so that an animal might rest from willful activity, for it is impossible to be on the move always.

Constantinus (Africanus, d. 1087) says in *Pantegny* that some sleep is natural and some unnatural—but no more of that for the time being. Sleep comes naturally from moisture of the temperate brain (*ex humiditate cerebri temperati*), as from a moist and clear smoke (*vt ex fumo humido et claro*) coming from the whole body up to the brain (*cerebrum*). And that smoke thickens the spirits and fills the sinews (*neruos*) and thus binds the wits (*sensus*). In the aforementioned book (*On the Greatness of the Soul*) Augustine says that sleep comes from the food that enters from without, or from a temperate humor within, which comes to the brain when it is divided and dissolved (*cum resoluitur in fumum . . . et ibi resolutus*). The cold part goes down and the heat passes upward; cold dropping down assuages the heat of the heart, and impedes its function. Augustine says, and Aristotle too, that the heart is the source of action (*principium operationum*), and all good and evil come from the heart. In sleep the powers of motion and feeling are at rest, while the spiritual and natural powers remain as they were before, as it is seen and known by pulse, breathing and digestion, for the best digestion occurs in sleep. When Avicenna describes sleep he says that, speaking generally, sleep is the turning back of the spirit from the limbs of feeling and motion (*ab instrumentis sensuum et motus*) to the source, whence the instruments of the spirits have their origin. Natural sleep is a reversion of the spirits from the depths (*cum profundatione*) that food and drink may be digested, as happens in the sleep of working men, in whom sleep is deep and sound because of the excessive dispersion of the vital powers (*propter superfluitatem resolutionis spiritus*). Nature desires an increase in the essence (*substantia*) of the vital powers, and so buries them deep in the inner recesses and hides them there. And so in these the sleep is sound and long. ([Trevisa]: And in that manner slept Hezekiah.) [Cf. 2 Kings 20:21. For "Ezechias" the editors would read "Ezechiel," and cite Ez 4:8 (Seymour 1992, p. 85).] In like manner sleep those who are purged (*euacuati*) with laxatives and medicines, for much of the essence of the vital spirit is dispelled with the excess bodily fluids (*resoluit enim plurimus de substantia spiritus cum superfluitatibus*). This sleep is profitable and restores to them their strength and power, as Avicenna says.

Thus says Aristotle in book 3: sleep is proper to every animal in good health, though in some it is very light and imperceptible (*valde occultatus*). From this it is known that the material cause of sleep is a diffuse smoke given off by the body (*fumus indigestionis a corpore resolutus*); the formal cause is in the head at the common wit (*in capite apud communem sensum*) that is the source of feeling of the sinews (*et originem omnium neruorum sensibilium*) that are stopped and bound, and so the animal rests and all the members are comforted. Constantine says that the process of sleep varies in two ways, depending on the quantity and greatness of the matter that is found in the body. Concerning the quantity of the matter, if there is too much the power of digestion fails and the body becomes moist and cold, since humor is broken and dissipated, and so heat is quenched, and phlegm is increased while natural heat decreases. And if there is not enough matter the power of digestion fails and the body becomes dry. And if the food is moderate, it is well digested and the body is fattened, the heart comforted, natural heat increased, humors made temperate, and the wit (*mens*) made clear. Also the operation of sleep varies according to the matter that is found. For if the matter is great and natural heat is dissipated, it is overcome and quenched (*Quia si materia fuerit multa calor naturalis debilis per somnum fit maiorum humorum resolutio, quam intrans calor naturalis vincitur et exteinguitur*).

Therefore it is required that those that take drinks *and those that have been bled* should not sleep lest there be so great dispersion of humors in sleep that nature cannot govern them (*Etiam potionatis ne dormiant precipitur ne si per somnum tanta fiat resolutio humorum que non possint a natura regi*). But if the food be temperate and the humors also, heat is gathered within during sleep and digests the food and drink, makes the humors temperate, and the body moist, hot, and fat.

From the aforesaid you may conclude that sleep gathers natural heat inward, cools the outer parts, draws blood from there, heats, feeds and comforts the inner parts, ripens and cooks what is impure and raw, and quiets and comforts the powers of feeling and motion. And if it is temperate in quality and quantity it relieves a sick man, and indicates that nature shall have the victory and mastery over the illness, and marks a good turning point. If sleep does the contrary, it is suspect. So says Constantinus.

VI, 25

Then in sleep take heed of the will of him that sleeps, for he disposes himself willingly (*voluntarie*) to sleep. For Avicenna says that sleep is nothing but a desire for rest in the power of feeling (*in vi sensitiua* = "in the nervous system"?). Also take heed of the shortness of sleep, for when a man disposes himself and lays him down to sleep, his purpose is to rise again soon. Also take heed of the coming together of one's strength in sleep (*virtutis in dormitatione vnitas*), for the strength that is dissipated in waking is gathered and joined together in the body of him that sleeps, as Avicenna says. Also take heed of the lack of feeling in one that sleeps, as is known by things that have been said before, that often it happens that a man sleeps so strong and so fast that he scarcely feels anything external, even if he is beaten. Also take heed of the sweetness of rest, for sweetness in sleeping makes him forget all kinds of labors that were and are. Also take heed of the security of him that sleeps, for while he sleeps he dreads not the presence of his enemy. Also take heed of the changing and diversity of his shape (*figure*) that sleeps, for he seems dead on the outside but alive within, pale without but ruddy within, cold without but hot within; without all the power of working is dissipated (*foris tota virtus in effigies . . . se diffundit*) as it is in two contraries, but within all the power gathers itself together. Also men should take heed of diversity in sleeping, for some animals sleep with eyes closed and the lids fast together, and all such animals have sharper sight than other beasts that sleep with open eye and unclosed, as Aristotle says. And therefore fish have feeble sight, for they do not close their eyes in sleeping. And as he says in book four, fish rest in sleep, but very little, for they wake suddenly and flee. See above in book five about the eyelid and the eye (chapters 5–8).

Also men take heed of dreams and fantasies, for while asleep, through the mingling of reason and delusion, the soul encounters many fantasies. And the soul knows somewhat by imagination the likeness and shape thereof, but has no full grasp of these things and fantasies. And therefore often when a man awakens he takes no heed of what he has seen in his sleep. Also men must above all take heed of the profit that there is in sleep, for if the sleep is kind and temperate, it gives to the body very many benefits, as it is said beforehand in the words of Avicenna and Constantinus, and especially because then there is good digestion, and the pure is separated from the impure; and the pure thing that resembles the body is joined to it, and what is impure is separated from the body by the operation of the expulsive power. Concerning bad and unnatural sleep, see below in book seven, on lethargy (chapter 7).

5

THE ENGLISH BIBLE

Much about that time, euen in our
King *Richard* the seconds dayes, *Iohn Treuisa* translated them [the Scriptures]
into *English*, and many *English* Bibles in written hand are yet to be seene
with diuers, translated as it is very probable, in that age.

—Preface to the King James Bible, 1611

This passage from the Preface to the King James Bible, "The Translators to the Reader," is perhaps the most prominent statement that
we have of the little-known belief that Trevisa translated the Bible into
English. Yet it is true that for nearly five hundred years this idea has
been debated back and forth by editors, historians, and students of the
Bible. Unfortunately, no decisive evidence has been brought forward,
and it therefore cannot be said that anyone has clearly established the
truth or falsity of the allegation quoted above.

My purpose in this chapter is, first, to evaluate the tradition which
says that Trevisa translated the Bible; second, to review some pertinent
facts about Trevisa's career; and, third, to suggest a new line of inquiry
that should be more profitable for future research, and may even lead to
the resolution of this interesting problem.

The Tradition

The first mention of Trevisa as translator of the Bible is made by
the printer William Caxton, who published Trevisa's translation of the
Polychronicon in 1482. In his Prohemye to this edition Caxton identifies
Trevisa as one who "atte request of thomas lord barkley translated
this sayd book [i.e., the *Polychronicon*], the byble and bartylmew de
proprietatibus rerum out of latyn into english." This was exactly eighty
years after Trevisa's death.

Next, in 1557, John Bale published his famous and highly influential
Catalogue of Illustrious British Writers, containing much information which

Note: This chapter is adapted from my "John Trevisa and the English Bible," *Modern Philology* 58 (1960): 81–98, which may be consulted for more detailed citation of sources.

is still of great value to the student of English literature. In this *Catalogue* John Trevisa finds a prominent place. Bale speaks of him as one famous for learning and eloquence, who labored to adorn the English tongue, and he particularly stresses two facts: that Trevisa was interested in history and antiquities, and that he was often severe in his criticism of monks and friars. From this it is easy to perceive that Bale, antiquarian and Protestant pamphleteer, saw in Trevisa a kindred spirit. He then proceeds to list his works as follows.

At the request of Lord Berkeley, Trevisa translated the whole Bible, the Old as well as the New Testament. The Bible is in two books, and Bale gives the *incipit*, "Ego Ioannes Treuisa, sacerdos." He then adds an impressive list of other works by Trevisa, citing first the *De Proprietatibus Rerum*, *Polychronicon*, *Dialogue on Translation*, and the *Polychronicon* continuation, all with *incipits*; these are followed by *Gesta Regis Arthuri*, *Brytanni descriptionem*, *Hyberni descriptionem*, *De memorabilibus temporum*, and "many others he made or translated." The latter works all lack *incipits*, being identified only as consisting of one book each (*Lib. 1*).

It is evident that the reader who takes Bale at his word is bound to be impressed by Trevisa's accomplishments. Here is a writer who has translated the entire Bible, a universal history (and added a continuation of fifty-five years!), a huge encyclopedia, and many other compositions and translations. Most important for our purposes is that Bale quotes the opening lines of Trevisa's translation of the Bible, so as to invite us to make the inference that he had seen the manuscript himself.

Fortunately, however, we do not have to take Bale at his word. In gathering materials for his *Catalogue*, Bale compiled an *Index* containing an alphabetical list of authors in which he inserted the information he gathered from time to time. This *Index*, of course, was not compiled with a view to publication in that form; hence it is often illuminating to compare it with Bale's published catalogue. This is especially true as regards the entry on Trevisa. Looking at the *Index*, we find that Bale listed the *Polychronicon*, the Bible, *De Proprietatibus Rerum*, the *Dialogue on Translation*, a preface to the *Polychronicon* on translation (*opus translationis*, i.e., the epistle to Lord Berkeley), and the *Polychronicon* continuation. These titles correspond to the ones given, with *incipits*, in the published *Catalogue*. But there are three important differences, all related to the biblical entry. First, in the *Index* the Bible is described as consisting of only *one* book (*li. i*); second, there is no *incipit*; and, third, the opening words of the *opus translationis* ("Salutem et honorem digno atque honorabili domino meo Thome Barkeley, Ego Ioannes Treuisa, etc."), suppressed in the printed *Catalogue*, bear a suspicious resemblance to the *incipit* there assigned to the Bible ("Ego Ioannes Treuisa, sacērdos"). Hence we may conclude, I think, that at some time prior to the publication of the *Catalogue* in 1557, Bale transferred a portion of the *opus translationis incipit* to the biblical entry, thus giving the latter an appearance of solidarity. Then, to exalt still further his hero's accomplishments, Bale in his *Catalogue* credits Trevisa with the apocryphal *Gesta Regis Arthuri*, etc., a list of titles derived largely from the Caxton entry in his *Index*.

The effect of this inflation of Trevisa's reputation—so great was the influence of Bale's *Catalogue*—has lasted for over four hundred years. It is indeed very likely that the King James translators based their statement on Bale's authority; and the same can be said, I think, for the somewhat earlier entry in Holinshed's Chronicle (1577): "Iohn Treuise a Cornish man borne, and a secular Priest & Uicar of Berkeley, he translated the Byble, Bart. de Proprietatibus, Polichron of Ranulfe Higeden, and diuerse other treatises."

At least a half-dozen writers in the seventeenth century refer to Trevisa as translator of the Bible, and they all either cite Bale as their authority or reveal in some way that they are ultimately indebted to him for their information. John Pits's entry for Trevisa is practically a transcript of Bale, with just enough changes in wording to give it an appearance of originality. John Smyth of Nibley, the historian of the Berkeley family, writing about the year 1622, takes most of his information straight from Bale and acknowledges his indebtedness. And so it goes through the remainder of the century in the writings of Ussher, Fuller, Wharton, the Latin edition of Anthony Wood, and the manuscript of Dr. Richard Parsons (Bodleian MS Rawlinson B323). The paramount influence on all these authors was quite obviously John Bale.

Two of these men, however, show in their comments that they did some independent thinking on the subject. Thomas Fuller, in his *Church History of Britain* (1655), has an important statement on Trevisa. It should be noted, first, that Fuller had devoted considerable study to Trevisa and had read more about him than any of the earlier authorities we have considered. He specifically acknowledges indebtedness to Carew's *Survey of Cornwall* (1602), Bale, Pits, and the *Polychronicon* itself (probably in

Caxton's edition), and it is evident from his reference to the Apocalypse written on the roof and walls of Berkeley Chapel that he has seen Smyth's manuscript history of the Berkeley family. Furthermore, in his *History of the Worthies of England* (1662), published in the year after his death, Fuller speaks in still more detail of Trevisa's translation of the Bible, giving the impression that he has studied it and compared it with Wyclif's:

> Some much admire he would enter on this work, so lately performed (about fifty years before) by John Wickliffe. What was this, but, *actum agere*, to do what was done before? Besides, Wickliffe and Trevisa agreeing so well in their judgments, was it not much he would make a re-translation. Such consider not, that in that age it was almost the same pains for a scholar to translate as transcribe the Bible.
>
> Secondly, the time betwixt Wickliffe and Trevisa was the crisis of the English tongue, which began to be improved in fifty, more than in three hundred years formerly. Many coarse words (to say no worse) used before are refined by Trevisa, whose translation is as much better than Wickliffe's, as worse than Tyndal's. Thus, though the fountain of the original hath always clearness alike therein, channels of translation will partake of more or less purity, according to the translators age industry, and ability.

What are we to make of this? I am inclined to believe that Fuller had recognized the existence of the two versions of the Wycliffite Bible; that he believed the earlier one (now attributed in part to Nicholas Hereford) to be the work of Wyclif himself and the later one (now dubiously attributed to John Purvey) to be Trevisa's translation. In claiming that the latter was made at the instance of Thomas Lord Berkeley, Fuller was simply following Bale.

Henry Wharton is the other seventeenth-century scholar who seems to have given considerable thought to Trevisa and the Bible. He is generally credited as the first to have perceived the two versions of the Wycliffite Bible (though I think Fuller anticipated him in this) and to have seen them in their correct chronological relationship. Like Fuller, he believed Wyclif to be the author of the earlier version, and on one occasion he even suggested Trevisa as the translator responsible for the later version.

Thus we see that the two writers in the seventeenth century who studied the problem at firsthand (both competent scholars in their day) thought that Trevisa translated the Bible and entertained the idea that his text might have been what we call the later version of the Wycliffite Bible. They also believed, thanks to Bale's influence, that the translation was done at the instigation of Thomas Lord Berkeley. Yet Wharton realized that the Preface found in some manuscripts had a distinctly Lollard inflection; and this may be the reason that he seems to waver between two theories: (1) that Trevisa was responsible for the "Purvey" translation, and (2) that Trevisa's translation is yet to be discovered in manuscript, while the author of the later Wycliffite Bible remains anonymous.

Early in the eighteenth century we find, for the first time, a skeptical attitude toward the Trevisa translation. Humphrey Wanley, well-known antiquary and compiler of *A Catalogue of the Harley Manuscripts in the British Museum*, had this to say (2:320):

> As to the Bible's being wholly translated by our author Trevisa; I perceive it mentioned by Caxton; from him by Bale and Pits, who give the beginning of the Preface thereunto; from Bale, Primate Usher takes the notion; and at length Mr. Wharton . . . believes it may be still extant: it relating not to the book in hand [i.e., Harleian MS 1900], I shall say no more but this; I shall be very glad to see one of them.

Another skeptic during this period seems to have been John Russell, minister of Poole in Dorsetshire, who was at work on an edition of the Wycliffite Bible. Though he never brought out his edition, there is evidence that Dr. Russell planned to write a formal refutation of Wharton's idea that Trevisa may have been the author of the later version. Some of his criticisms of Wharton survive in Le Long's *Bibliotheca Sacra* and are referred to in Oudin's *Commentarius*.

But certainly the most knowledgeable person to consider the Trevisa question in the eighteenth century was Daniel Waterland, who was greatly interested in the history of the English Bible. He did not have the leisure necessary to publish extensively on the subject, but instead he placed all his knowledge at the disposal of John Lewis, whose edition of the (so-called) Wycliffite New Testament appeared in 1731. Waterland's own reflections on Wharton's theories first appear in his *History of the Athanasian Creed* (1724), where he expresses a mild skepticism, while at the same time he allows the possibility that Wharton might be right. He gives weight to Wharton's test for distinguishing the Wycliffite from the "common" version (the frequent insertion of doublets or synonymous words) and attaches importance to the different rendering of the same passage in the two versions (e.g., Luke 2:7). Unfortunately, Waterland goes on to assume that the "common version" (i.e., what is now known as the later version) is by Wyclif, a view rejected by modern scholars. Then he adds (p. 80):

> Perhaps he [Wyclif] might give two editions of it; or else Trevisa's may be little more than Wycliff's version, corrected and polished with great liberty, both as to sense and expression, where it appeared needful.

Further reflections of Waterland appear in his letters to the aforementioned John Lewis, written during the period 1727–29. These letters are very interesting and reveal the progress of Waterland's thinking as he came to reject Trevisa as translator of the "common version" and seized on John Purvey as the most likely candidate. This theory of authorship proved to be highly influential, for it was later adopted by Forshall and Madden in their edition of the Wycliffite Bible in 1850.

Meanwhile, echoes of the traditional ascription of a biblical translation to Trevisa continue to be heard. Thomas Tonkin, who by 1739 had collected materials for a new edition of Carew's *Survey of Cornwall*, reaffirms Trevisa's claim in words that are reminiscent of Fuller's account in his *History of the Worthies of England*. William Borlase, in his *Collectanea*, a manuscript book of notes from which he compiled his two volumes dealing with the antiquities and natural history of Cornwall, refers to Wharton's theory, citing Dr. Waterland's *History of the Athanasian Creed*. Similar entries occur in Tanner, *Bibliotheca Britannico-Hibernica* (1748), Fabricius, *Bibliotheca latina mediae et infimae aetatis* (1734–36), and, finally, in Bigland's *Gloucester* (1791).

It remained for Thomas Dibden, who in 1810 undertook an extensive revision of Ames's *Typographical Antiquities*, to initiate a new phase in the quest for Trevisa's translation. Dibden's investigations are sufficiently recounted by Wilkins and Perry. Suffice it to say here that his inquiries launched a search of the records in the muniment room of Berkeley Castle (where Trevisa had been chaplain and vicar of Berkeley) which lasted through the nineteenth century and reached as far abroad as the Vatican Library in Rome. This whole investigation, of course, was predicated on what we have seen to be the dubious assumption that Trevisa made a separate translation of the Bible for Thomas Lord Berkeley. It is ironical to see how Bale's enthusiastic padding of Caxton's statement continued to dictate the course of investigations after more than three hundred years.

While the search for the Trevisa translation was still in progress, Forshall and Madden published their splendid edition of the Wycliffite Bible. As we have seen, these editors, following Waterland, were convinced that Purvey was responsible for the later version, together with the Prologue, and it is therefore not surprising that they dismiss Trevisa's claim without seriously considering it. Their argument in favor of Purvey, however, was strongly attacked by Alfred W. Pollard in his *Fifteenth Century Prose and Verse* (1903). Pollard explains Forshall and Madden's preference for Purvey as follows (p. xxii):

> The readiness with which the conjecture [of Waterland] was accepted [by Forshall and Madden] can only be accounted for by the desire to make the work of translation centre at Lutterworth instead of, as I believe to be the case, at Oxford. It seems to be considered that we shall be robbing Wyclif of his due unless the translations are connected with him as closely as possible.

Then, after making some speculations of his own, Pollard concludes (p. xxiv):

> At any rate, William Caxton seems a better authority than an eighteenth-century divine as to the authorship of a translation made only a few years before he was born. We know that Trevisa was what we may call a professional translator, well equipped for his task; and we find him in the preface to the *Polychronicon* discussing the translation of the Bible in a strikingly similar spirit to that in which it is discussed in the Prologue to one of the translations which have come down to us. It is to be hoped that the subject may receive further investigation, and that without the importation of theological bias.

Pollard's views did not long remain unchallenged. Alice Greenwood, in her chapter dealing with Trevisa in the *Cambridge History of English Literature* (vol. 2, chap. 3), rejects his theories, though she attempts no real exploration of the problem and even seems to credit the notion that Trevisa did a private translation for his patron. In 1920, however, Margaret Deanesly, in *The Lollard Bible*, seriously attacked Pollard's position. Citing his suggestion (in *Records of the English Bible*, 1911, p. 2) that Trevisa perhaps finished Hereford's translation after Baruch 3:20, she has this to say in reply (p. 300, n. 2):

> But (1) there is no positive evidence of this. (2) It is most unlikely that, if Trevisa took no part in the translation up to Baruch iii.20, he would attach

himself to the Lollard scholars in the work *after* the attack on them in 1382; such a work would have been undertaken only by one thoroughly in sympathy with them.

Miss Deanesly then goes on to suggest, with considerable perceptiveness, that all the many assertions concerning Trevisa's Bible are traceable to Caxton and that even Caxton's statement is merely an inference based on his reading of Trevisa's *Dialogue on Translation*. Thus we are asked to conclude that Pollard's theory had been anticipated by Caxton and that both are wrong. Whether we accept this part of Miss Deanesly's contention or not, it must be admitted that she has here managed an argumentative tour de force.

Without trying fully to evaluate Miss Deanesly's refutation of Pollard, I find that there are two points in her discussion that suggest closer agreement with Pollard than might at first be apparent. One of these is her suggestion that Trevisa's *Dialogue on Translation* may reflect interest in the debate over the lawfulness of translating the Bible (p. 250):

> The absence of reference to the Wycliffite translations may shew merely that by 1387 they were not yet widely enough circulated to have reached Trevisa: but it is much more likely that the raising of the question of biblical translations in the *Dialogue*, was due to the fact that the lawfulness of the Wycliffite translation was already in debate. In any case, Trevisa knew of no recognized Middle English translations to instance.

The other point is her apparent belief that the actual work of translation (at least on the earlier version) was being carried out at Oxford University. It will be recalled that this was one of the points stressed by Pollard.

After Miss Deanesly's book appeared in 1920, there was for some time no serious independent study of the possibility that Trevisa translated the Bible into English. A. J. Perry reviewed the controversy but offered no opinion. Fristedt, in his valuable ongoing study of the Wycliffite versions, first leans toward Purvey and later toward Trevisa (*The Wycliffe Bible*, 3 vols., Stockholm, 1953–73). In short, once again the search for Trevisa's translation has ground to a halt, and the only evidence that we have concerning it, after nearly five hundred years, is the simple statement of William Caxton: "Treuisa . . . translated . . . the byble."

On the other hand, it is possible that the arguments of Pollard and Deanesly suggest a new approach to the problem. Both these scholars seem to agree that the earlier Wycliffite Bible was translated at Oxford University, and both allow that Trevisa, in his *Dialogue on Translation*, seems conscious of the argument over translating the Bible which the Oxford project evoked. The time has come, it seems to me, for an examination of some of the facts of Trevisa's life, particularly as they relate to his tenure as a fellow of Queen's College, Oxford, in the 1370s.

The Trouble at Quenehalle

Queen's College in Oxford (better known in those days as "Quenehalle") was founded by Robert de Eglesfield in 1341. It soon occupied a modest place in the life of the university, although in 1361 it was nearly wiped out by the devastations of the second occurrence of the great plague. At this crucial moment the new provost, Henry Whitfield, began to build up the college until in the 1370s it became a thriving center of study. In 1361, Henry de Hopton, William Trevelles, and William de Wilton were admitted as fellows. Six years later came Thomas Carlisle, who was destined, as we shall see, to succeed Whitfield as provost. Then in 1369 three new men, all of them important, were admitted as fellows of the college: William Middleworth, Nicholas Hereford, and John Trevisa. Middleworth had been expelled with John Wyclif from Canterbury Hall in the same year (1369); Hereford, of course, is well known as one of the Wycliffite translators of the Bible; Trevisa (along with Middleworth) had been a fellow of Exeter College in the 1360s. In 1372 came William Frank, who had been expelled from Exeter after a disputed election there in 1371. Shortly thereafter another former Exeter student, Robert de Lydeford, was admitted to Queen's, along with Richard Thorpe, about whom little is known. Finally, in 1374, John Wyclif rented a room in Queen's College where, according to R. H. Hodgkin (1949, p. 32), he probably remained until 1381.

One of the most striking things about this sudden influx of scholars into Queen's in the 1370s is the number of fellows who came there from Exeter College. Middleworth, Trevisa, Frank, and Lydeford all were Exeter men; and it is perhaps significant that the provost of Queen's, Whitfield, seems to have had some ties with Exeter College, having been appointed as visitor there by the bishop of Exeter on three different occasions. Thus by 1376 the Queen's College, which had been founded by Eglesfield especially on behalf of students from the northern counties of Cumberland and Westmorland, was rapidly being overwhelmed by a wave of intruders from the southern and western counties of England. Fellows like Thomas Carlisle, a northerner, were in grave danger of becoming a minority voice in the affairs of the college. With this background in mind, we must now attempt briefly to trace the history of a controversy which erupted at Queen's in 1376 and raged unabated for nearly four years.

On 6 January 1376, Carlisle was elected provost of Queen's College, replacing Henry Whitfield. This election seems to have been disputed, however, and the southern faction responded by naming William Frank, one of the transfers from Exeter, as provost in defiance of Carlisle's election. As a result of this the archbishop of York was called in to settle the dispute. But the archbishop seems to have met with violent resistance from some of the fellows, for it soon became necessary to obtain an order from the king, commanding them to be obedient to the statutes of their college, and not to obstruct the archbishop in the performance of his duties. This order was dated 18 November 1376. Shortly thereafter, on 27 November, Alexander Neville, archbishop of York, appointed a commission, consisting of Thomas de Salkeld, Henry de Ingelby, William Aston, and William Neubald, to investigate and settle the matters in dispute.

The efforts of Archbishop Neville to settle this dispute appear to have failed completely. The matter was therefore transferred to the Chancery, and King Edward, on 13 May 1377, required the sheriff and mayor of Oxford to obtain the statutes and regulations drawn up by Eglesfield and send them under their seals to the Chancery. The college appears, however, to have given the sheriff merely a *copy* of the statutes, and the chancellor of the new king, Richard II (Edward III having died in June 1377), was compelled to require that they hand over Eglesfield's original statutes. He then issued a ruling, dated at Westminster, 6 January 1378, which reads in part as follows:

> The article about the election of Fellows, upon which in the first instance the whole dissention grew up (*super quo primitus tota inolevit dissencio*), he thus declares, that as often as one or two fit person or persons of the family of Robert de Eglesfield, or else of the counties of Cumberland or Westmorland, shall have been duly elected Fellows, then the said Provost and Scholars shall be bound to elect as many from places in which the said College possesses

benefices, if fit men according to the form and content of the statutes can be found; otherwise from the most sufficient and fit men they can find in the University.

The king's ruling was a clear victory for the northern party, and the southerners must have been expelled immediately. This was in January 1378. But the battle was not over. The southern faction seems to have been prepared for an adverse decision, for at some time prior to 10 January 1378, they had carried off the college seal, together with miscellaneous properties belonging to the college, and apparently continued to transact official college business, conduct services, and pursue their studies in calm defiance of the royal decision. Carlisle had won a legal victory, but he had no proper college over which to preside. The seriousness of this schism is evident in the tone—at once threatening and conciliatory—of the chancellor's order, dated 10 January 1378, four days after the decision favoring Carlisle, in which the chancellor offers to readmit the expelled fellows.

This royal appeal, however, seems to have fallen on deaf ears, and the southerners maintained possession of the college seal, keys, papers, plate, and books. Up to this point in the controversy we have been left in the dark as to who these "southerners" were. But now, in a grim effort to force a settlement of this affair, the sheriff of Oxford begins naming names. In a royal writ dated 1 February 1378, the sheriff is ordered to take Richard Thorpe, William Middleworth, and others, and force them to restore the common seal of Quenehalle. On 27 March of the same year Frank, Middleworth, Thorpe, and any others who had carried off properties of the college, were ordered to be arrested. The same three men are named in an order to the sheriff and his deputies dated 6 April.

The most elaborate effort to settle this controversy appears to have been made on 13 May 1378, when an indenture was drawn up in the presence of the sheriff of Oxford, Edmund de Stonore, attesting the transfer of the college seal, papers, plate, and certain books from William Frank by the hands of Robert Hodersale. The importance of this indenture can scarcely be exaggerated. We shall return to it in a moment. Meanwhile, it is sufficient to note that, although the indenture attests the transfer of possessions of the college from Frank to Carlisle, a little over a year later, on 26 June 1379, a jury is ordered to investigate the dispute (CCR 1377–81, p. 258):

To the chancellor and proctors of Oxford university. Order by true men of the town to make inquisition to whose hands are come the charters, books, jewels, muniments, goods and chattels of the college called the Quenehalle, which were taken and carried away by certain of the scholars now removed, and were lodged and pledged in diverse places in the town, by whom, on what pretense, where, how and for how much they are pledged, and the description thereof, to arrest and keep the same in safe custody, and from time to time to certify their action in chancery, that by advice of the council the king may deal according to reason in the matter; as a prolonged dispute between the scholars was late pending before the king and council, and certain scholars in whom greatest defaults were found, and who are removed, have taken charters etc. as aforesaid that the same might be for ever withdrawn from the college and dispersed.

It is quite evident from the wording of the order just quoted that Frank, the "anti-provost," and his cohorts were still holding out, more than three years after the duly constituted election of Carlisle. Very likely it was at about this time that the chancellor of the University of Oxford ordered Frank to appear before him at the first hour in St. Mary's. Whether he actually put in an appearance is not clear. I would tend to doubt that he did.

We have nearly reached the end of this remarkable controversy. But there are two more orders related to it that are important (1) in showing that the dispute flared as late as February 1380 and (2) in revealing the names of other men in the southern faction who had been expelled along with Frank, Middleworth, and Thorpe. The first of these instruments is dated 20 October 1379 (CPR 1377–81, p. 470):

Comission of oyer and terminer to the chancellor of the university of Oxford for the time being, Master John de Bloxham, Master Thomas Walleworth, Master John de Colton and Master Robert Dix, after enquiry at Oxford into the complaint of Master Thomas de Karlell [i.e., Carlisle], Provost of "Quenehalle" and the scholars of that college, that Master Henry Whitfield, late provost, and Master William Fraunk, Master Robert Lydeford, and Master John Trevisa, late scholars and fellows thereof, who have been excluded therefrom for their unworthiness (*exigentibus demeritis*), refuse to account for certain moneys of the college that came to their hands as well before the cession of the said Henry and the exclusion of the other three as after, and have taken away charters, books, jewels and muniments, besides goods belonging to the college.

The same men are accused in a similar commission dated 7 February 1380, in which the following additional instructions appear:

The commissioners are to proceed by sworn examination of both parties and other scholars of the University and to compel restitution.

Thus it appears that the southern faction—at least those who remained unmoved by the shower of writs, mandates, and commissions—consisted of Frank, Middleworth, Thorpe, Lydeford, Trevisa, and Provost Whitfield himself, and that these men held out for over four years against the legal onslaughts of Carlisle.

Unfortunately we cannot be sure how this controversy was resolved. If we are to believe Anthony Wood, Whitfield himself restored the stolen property to Carlisle. We do know that a pardon of outlawry was granted to William Middleworth (for not appearing to render chattels to Carlisle) on 1 May 1380. By this time Whitfield had become archdeacon of Barnstaple and seemed to harbor no malice. Middleworth was again in good standing, remaining as fellow until 1383, and later renting rooms in the college. Of the subsequent fortunes of William Frank, little is known. He last appears in the Queen's College long rolls in the fiscal years 1379–80. Still less can we be sure of the later activities of Richard Thorpe and Robert Lydeford. And the last reference to Trevisa in the long rolls of Queen's College—for the period of this controversy— appears under the year 1378–79. We have no certain knowledge of his whereabouts or activities from 1378–79 to 1382–83. From these dates it is evident that the backbone of southern resistance was broken in 1378 or 1379 and that the stubborn group had dispersed or submitted by the summer of 1380. Other men present immediately before or during the dispute, but not mentioned in any of the documents connected with it, were Wyclif and Hereford. Both of these scholars appear to have left the college some time in 1380–81.

Conclusions

What were these scholars doing at Queen's during the time of this controversy? Wyclif, we may be sure, was busily engaged in writing some of his numerous controversial pieces, particularly his *De Eucharistia*, completed in 1379. Nicholas Hereford was doing his share of the translation of the Bible. What program of studies were the other scholars pursuing? It is tempting to conclude, somewhat grimly, that their time was fully occupied in legal maneuvering. On the other hand, the very controversy which we have been considering supplies us with some valuable evidence of their scholarly interests. I refer, of course, to the

indenture drawn up in the presence of Edmund de Stonore on 13 May
1378. This indenture begins with a list of the possessions of the college
which the rebels were turning over to Carlisle: (1) the seal, (2) seven
indentures concerning the choice of books of the college (1372), (3) a
gilded silver chalice, with a paten with a chasuble for the same, a piece
of plate with cover and chasuble, and a mazer with a silver cover bound
to it with a chasuble for the same. But the most informative part of
the indenture is its list of books the southerners had carried off. These
books are listed by title and even identified, with great precision, by the
opening word or phrase of the second folio of each. I give the list in its
entirety (Stainer, *Compoti*, II, no. 2118):

ITEM		SECUNDO FOLIO
1.	Unum librum Catholican	unde colum
2.	Sextum decretalle cum omnibus doctoribus	fervore caritatis
3.	Unum bibliam	celi ezecheli
4.	Moralia beati Gregorii super Joob	quo ordine
5.	Doctorem subtilem	figure
6.	Concordancia	abra
7.	Crisostomum super Matheum	lum spiritus
8.	Augustinum de civitate Dei	corum
9.	Doctorem de Lira in parte super proverbia Salomonis	incomparatione
10.	Liram super salterium	dominum sedentem
11.	Polucranica Cestrensis	navigabil'
12.	Manipulum florum	quisque
13.	Librum super Genesim a diversis tractatoribus	set bona facere
14.	Originalia Augustini	ac sibi
15.	de eleccione predicti Will. Frank unum par decretorum	aliter agentes
16.	Thomam super quartum sententiarum	scilicet sol effectus
17.	Adamentem	facere
18.	Magistrum sententiarum	ponis
19.	Ricardus de sancto Victore de trinitate	aliter
20.	Tabulam philosophie et theologie	asiua
21.	Sententia Augustini de libro retractacionum	naut ut sit
22.	Sanctum Thomam super primum sententiarum	ipso factis

23. Reportorium Magistri Willielmi
    Duraunt . . . . .3 j in P
24. paruum librum rubium de
    preposissionibus . . . . .revocat

It was a rare good fortune indeed that preserved for us this list of
books taken from the Queen's College in the late 1370s. These books
are of the utmost importance to anyone interested in the literary career
of John Trevisa. The only scholar to my knowledge who has connected
Trevisa with this list is R. H. Hodgkin, who writes in his history of the
Queen's College as follows (pp. 37–38):

> Among the frequenters of the college, in addition to Nicholas of Hereford,
> was a less solemn pioneer of English prose, John Trevisa, the translator of
> Higden's *Polychronicon* and of other works, who had come to Queen's in
> the same year as Middleworth and Hereford, and was probably their friend,
> since all three had been fellows at Stapledon Hall. . . . But his [Trevisa's] poor
> record in finance and his removal of the *Polychronicon* from the library in 1377
> may be forgiven him for the amends which he made by translating the book.

Hodgkin is undoubtedly correct in seeing more than coincidence in
the fact that Trevisa and his colleagues carried off the *Polychronicon* and
that Trevisa subsequently made a translation of the same book. But it
is also interesting to observe the other books on this list. That Trevisa
knew Nicholas of Lyra's commentaries on the Bible is scarcely open to
doubt. In a note about Noah's ark, for example, which he adds to his
translation of the *Polychronicon*, we find (II, 235):

> Here me may wondre how þe wyndowe was i-made byneþe in þe side of the
> schippe for comynge yn of water. Doctor de Lyra meueþ þis doute. . . .

The *Polychronicon*, however, seems not to have been translated by
Trevisa until about 1385–87. What was he doing at Queen's in the
1370s? I suggest that he worked with John Wyclif, Nicholas Hereford,
and probably others, on a translation of the Bible. Here we have a man
who was living in the same college with one of the known translators,
who was said by Caxton to have translated the Bible, who defended
such translations in his known work, and who removed from Queen's
College a Bible, a Latin dictionary, a concordance, Gregory's Morals on
the Book of Job, pseudo-Chrysostom on Matthew, two commentaries
of Nicholas of Lyra, and a commentary on Genesis. It is also possible,
as suggested to me by Ralph Hanna, that number 14 in the sheriff's list

is a version of the index to the fathers prepared by Robert Kilwardby while he was a student, the *Tabulae super Originalia Patrum*, or at least that portion which indexes St. Augustine's *City of God* (see Beryl Smalley, *English Friars and Antiquity*, p. 62, nn. 1, 2).

Furthermore it is possible, I think, to show that Trevisa was at times unusually conscious of alternative translations of biblical texts. In one of his additions to the *Polychronicon*, for example, he refers to the parable of the wheat and tares (Matt. 13:25) as the "ensaumple of whete and of eure, that som men clepeth darnel" (VII, 525). It is perfectly clear from this statement that Trevisa prefers "eure" for the Latin *zizania*, but it is equally obvious that he knows "som men" who insist on translating "darnel." If we turn to the earlier version of the Wycliffite Bible as printed by Forshall and Madden, this is what we find: "But, when men slepten, his enmye came, and sew aboue dernel, or cokil, in the midil of whete, and wente awey" (IV, 34). It should be understood that I do not cite this one passage as constituting proof in itself that Trevisa was one of the committee of translators but only as an example of the kind of evidence in his known work which points in that direction and one which scholars have hitherto overlooked.

To the suggestion that Trevisa was one of the Wycliffite translators, however, it may be objected that he was not a follower of Wyclif. This is perfectly true. Trevisa was not a Wycliffite, if by that term we mean a man who accepted all the reformer's doctrines and simply followed where he led. The two men seem to have differed, for example, on the question of the fate of the righteous heathen, and it is doubtful whether Trevisa would be able to read with equanimity Wyclif's *De Eucharistia*, completed in 1379. That Wyclif had friends and colleagues who nevertheless differed firmly with him on matters of doctrine is well attested by passages in his *De Ecclesia* (1378) and elsewhere. Trevisa may well have been one of these intellectually independent friends. To force Trevisa into the category of enemy or devotee is to subject him to a post-Reformation distortion.

Once we understand the limits of Trevisa's agreement with Wyclif, it is then pertinent to remember that he was indeed influenced by the latter. Bale long ago pointed out Trevisa's severity with monks and friars (as witnessed in the *Polychronicon*), and of course the fact that Trevisa translated FitzRalph's sermon against the friars reveals a common ground of agreement with Wyclif's later attitude. Wyclif's "favorite historian" was Higden; Trevisa translated Higden's *Polychronicon*. Nicholas of Lyra became a favorite Lollard commentary; Trevisa is acquainted with and uses Lyra. Of course these things could conceivably be the result of coincidence of interests and attitude; but even after the condemnation of Wyclif's heresies in 1382, Trevisa does not hesitate to comment on "possessioners" in a way that would have been quite acceptable to Wyclif (*Polychronicon*, VI, 465–67):

> And now for þe moste partie monkes beeþ worste of alle, for þey beþ to riche, and þat makeþ hem to take more hede aboute secular besynesse þan gostely devocioun; þerfore, as it is i-seide bifore in 4° libro in þe 26 capitulo, by Ierom, seþþe holy cherche encresede in possessiouns hit haþ decresed in vertues. þerfore seculer lordes schulde take awey the superfluyte of here possessiouns, and ȝeue it to hem þat nedeþ , or elles whan þey knowen þat, þey beeþ cause and mayntenours of here euel dedes, seþþe þey helpeþ nouȝt to amende hit while it is in hir power, what euere couetous preostes seyn. For it were almesse to take awey þe superfluite of here possessiouns now, þan it was at þe firste fundacioun to ȝeve hem what hem nedede.

With all the available facts before us, I now take the liberty of reconstructing the circumstances and chronology of the translation of the first Wycliffite Bible. Some time after the arrival at Queen's of Hereford, Trevisa, and Middleworth, perhaps as early as 1372, work on the translation was begun. Wyclif, the prime mover of this project, rented a room at Queen's in 1374, though I would hesitate to say to what extent he involved himself in the actual task of translation. The work may have continued to as late as 1378–79, when, as we have seen, the legal assaults of Carlisle began to break up the "southern" faction and force the dispersal of their books "in diverse places in the town" of Oxford. The legal issue in this dispute, as has often been pointed out, was the interpretation of the founder's stipulation regarding the admission of northerners into the college and the consequent contested election of a provost; but I think it would be naive in the extreme to suppose that this fact rules out the possiblity of a deeper motive for the controversy. Academic disputes often display a surface calm, or at least a legal decorum, beneath which may lurk the most profound ideological conflict. Anthony Wood knew this when he indulged in his famous speculation on the cause of the "scandal" at Queen's: "whether upon account of heresy or election of a Provost I know not." On this point I dare not go further than Wood.

Whether Trevisa, after 1378–79, ever again worked on a translation of the Bible (i.e., the later version) is a separate question which I do not now wish to consider. I can see no real evidence that he did. By the time of his expulsion from Queen's, if not earlier, he had become established as chaplain and man of letters for Thomas Lord Berkeley in Gloucestershire, and the new requirements of this position, not to mention his duties as vicar of Berkeley, must have had a considerable effect on his literary interests and his whole way of life. He rented rooms in Queen's College in the 1380s and 1390s, but there is no evidence of the formation there of a new congregation of scholars equivalent to the famous gathering at Queen's in the 1370s.

Trevisa must have begun his translation of the *Polychronicon* by 1385, and he completed it, as we know, in 1387. His *Dialogue between a Lord and a Clerk upon Translation*, to which we have had occasion to refer, was no doubt written during this period. It is prefixed to his translation of the *Polychronicon* and serves as a kind of preface to that work. By way of conclusion, I wish to quote a passage from this dialogue, for I believe that it cannot be fully appreciated unless we realize that its author is not only defending English translations in general but is also carefully defending his own earlier role as a translator of the Wycliffite Bible (modernized from Waldron's edition, 1988):

The Clerk The Latin is both good and fair. Therefore it needeth not to have an English translation.

The Lord This reason is worthy to be plunged in a plod and laid in powder of lewdness and of shame. It might well be that thou makest this reason only in mirth and in game.

The Clerk The reason must stand but it be assoiled.

The Lord A blear-eyed man, but he were all blind of wit, might see the solution of this reason; and though he were blind he might grope the solution, but if his feeling him failed. For if this reason were aught worth, by such manner argument men might prove that the three score and ten [i.e., translators of the Greek Septuagint] and Aquila, Symachus, Theodocion, and he that made the fifth translation, and Origines were lewdly occupied when they translated holy writ out of Hebrew into Greek; and also that Saint Jerome was lewdly occupied when he translated holy writ out of Hebrew into Latin, for the Hebrew is both good and fair and written by inspiration of the Holy Ghost; and all these for their translations be highly praised of all Holy Church. Then the foresaid lewd reason is worthy to be powdered, laid a-water and ysoused.

Also holy writ in Latin is both good and fair, and yet for to make a sermon of holy writ all in Latin to men that can English and no Latin, it were a lewd deed, for they be never the wiser for the Latin, but it be told them in English what it is to mean; and it may not be told in English what the Latin is to mean without translation out of Latin into English. Then it needeth to have an English translation, and for to keep it in mind that it be not forgotten, it is better that such a translation be made and written than said and not written. And so this foresaid lewd reason should move no man that hath any wit to leave the making of English translation.

The Clerk A great deal of these books standeth much by holy writ, by holy doctors, and by philosophy; then these books should not be translated into English.

The Lord It is wonder that thou makest so feeble arguments, and hast gone so long to school. Aristotle's books and other books also of logic and of philosophy were translated out of Greek into Latin. Also at praying of King Charles, John Scott translated Deny's books out of Greek into Latin. Also holy writ was translated out of Hebrew into Greek and out of Greek into Latin, and then out of Latin into French. Then what hath English trespassed that it might not be translated into English? Also King Alfred, that founded the University of Oxford, translated the best laws into English tongue, and a great deal of the Psalter out of Latin into English, and made Wyrefrith, Bishop of Worcester, translate Saint Gregory's books, the dialogues, out of Latin into Saxon. Also Caedmon of Whitby was inspired of the Holy Ghost, and made wonder poesies in English nigh of all the stories of holy writ. Also the holy man Beda translated St. John's gospel out of Latin into English. Also thou wotest where the Apocalypse is written in the walls and roof of a chapel, both in Latin and in French. Also the gospel, and prophecy, and the right faith of holy church must be taught and preached to English men that can no Latin. Then the gospel, and prophecy, and the right faith of holy church must be told them in English, and that is not done but by English translation. For such English preaching is very English translation, and such English preaching is good and needful; then English translation is good and needful.

Postscript (1993)

The opinions expressed in this chapter go back more than thirty years, but I have found no evidence since my original article was published to question its conclusions as to Trevisa's probable role as a translator of the Early Version of the Wycliffite Bible. Concerning the role of Wyclif himself, see Michael Wilks (1975); concerning the increasingly doubtful role of John Purvey, see Anne Hudson (1981). The idea that Trevisa translated the Bible into Cornish appears to be as groundless as I surmised it to be in *Modern Philology* in 1960 (p. 86, n. 26), without having at that time laid eyes on the "Heraldic and parochial collections" of Dr. Borlase. I have since found Borlase's "Memorandums in Heraldry" (1740) in the Morrab Library, Penzance, and it contains nothing to support the claims of the writer of the article of the *Quarterly Review* for 1875. For a more recent survey of the circumstances of the making of the Wycliffite Bible, consult Hudson (1988), who postulates a later date for the beginning of work on this translation (1380) for reasons that are not entirely clear to me (pp. 246–47, 395–97). See my review in *Studies in the Age of Chaucer* 12 (1990): 296–305 (esp. p. 302).

Recently I was fortunate enough to obtain from the Keeper of the Archives, Queen's College Oxford, Mr. John M. Kaye, a critique of my reading of the evidence in the long rolls concerning the expulsion of Trevisa and his colleagues from the college in 1376, together with some new evidence. With his kind permission, I am including his statement here as the latest word on this complex and controversial subject:

> My own interest in the [dispute in Queen's] is only incidental to the book which I am writing, because I am attempting to cover the period 1450 to about 1700 (the most interesting period from the point of view of the college estates and finances) and not going back to the foundation of the college in 1340. However, in view of the importance of the policy of Provost Carlisle and his successor, Whelpdale, of finding means to turn the college into an almost closed foundation, (i.e., closed to all but natives of Cumberland and Westmorland) I found it necessary to go back in this instance to the affairs in the 1370s. In your account of the matter, in *Modern Philology*, you broadly followed what I hope I may, without disrespect, call the Magrath line. I have made several tentative amendments to this, namely:

> [1] I do not think that Provost Whitfeld was expelled, but that he resigned voluntarily, at some time after [Alexander] Neville [Archbishop of York, as Visitor], had issued his 1376 commission to settle the *lites et discordias* etc.

> [2] Neville incidentally had no right to settle the dispute, because the Statutes gave the Visitor power to intervene only in a case wherein the provost was opposed by all or a majority of the fellows: in other cases the provost was to settle disputes himself. As Carlisle was the only fellow in the college from Cumberland or Westmorland (Magrath refers incorrectly to a "Northern Party") it is difficult to see how the Archbishop could have justified his action.

[3] Shortly after Whitfeld's resignation, the fellows elected Frank to succeed him. This was perfectly lawful, under the Statutes, as Frank was a master of arts and one of the existing fellows. However, Neville refused to confirm his election, and insisted on confirming Carlisle as provost on 6 January 1376/7. Neville's confirmation speaks of Carlisle as having been "duly elected," but this is not likely to have been the case, as Frank was the person responsible for the said dissensions. The result was that, for about a year, the college had a so-called provost, confirmed as such by the Visitor, who was powerless to act because the fellows did not support him, and an "anti-provost," who, though not confirmed by the Visitor, was recognized as provost and in fact named as such in a document dated 3 September 1377. The fact that Frank was, and that the fellows considered him to be, the rightful provost is consistent with his having in his possession the college seal and muniments etc., which later on he and the fellows were compelled to surrender by legal action.

[4] At some point in the year January 1376/7 to January 1377/8 Carlisle's provostship was ratified by the Chancery, and Frank, with some fellows including Lydeford and Trevisa, expelled. This was presumably done by the authority of the Crown, with the concurrence of Archbishop Neville, but the precise date of the expulsion, and the precise manner in which it was brought about, are unknown. The relevant documents do not mention any other fellows, other than those named above, to have been expelled, so it is not clear whether Middleworth and Thorpe were expelled too; they may have resigned voluntarily, but they certainly disappeared at the same time as the rest. The missing long rolls 1375–7 would have been crucial here.

[5] The Chancery Decree of 1378 had no retroactive effect, and related to the forthcoming election at which it was necessary to replace the expelled fellows: by my reckoning, there were at most two fellows left in the college (Hereford and Hodersale), and perhaps only one (Hereford) because Hodersale does not appear in college records until the financial year beginning 11 June 1378. However, as the Decree began with the word *Quoties*, it was probably meant to be put into effect at all future elections.

[6] The said Decree cannot really be interpreted, as Magrath did, as a "victory for the northern party", because it made it plain that, in an election of (say) four fellows, only "one or two" might be chosen from founder's kin or from Cumberland and Westmorland, and "one or two" from places in which the college had possessions (e.g. Berkshire, Hampshire, Oxfordshire) or, failing those, from the University at large. (In fact, in a mass election of five fellows made in 1391 only one was from the "Two Counties"). The task which confronted Carlisle, and after him Whelpdale, was not, how to make use of

the Decree, but how to get round it so as to avoid having to take into the college more than an occasional fellow not born in the Two Counties.

[7] I recently came across a bit of evidence which doesn't fit the rest: noticing that Magrath does not give the date on which Archbishop Neville confirmed Carlisle as provost, I did what I ought to have done long ago, i.e., consult his register (of which there is a microfilm in the Bodleian). To my surprise, I found that Neville (folio 102v) confirmed Carlisle as early as 6 January 1376/7, his confirmation clearly stating that Carlisle had been elected by the fellows! I shall have to give more consideration to this: it may be that Neville had been asked to confirm Frank and had refused to do so, thus compelling the fellows to hold a new election. But if this were the case, why did they refuse to acknowledge Carlisle as provost, and proceed to ally themselves with Frank? At the moment I can't think of an answer.

Yours sincerely,

John M. Kaye

Appendix I
Westbury-on-Trym Controversy

1. PRO SC 8/148/7355

A nostre tresredoubte seignur le Roi et a son tressage conseil pleint Robert Dean de l'esglise Collegial de Westbury en le counté de Gloucestre de John Poleyne, esquier de Thomas Berklé de Bereklé, chivaler, de ce que le dit John ove grant nombre de gentz armez et araiez en habergeons, esperes, Bokelers, Daggers, bastons, arkes et setes, coillez en routes, a feore de guerre, contre la pees nostre dit seignur le Roi, l'estatut de Northampton et autres estatuiz et ordinances en tiuex cas purveux, viendrent a Westbury suisdit, l'endemain proschein apres le seint Trinité, l'an nostre dit seignur le Roi xi, a neot, et ly assegeront illoeques et le mesoun le dit Dean et les hus debreseront et en sa chambre par mesme la force entreront et le dit Dean en son lit gisant pristrent et hors de sa meson lui treront en la Rue, desirantz ses draps et illoeques a lui assaut firent, bateront et naufreront et maliciousement treteront, issint q'il fuist en dispoir de sa vie et puis ly enprisonerent et ly manaseront d'occire Issint que pur doute de mort it promyst de faire fyn ovesqȝ ly et de doner toutz ses biens de ly suffrer avoir sa vie. Et puis le dit John [Poleyne], John Trevysa, John Breton, Richard Curteys et John Smyth de Westbury, des queux il se plaint en mesme le manere, ove grand nombre de gentz coillez en route, armez et araiez en feore de guerre en manere de insurreccioun, le lundy le xiime jour de ffevever, l'an nostre dit seignur le Roi xiime, viendrent a Westbury suisdit et illoeques la meson le dit Dean et ses hus debreseront et forciblement entreront encontre la pees et les statutz suisditz pur ly querre d'occire et . . . ses servants, asaut firant, bateront, naufriront et malement treteront et ses biens et chateux a la valu de xl livres pristront et enproterent et autres grandz oppressions, affraies et grevances lui firent en contempt nostre seignure le Roi, en oppressions, affraies et malveys ensample de tote la pais et as damages le dit suppliant de C livres, dont it prie remedie d'estre ordine par nostre seignur le Roi et son dit conseil, pur dieu et en oevere de charité a cause que le dit suppliant ne poet avoir droit ne recoverer par la comune ley devers eux pur ce que le dit John Poleyn est cy grand maintenour des quereles et taunt endose de grand seignurie en la pais suisdit.

2. PRO SC 8/84/4193

A tresreverent et tresnoble seignur le caunceller nostre seignur le roy soy pleynt Meistre Thomas Cone provender del provendre de Wodeford en lesglise collegial de Westebery en le conte de Glouc' sibien pur nostre dit seignur le

roy come pure luy mesme qe Johan Trevysa et Johan Poleyn son meyntenour
le xvi jour de feverer lan du regne nostre dit seignur le roy xii leveront tout la
paiis per xv lieux envyron per cornes sonantz come encountre enemys du roy
et de roialme ove nombre dez gentz de ccc et plus armes et araiez a feore de
guerre ove haburjons paletz espees bokelers arkes tenduz et setes en manere de
insureccion viendront a lesglise de Westbury suisdit en lastall ou dit provendrer
est et illeoqes un Robert Banak son viker occupiant le dit estall enfestinez divine
service bateront et malement treiteront et de la luy et trieront per les jambes
et pees tange al hus de mesme esglise desirantz ses drapes et daggers traiez et
espees nues et mys a ses costes et son dors qil fuist mys en graunt affray et peril
de sa vie et illeoqes un Walter et Thomas ses servantz en son service esteantz et
trovez bateront naufreront et de dit Walter sank traieront dein le dite esglise per
qoy mesme lesglise estoit defame come polute issint qe nule divine service ne
sacrement de seint esglise nont este fait ne use depuis encea et auxi un William
Colerne et Johan Rothewell ses servantz illeoqes trovez ensemblement ove le
dit viker pristeront et amesneront tange al chastel de Berkeley et illeoqes les
enprisonerent per un dim jour et une noet entier et deilleoqes les amesneront a
Glouc' et illeoqes les enprisonerent per x jours et plus tange qils feurent deliverez
per brife nostre seignur le roy et a dit xvi jour de feverer entreront a Wodeford
en le corps du dit provendrer ove le dit nounbre dez gentz et le corps del dit
provendrer forciblement unqore teignont en manere de guerre sibien envers le
dit provendrer come devers le viscount del dit counte eiant poair per brief nostre
dit seignur le roy doustier et arestier toutz ceux qi veignout en la manere suisdite
encountre lestatutz de Northampton et autres estatutz et ordinances en la dit cas
purveuz non obstant qe le dit viscount ad maunde per diverse temps a Wodeford
suisdite ses minestres doustier les ditz mesfaisurs et rebelles ou de les arestier per
vertue de les ditz briefs les quex le dit mandement oiez et liez devant eux
overtement et bien entenduz responderont as ditz ministres rebelliousment et
cruelement qe pur mandemant du roy viscont ou de nul autre vivant ne voillent
voider le dit corps del provendrer ne sooffrer destre arestez ne soy rendre forsque
al dit Johan Poleyne lour meistre et dustre en la querele suisditz encontempt du
roy et en oppression affray et malveyse example del paiis et en areressement et
damage del dit suppliant de cynk cent livres dont il prie remede pur dieu et en
oevre de charite a cause qe le dit suppliant ne poet avoir droit ne recoverer per
la comune ley envers le ditz Johan Trevysa et Johan Poleyne son meintenour en
le dit querel pur ces qe le dit Johan Poleyne est tant endose de graunt seignurie
et aliance et comune meintenour des querels en la paiis suisdit.

3. PRO KB 27/512/Rex m. 17
Adhuc de Termino Pasche.
Glouc.

Alias coram Thoma de Berkele et sociis suis, custodibus pacis domini Regis et
Justiciis suis ad diversas felonias et transgressa in Comitatu predicte audiendas et

terminandes assignatis, extitit presentatum quod Robertus Taillour, Capellanus, Willelmus Colerne et Johannes Rothewell cum diversis aliis multis ignotis, in dispectu et contemptu mandati domini Regis et proclamacionis predicte armati, apud Berkeley potencialiter modo guerrino die Martis proximo post festum Sancti Petri anno regni Regis Ricardi secundi post conquestum duodecimo apud ecclesiam colligiatam de Westbury accesserunt, videlicet in locum habitacionis Magistri Johannis Trevisa, Canonici dicte ecclesie et prebendarii prebende de Wodford in eadem ecclesia extiterunt per unum diem et unam noctem et ibidem diversos insultus Johanni Boteller, procuratori et seruienti dicti Magistri Johannes Trevisa in possessione existentis de dicta prebenda de Wodford ac aliis diversis hominibus fecerunt, et tales terrores populo domini Regis in partibus illis perpetrarunt, quod nullus audax erat interim ad domum suam commorare. Et hoc ex precepto et excitacione Roberti Wattes, Decani ecclesie predicte, qui quidem predicti Robertus Taillour, Capellanus, Willelmus Colerne et Johannes Rothewell habuerunt ibidem diversas armaturas ad valenciam quinque marcerum, videlicet unam loricam, duos arcus, duas garbas sagittarum, duos gladios, duo boclerio, et vnum polax, que quidem armature arestate fuerunt et dimisse in custodiam dicti Roberti Wattes ad requisicionem suam, inde domino Regi responsit. Quod quidem indictamentum dominus Rex inter alia coram eo venire fecit terminandum. Et modo scilicet die sabati proximo post mensem Pasche isto eodem termino coram domino Rege apud Westmonasterium venerunt predicti Robertus Taillour, Willelmus et Johannes Rothewell in propriis personis suis et allocati sunt qualiter de premissis sibi inpositis se velint acquietare. Qui dicunt . . .

TRANSLATIONS

1.

To our very dread lord the king and to his very wise council complains Robert dean of the Collegiate Church of Westbury in the county of Gloucester of John Poleyne, squire of Thomas Berkeley of Berkeley, knight, of this that the said John with a great number of men armed and arrayed with habergeons, swords, bucklers, daggers, sticks, bows and arrows, riotously assembled in manner of war against the peace of our said lord the king, the statute of Northampton and other statutes and ordinances in such cases provided, came to Westbury aforesaid the morrow of the feast of the Holy Trinity the eleventh year of our said lord the king [25 May 1388] by night and besieged him there and broke open the doors and entered by force into his chamber and took the said dean lying in his bed and dragged him out of his house into the street tearing his clothes and there assaulted, beat, wounded and maltreated him so that he was in despair of his life and then imprisoned him and threatened to kill him so that for fear of death he promised to come to terms with him and to give all his goods to suffer him to have his life.

And then the said John [Poleyne], John Trevisa, John Breton, Richard Curteys and John Smyth of Westbury of whom he complains in the same manner followed by a great number of men riotously assembled, armed and arrayed in warlike fashion in a manner of an insurrection the Monday February 12th, the 12th year of our said lord the king [1389] came to Westbury aforesaid and there broke into and forcibly entered the house of the said dean and his doors, against the peace and the aforesaid statutes in order to kill him, and assaulted, beat, wounded and maltreated his servants and took and carried away his goods and chattels to the value of 40 pounds and committed other great oppressions to his cost and damage in contempt of our lord the king to the oppression, terror and bad example of the whole country and to the damage of the said suppliant to the amount of 100 pounds for which he prays that a remedy may be ordained by our lord the king and his said council for God and as a work of charity, because the said suppliant cannot have justice nor recover against them by the common law because the said John Poleyne is so great a maintainer of quarrels and so much encouraged by the great lords in the aforesaid country.

2.

Master Thomas Cone, prebendary of the prebend of Wodeford in the collegiate church of Westbury, in the county of Gloucester, complains to the very reverend and very noble lord chancellor of our lord the king, for our said lord the king as well as for himself, that John Trevysa and John Poleyn, his maintainer, on the xvi[th] day of February in the twelfth year of the reign of our said lord the king [1389] did raise the whole country for fifteen leagues around by sounding horns, as though against enemies of the king and of the realm, with persons to the number of three hundred or more armed and arrayed in warlike fashion with habergeons, pikes, swords, bucklers, drawn bows and arrows, in the manner of insurrection, (and) came to the said church of Westbury to the stall where the said prebendary is, and there did beat and mistreat one Robert Banak, his vicar, occupying the aforesaid stall adorned (for) divine service, and from there they did drag him by the legs and feet up to the door of the same church, tearing his clothes, and with drawn daggers and bare swords placed against his sides and his back so that he was placed in great fright and peril of his life, and there they did beat and wound one Walter and Thomas, his servants, being in his service and found there, and drew blood from the said Walter within the said church, on account of which the same church itself was declared polluted, so that no divine service nor sacrament of holy church have been performed or used since then, and also they did seize one William Colerne and John Rothewell, his servants found there together with the said vicar, and did take them as far as Berkeley castle and there they did imprison them for one half day and one whole night, and from there they did take them to Gloucester and there imprison them for ten days and more, until they were set free by brief of our lord the king. And on the said xvi[th] day of February, they entered at Wodeford into the grounds of the said prebendary with the said number of persons, and still hold by force the grounds of the said prebendary in warlike fashion both against the said prebendary as well as against the lord-lieutenant of the said county, empowered by brief of our said lord the king to remove and arrest all those who come in the above stated way, against the statutes of Northhampton and other statutes and ordinances provided in the said case, notwithstanding that the said lord sent word at diverse times to his ministers at the above-mentioned Wodeford to remove the malefactors and rebels or to arrest them in virtue of the said briefs, who, the said word heard and read before them openly and well understood, answered the said ministers rebelliously and cruelly that for summons of the king, lord, or any other living person they did not wish to leave the said grounds of the prebendary nor submit to being arrested nor to surrender except to the said John Poleyne their master and leader in the above-mentioned quarrel, in contempt of the king and in oppression, affright and bad example to the land and in arerissement and damage of five hundred pounds to the said suppliant, for which he begs remedy for God and as a charitable work, because the said suppliant cannot have justice nor recovery through common law from the said John Trevysa and John Poleyne his maintainer in the said quarrel, because the said John Poleyne is so encouraged by great lordship and alliance and a common maintainer of quarrels in the above-mentioned land.

3. Gloucestershire

At another time, before Thomas of Berkeley and his associates, keepers of the peace of the lord king and his justices, who were assigned to hear and settle various felonies and crimes in the above-mentioned county, it then happened that Robert Taillour, Chaplain, William Colerne, and John Rothewell with many various other unknown persons, having armed themselves in disrespect and contempt of the aforesaid mandate and proclamation of the lord king, at Berkeley on a Tuesday next [23 Feb] following the feast of St. Peter [= cathedra petri, 22 Feb] in the twelfth year of the reign of king Richard the second after the conquest [1389], did forcibly enter in a warlike manner the collegiate church of Westbury [-on-Trym], occupying the place of habitation of Master John Trevisa, Canon of the said church and prebendary of the prebend of Woodford; they remained in the same church for a day and a night, and moreover they made various insults to John Boteller, the steward and servant of the said Master John Trevisa in regards to possession of the income of the said prebend of Woodford and to various other people, and they perpetrated such terrors on the people of the lord king in those parts that no one was brave enough at the time to stay in his own home. And this by order and incitement of Robert Wattes, Dean of the above-mentioned church, that indeed the above-mentioned Robert Taillour, Chaplain, William Colerne, and John Rothewell were supplied moreover with various arms to the value of five marks, namely a breastplate, two bows, two quivers of arrows, two swords, two bucklers, and a poleax, and these arms had been confiscated and placed in the custody of the said Robert Wattes at his request, when he made his petition to the lord king. Which indictment among other things the lord king decided would be settled in his presence. And in due time, that is on the first sabbath following the paschal month in that same term [2 May 1389] before the lord king at Westminster came the aforesaid Robert Taillour, William (Colerne) and John Rothewell in their own persons and they declared how they were unwilling to remain quiet concerning the allegations made against them. They say . . .

Appendix II
Authorship of Piers the Plowman

The following citations are intended to illustrate the application of my hypothesis that Trevisa wrote the B and C versions of *Piers the Plowman*. Catchwords are used to suggest the period or aspect of his life reflected in the passage. Passus and line numbers are from W. W. Skeat's parallel text edition in two volumes (Oxford, 1886), B text unless otherwise indicated. Further references are given in a note at the end.

travel   V 251–52: Lombardes lettres. See *Review* 2:247 (note to C VI 246). Trevisa traveled abroad more than once, and made use of Lombards' letters in doing so (CCR 1392–96, p. 524).

London   X 78–79 (from Schmidt's B text; not in Skeat): (*Review* 2:219) "For God is deef nowadayes and deyneth noght his eres to opene, That girles for hire giltes he forgrynt hem alle." These lines are in B MSS RF only and appear to be added at a later date (though Kane-Donaldson and Schmidt think not). See the continuation of Higden's *Polychronicon* by the Monk of Westminster (RS ix 14) July 1382: "Eodem tempore fuit epidemia Londoniae sed maxime puellarum et puellorum." In the C text (when this epidemic was presumably no longer in the headlines) "girles" is replaced by "good men" (C XII 62).

Oxford   X 256–90: Critique of bishops (dobest), directed especially against Thomas Brinton for lending his prestige to the Black Friars Council (summer of 1382) and perhaps especially for his prominent role as an inquisitor at Oxford in preparation for Archbishop Courtenay's convocation there on 13 November 1382. See *Review* 2:230–1, 248–49.

Berkeley   X 312–13:
"Litel had lordes to done to ȝyue londe fram her heires To religious that haue no reuthe though it reyne on here auteres." This concern for how lords dispose of their lands befits a man who was chaplain to Thomas IV, Lord Berkeley. See *Traditio* 18:314, n. 99; *Review* 2:245–46. And see esp. XV 310–36.

Oxford   XI 49–102: A primary purpose of the B-continuation (XI–XX) is to expose the self-serving practices of the friars. Trevisa translated

241

FitzRalph's *Defensio Curatorum*, and makes his view of the friars quite clear in notes to his translation of the *Polychronicon*.

Berkeley · XI 191–209: The poor and uneducated do not have a monopoly on virtue. Having a wealthy patron tends to inhibit hasty generalizations about wealth and poverty (cp. A text).

priest · XI 274–308: Critique of the priesthood. One might say that the criticism of the friars (XI 49–102) is here balanced with a rebuke to secular priests. But one only has to read the two passages to see that the friars are denounced, whereas priests are subjected to in-house criticism. The author clearly writes as an experienced and concerned parish priest.

Cornwall · XI 332–353: God's Creation (animals and birds) from the Cornish *Ordinalia*, *Origo Mundi*, 123–34. *Medieval Studies* 23:91–125; *Speculum* 44:309; *Review* 2:233–34. John Trevisa was a Cornishman. Several words in BC have as yet no satisfactory etymologies: see, e.g., "goky" (XI 299–300) and note *MED*.

personal · XII 20–24: The value of recreation. See Kane in *New Perspectives in Chaucer Criticism* (1981), 1ff.; Trevisa's translation of "Anglia plena jocis, gens libera digna jocari" *Poly.* RS ii 19, and comment thereon by R. H. Hodgkin, *Six Centuries of an Oxford College* (1949), p. 38, contrasting Wyclif's and Trevisa's views; and Glending Olson, *Literature and Recreation in the Later Middle Ages* (1982), p. 94, n. 6.

Priest · XII 175–85: Introspective passage on how a priest meets his own spiritual needs in comparision with the layman who is dependent on the expertise of his confessor.

personal · XII 257–9, XV 132–41, XX 287–91: False executors. For Trevisa's performance as an executor, see *Traditio* 18:305–6.

Oxford · XIII 21–214: Satirical portrait of the Dominican William Jordan (Oxford convent ca.1350–68). See M. E. Marcett, *Uhtred de Boldon, Friar William Jordan and Piers Plowman* (1938); *Review* 2:235–6; *Poly.* i 77. On the possible influence of Uhtred (Jordan's opponent) on C XVIII 123–24, see G. H. Russell, *JWCI* 29:101–16. Russell wonders why this allusion to the clear vision would appear in C and not B, when the discussion took place in 1366; it is worth pointing out in this connection that Uthred returned to Oxford in 1383 (A. B. Emden, *BRUO* 1:212) at which time Trevisa also was there.

Oxford   XIII 108–9: Alluding to the recruiting practices of the friars, criticized by FitzRalph in *Defensio Curatorum*, translated by Trevisa EETS OS 167, p. 56. *Review* 2:236.

travel   XIII 384–99: Worldly merchant plans his overseas transactions while attending Mass, sending his servants to Bruges or to Prussia "to marchaunden with monoye and maken her eschaunges" (XIII 394). For Trevisa's experience with the exchange rate at Breisach see *Poly.* vi 259.

Berkeley   XIII 410–57: Branches of Sloth. Instead of minstrels, lords should include at their feasts the poor, the learned, and the ill or afflicted.

Cornwall   XIV 224–28, 238–43: The efforts of Wrath and Covetousness to overcome the poor are envisioned as a wrestling match. The neck hold (238–39) is the opening position: see B. H. Kendall, *The Art of Cornish Wrestling*, p. 3. See *YES* 7:36.

XV 68–144   Balanced criticism (cf. XI 274–309 above) of friars (68–86) and priests (87–144), the latter clearly in-house and presented with a strong consciousness of potentially hostile colleagues (in this connection see also XV 381, 412, and 487).

Oxford   XV 115: Quotation of Pseudo-Chrysostom on Matthew, from memory. See Skeat, ii 217–18; *MP* 58:94, item 7 and n. 68; *Review* 2:258.

Oxford   XV 365–82: Decay of education undermines the priesthood. Children no longer learn French in grammar school (365–69). See Skeat, 2:227; *Poly.* ii 161; *Review* 2:245. Students no longer know how to respond to a quodlibet; the author "dare not say it for shame" (p. 376) because this is his world. How far did Trevisa progress with his education? Emden lists only the M.A.; John Shirley (ca. 1422) says "maystre Iohan Trevysa Doctour in theologye" (BL Add. 16165, fol. 94r).

Oxford   XV 383–88, 483–94, 532–38, 572–601: Conversion of Saracens and Jews. The poet's expanded horizon here may come from FitzRalph, *Summa in Quaestionibus Armenorum*, esp. books xviii, xix. See Walsh, *Fitz-Ralph* (1981), p. 174.

Oxford   XV 389–408: Mohammed and the dove. See *Poly.* vi 19–21.

Oxford   XV 501–31: Donation of Constantine. See *Poly.* v. 131 and *Review* 2:259.

London   XV 555–56. A prelate who followed the example of St. Thomas à Becket: Simon Sudbury, archbishop of Canterbury, murdered by a mob during the Peasants' Revolt in June 1381. See *MP* 77:158–59; *Review* 2:221–22, 259.

London   XVII 203–350: Spiritual status of participants in the Peasants' Revolt. See *Review* 2:262–63.

Cornwall   XVIII 31 "likth" (and XII 145 "hexte"): A southwesternism. See *Review* 2:223.

Bible   For Trevisa as translator of the Bible see Chapter 5 above. The following passages relate to this issue:

Bible   C XII 97: "And of Scripture the skylful and scryuaynes were trewe." See *Review* 2:253.

Bible   XII 147–8: "Ne in none beggares cote was that barne borne
                    But in a burgeys place of Bethlem the best."
See WB EV Luke 2:7; *Review* 2:235, 257. I believe Trevisa's assciation with the Wyclif Bible project to be with EV only.

Bible   XVIII 53 (CXXI 53): A crux in the passion narrative (Matt. 27:34, Mark 15:23, Luke 23:36, John 19:28–30). See *YES* 7:38, *Review* 2:263.

Bible   XVIII 109 (CXXI 114): A crux in the interpretation of Dan. 9:24. See *YES* 7:38, *Review* 2:237–38, 263.

Cornwall   XVIII 324–401: The guiler beguiled: for a comparison of this theme in *Piers* and in the Cornish *Ordinalia*, see Robert Longsworth, *The Cornish Ordinalia* (1967), chap. 4.

Oxford   XVIII 377–85: The extent of Christ's mercy: Trevisa's note on the two hells in *Poly.* vi 461. See *Review* 2:263–64.

Cornwall   XIX 4–14: The Ascension. See *Review* 2:265, and the depiction of the Ascension at the end of the Cornish *Resurrexio*.

personal   XIX 314–25: The building of Piers's barn. See accounts of Exeter College Oxford for L.V. 1363: Item per compot. de xij d solut. pro conductione duorum equorum quando Rector et Johannes Trewyse fuerunt apud West Wyttenham ad componendum cum firmariis pro horreo faciendo.

Oxford   XX: Siege of barn of Unity by Antichrist: the emotional source of this dramatic ending of the poem may be found in the poet's reaction to the crisis of Oxford University in 1382, when those agents of Antichrist (the friars) won a great victory over the secular faculty by means of the Black Friars Council and the subsequent

visitation by Archbishop Courtenay in November 1382. See "Poetry and the Liberal Arts: The Oxford Background of *Piers the
Plowman*," *Arts Libéraux et Philosophie au Moyen Age* (Montreal and
Paris, 1969), pp. 715–19. For the specific critique of the friars,
FitzRalph's *Defensio Curatorum* should again be consulted. And
notice the references to the "wise teachers" of Holy Church who
are the embattled seculars (esp. xx 299–301).

Bible   XX 1–50: The character Need has very complex biblical roots.
See Robert Adams in *Traditio* 34:273–301, especially on the importance of Job 41:13b as interpreted by Gregory in his *Morals*:
"need (egestas) goeth before his face" (AV 41:22b has a different
reading). This same verse is discussed by Trevelles in a determination on the infallibility of biblical prophecies concerning
Antichrist and the Judgment, and the same commentary by Gregory is invoked to interpret it. William Trevelles was Trevisa's
colleague at Queen's College, but considerably senior to him,
having incepted as doctor of theology by 1368. It is quite possible
that Trevisa attended lectures by Trevelles while the latter was a
regent master, perhaps in 1369–70. Later the Queen's College
long rolls record the expenditure of xx d "pro Trevisa & Trevelles" (1385–86). The substance of Trevelles's determination was
noted down, probably by John Malverne a Benedictine, in Worcs.
Cath. MS F.65, fol.5. (See Chapter 2 above, "The Curriculum,"
pp. 72–75.)

NOTE

The above examples should be understood in light of my general approach
set forth in *Piers the Plowman: Literary Relations of the A and B Texts* (University
of Washington Press, 1961). Other relevant articles and reviews are in *Modern
Philology* 50:5–22, 58:81–98, 212–14, 71:393–404, 77:158–59; *Modern Language Quarterly* 20:285–87, 24:410–13, 32:243–54; *Mediaeval Studies* 23:91–125;
Traditio 18:289–317; *English Language Notes* 3:295–300; *Speculum* 44:308–10;
Yearbook of English Studies 7:23–42; 11:224–26; *Review* 2:211–69. YES 7:23–42
(cited a few times above) reviews the Kane-Donaldson edition of the B text
(1975); *Review* 2:211–69 (cited frequently above) treats the B and C texts edited
independently by Schmidt and Pearsall, both published in 1978.

By way of conclusion let me say that colleagues in the field of *Piers Plowman*
studies have treated me kindly. After all, it might have been tempting to brand
me as a Baconian, but they have not done so, and for that I am grateful. Their
silence I interpret as respectful but skeptical. One of the few scholars to address
the question directly in recent years has been John M. Bowers in his book *The

Crisis of Will in Piers Plowman (1986). In the opening chapter he develops a hypothesis that the poet's education went no farther than a cathedral school, perhaps that of Worcester, which was not far from the Malvern Hills mentioned in the poem. In arguing against the suggestion that the author was educated at Oxford, Bowers remarks "the reader of *Piers Plowman* is forced to conclude that the poet was very much *un*like John Trevisa" for the following reasons (p. 18):

> the B-poet shows no signs of being a foreign traveler, admits to behaving contemptuously to social superiors such as Lord Berkeley would have been, and betrays little of the encyclopedic lore to be gained from Bartholomeus or the historiographical method to be found in Higden. . . .

Since offering my Trevisa hypothesis I have tried to avoid defending it at every turn, but let me now make an exception to this rule and comment briefly on Bowers's argument. First, to the assertion that the B poet shows no signs of being a traveler, I respond by asking what signs would be required beyond his references to "Lombardes lettres" (V 251–1), the monetary transactions in Bruges and Prussia contemplated by the worldly merchant who exemplifies covetousness on Haukin's coat (XIII 392–99), and the references to Rochmadore (XII 37) and Pamplona (XVII 252)?

Second, it is the Dreamer, not the B poet, who "admits to behaving contemptuously to social superiors." Such a blurring of the distinction between Dreamer and author would never be tolerated in Chaucer studies, and it is even more important to guard against it in "Langland" studies where the practice is rampant. But even if we tolerated it in this case, what is to be done with those numerous passages in the B text reflecting aristocratic interests? (See this Appendix, "Berkeley" for examples.)

Third, Bowers sees little evidence of the method of Higden or the lore of Bartholomeus in the poem. As regards the former, I am at a loss, since he makes no attempt to invalidate my numerous examples of connections between the B text and the *Polychronicon* both as regards the general structure of the B-continuation and its poetic details (Fowler 1961). As for Bartholomeus, we should not be surprised at the absence of his lore from the B text, written at least a decade before the translation of the *De Proprietatibus Rerum* was undertaken.

Finally, Bowers is skeptical that one person could have had time to write *Piers the Plowman* and also translate so many works. Of course no one can provide a certain answer to such an objection, and I should add that my theory of authorship remains just that: a theory. But that theory includes a hypothetical chronology: Trevisa's shorter translations were probably completed during his stay in Exeter College (1362–69); his help with the Wyclif Bible occurred at Queen's during the period 1370–78; revision of *Piers the Plowman* was undertaken following his expulsion from Queen's in the years 1378–83; the *Polychronicon* translation was completed in 1387; translation of the *De Regimine*

Principum of Aegidius Romanus probably belongs to the period 1388–92 along with the C revision of *Piers the Plowman* accomplished during that same time; and finally the encyclopedia of Bartholomeus was translated during 1394–99.

In reciting the above chronology I may sound a bit more confident than I am. But in the midst of so much uncertainty, it is probably best to be decisive. My theory that John Trevisa was responsible for the B and C versions of *Piers the Plowman* may indeed be improbable; the only thing *more* improbable, in my opinion, is the theory that they were written by William Langland.

Bibliography

PRIMARY SOURCES

English Manuscripts

Trevisa's translations are listed below in estimated chronological order (ca. 1362, etc.); the few exact dates are based on actual references in the documents. The roman numerals in parentheses following each entry show the date of each manuscript by century using a modification of the system found in N. R. Ker (1969–92, 1:vii): superscript numerals indicate quarter centuries.

Gospel of Nicodemus (ca. 1362–72)
London, BL Additional 16165, fols. 94–114 (xv$^{1/2}$)
Salisbury, Cathedral Library 39, fols. 129v–47 (xv^3)
Winchester College 33, fols. 74–93v (xv^3)

Defensio Curatorum (ca. 1362–72)
London, BL Harley 1900, fols. 6–21 (xv in.)
London, BL Stowe 65, fols. 205v–17 (xv in.)
London, BL Additional 24194, fols. 8–21 (xv^1)
Cambridge, St. John's College 204, fols. 5–18v (xv^1)
Manchester, Chetham's Library 11379, fols. 5v–18v (xiv/xv)
San Marino, California, Huntington Library HM 28561, fols. 5v–20v (xv med.)

Dialogus inter Militem et Clericum (ca. 1362–72)
London, BL Harley 1900, fols. 1–5v (xv in.)
London, BL Stowe 65, fols. 202–205v (xv in.)
London, BL Additional 24194, fols. 4–8 (xv^1)
Cambridge, St. John's College 204, fols. 1–5 (xv^1)
Manchester, Chetham's Library 11379, fols. 1–5v (xiv/xv)
San Marino, California, Huntington Library HM 28561, fols. 1–5v (xv med.)

Dialogue between a Lord and a Clerk on Translation and *Epistle . . . unto Lord Thomas of Barkley upon the Translation of Polychronicon* . . . (ca. 1387) written by Trevisa and prefaced to *Polychronicon* translation. Manuscripts classified by Waldron (1990).
London, BL Cotton Tiberius D. vii, fols. 1–2v (xiv/xv)
London, BL Harley 1900, fols. 42–43v (xv in.)
London, BL Stowe 65, fols. 217–18 (xv in.)
Glasgow, University Library Hunterian 367, fol. 1 (*Dialogue* only) (xv med.)

248

San Marino, California, Huntington Library HM 28561, fols. 41–42v (xv med.)
Princeton, University Library, Taylor MS, fol. 8v (*Epistle* only) (xv3)

Polychronicon (1385–87). Manuscripts classified by Waldron (1990).

Subgroup 1
London, BL Cotton Tiberius D. vii, fols. 3–296 (xiv/xv)
Glasgow, University Library, Hunterian 367, fols. 2–202v (xv med.)
London, BL Stowe 65, fols. 1–201 (xv in.)
Princeton, University Library, Taylor MS, fols. 9–225v (xv3)

Independently derived
Manchester, Chetham's Library 11379, fols. 35–178v (xiv/xv)

Subgroup 2
London, BL Harley 1900, fols. 44–310v (xv in.)
San Marino, California, Huntington Library HM 28561, fols. 43–319v (xv med.)
Caxton's 1482 print is derived from a lost manuscript belonging to this subgroup.

Subgroup 3
London, BL Additional 24194, fols. 36–262 (xv¹)
Aberdeen, University Library 21, fols. 12–171v (xv in.)
Liverpool, Public Libraries f909 HIG, fols. 13rb–220v (xv med.)
Cambridge, Corpus Christi College 354, fols. 1–182v (xv/xvi)
Oslo/London, Schøyen Collection 194, fols. 15–212v (*olim* Penrose 12) (xv¹)
Cambridge, St. John's College 204, fols. 34–280 (xv¹)
Princeton, University Library, Garrett 151, fols. 1–212v (xv¹)

Manuscripts extracts and fragments of Polychronicon
London, BL Landsdowne 210, fols. 67v–73 (extracts from II, III, V, VII, VIII)
Oxford, Bodleian Library, Rawlinson C. 86, fols. 31v–49v
Oxford, Trinity College 29 (extracts from II. 218–IV. 52, possibly copied from Caxton)
Edinburgh, National Library of Scotland, Asloan MS, fols. 77–86 (containing II. 5–7, 9, 11)
San Marino, California, Huntington Library HM 144, fols. 54v–64v (extracts from V, possibly in same hand as no. 17 above)

De Regimine Principum (ca. 1388–92?)
Oxford, Bodleian Library, Digby 233, fols. 1–182v (xv¹)

De Proprietatibus Rerum (completed 6 February 1398/9). Manuscripts classified by Seymour et al. (1975–88).

Bibliography

Subgroup 1
London, BL Harley 4789, fols. 1–286 (lacks 19 leaves; before 1430)
Oxford, Bodleian Library, e Musaeo 16, fols. 1–310 (imperfect; xv²)

Subgroup 2
London, BL Additional 27944, fols. 2–330 (ca. 1410)
New York, Columbia University Library, Plimpton 263, fols. 1–379 (ca. 1440)
New York, Pierpont Morgan Library M 875, fols. 1–337 (before 1430)

Subgroup 3
Bristol, City Library 9, fols. 1–137 (imperfect; xv⁴)
Cambridge, University Library, Ii. v. 41, fols. 2–343 (before 1450)
London, BL Harley 614, fols. 1–242 (lacks 1 leaf; before 1430)

Manuscript extracts and fragments of De Proprietatibus Rerum
London, BL Sloane 983, fols. 81–102v (epitomes of Books VII and XVII, ca. 1450; printed in Seymour 1969 and 1973)
London, BL Additional 45680, fols. 48–49 (Books XII. 7–10, XIII. 4–11, after 1450; printed in Bitterling 1977b)
Oxford, Bodleian Library, Ashmole 1481, fols. 92–94 (a *literatim* copy of no. 3 above, fols. 96ra–97rb) (Book VII. 57–59; printed in Seymour 1992)
Oxford, Magdalen College, Lat. 182, fols. 124v–26 (extracts from Book VIII. 9 and 11)
Tokyo, Keio University Library 170X. 9/5 (Books V. 1–2 and XVIII. 62–65; printed in Takamiya 1988)

Latin Manuscripts of Trevisa's Translations

Gospel of Nicodemus: Oxford, Bodleian Library, Bodleian 556, fols. 1–12, is close to Trevisa's exemplar: see Fowler (1988). Edited by H. C. Kim, *The Gospel of Nicodemus*, Toronto Medieval Latin Texts 2 (Toronto, 1973), based on Einsiedeln Stiftsbibliothek, MS 326. For a census of Latin manuscripts, consult Izydorczyk (1993), under Secondary Sources.

Defensio Curatorum: Oxford, Bodleian Library, Bodley 144 fols. 255–71. Fitz-Ralph's sermon diary: see Gywnn (1937), Walsh (1981). Editions in M. Goldast, *Monarchia S. Romani Imperii*, 3 vols. (Hanover, 1612–14), II. 1392–1410, and E. Browne, *Fasciculus Rerum Expetendarum et Fugiendarum*, 2 vols. (London, 1690), II. 466–86.

Dialogus inter Militem et Clericum, otherwise *Disputatio inter Clericum et Militem*: see diss. Erickson (1966) for list of manuscripts, to which add Oxford, Bodleian Library, Rawlinson G40 (B), fols. 32–38. Edition by Erickson (1967).

Polychronicon: San Marino, California, Huntington Library MS 132. This may be Higden's copy. See Taylor (1966) and Edwards (1978) for list of manuscripts.

Bibliography

De Regimine Principum: Oxford, Bodleian Library Hatton 15 appears close to the form of Trevisa's exemplar (to which I was alerted by the late N. R. Ker). For a study of the Latin manuscripts see diss. Briggs (1993; "English" in his title refers to provenance of the Latin manuscripts).

De Proprietatibus Rerum: see Seymour et al. (1992) for list of manuscripts.

Editions

Incunabula and Early Editions

Polychronicon. Westminster: Caxton, 1482.

Polychronicon. Westminster: De Worde, ca. 1495.

Bartholomaeus de proprietatibus rerum. London: Berthelet, 1535.

Batman uppon Bertholome. His Booke De Proprietatibus Rerum. London: East, 1592 (reprinted Hildesheim 1976, with introduction by J. Schäfer).

Modern Editions

Babington, C., and J. R. Lumby, eds. *Polychronicon*. 9 vols. Rolls Series (London, 1865–86).

Perry, A. J., ed. *Dialogus inter Militem et Clericum, Richard FitzRalph's Sermon, 'Defensio Curatorum' and Methodius, 'þe Bygynnyng of þe World and þe Ende of Worldes' by John Trevisa*, EETS 167 (London, 1925).

Pollard, A. W., ed. *Fifteenth-Century Prose and Verse* (London, 1903), containing a modernized English text of Trevisa's "Dialogue between a Lord and a Clerk on Translation" and "Epistle . . . unto Lord Thomas of Barkley upon the Translation of Polychronicon," pp. 203–10.

Seymour, M. C., et al., ed. *On the Properties of Things: John Trevisa's Translation of Bartholomaeus Anglicus, De Proprietatibus Rerum*, 3 vols. (Oxford, 1975–88).

Steele, R. *Medieval Lore from Bartholomaeus Anglicus* (London, 1895), modernized selections.

Waldron, R. A. "Trevisa's Original Prefaces on Translation: A Critical Edition." In *Medieval English Studies Presented to George Kane*, edited by E. D. Kennedy, R. A. Waldron, and J. S. Wittig (Woodbridge, Suffolk; Wolfeboro, N.H., 1988), pp. 285–99.

Episcopal Registers and Other Historical Documents

Berkeley, Glos. Berkeley Castle muniment room, box 14.12, "Tygembreth Manorium": rental roll (xiv/xv), general series.

Calendar of Close Rolls. London (Public Record Office). CCR.

Calendar of Institutions by the Chapter of Canterbury Sede Vacante. Edited by C. Eveleigh Woodruff and Irene J. Churchill. Canterbury, 1924. (KAS/RB8)

Calendar of Papal Registers (Papal Letters). V 1396–1404. CPR/L.

Calendar of Patent Rolls. London (Public Record Office). CPR.

Bibliography

The Episcopal Registers of the Diocese of Exeter. The Register of Edmund Stafford (A.D. 1395–1419). Edited by F. C. Hingeston-Randolph. London, 1886.

Gover, J. F. *The Placenames of Cornwall.* Copies on deposit in the Museum of the Royal Institution of Cornwall, Truro, and the National Library of Wales, Aberystwyth, 1948.

Inquisitions Post Mortem. XIV (1952), no. 10, pp. 7–12 [1374]. London: H.M. Stationery Office. Thomas de Bradeston. IPM.

Jeayes, Isaac Herbert. *Unpublished Catalogue in Berkeley Castle.* General Series. 3 vols. n.d.

The Liber Albus of the Priory of Worcester. Edited by James M. Wilson. Parts 1 and 2. Worcester Historical Society, 1919.

Libri Cancellarii et Procuratorum. Part 1 of *Munimenta Academica, or Documents Illustrative of Academical Life and Studies at Oxford.* Edited by Henry Anstey. 2 vols. Rolls Series 50. London, 1868.

Parsons, Richard. *Parochial Visitations of the County of Gloucester.* Oxford, Bodleian Library, Rawlinson B 323. (Parsons MS 5).

Public Record Office. PRO.
    Clerical Subsidy Rolls. PRO E 179 58/5 mm. 2–3 (1379).
    Ancient Petition. PRO SC 8/148/7355.
    PRO SC 2/161/74.
    PRO SC 8/84/4193.
    PRO KB 27/512/Rex m. 17.
    Treaty Roll. 75 14 Richard II m. 10 (1390).

The Register of John de Grandisson, Bishop of Exeter (A.D. 1327–1369). Edited by F. C. Hingeston-Randolph. 3 vols. London, 1894–99.

The Register of Wolstan de Bransford, Bishop of Worcester, 1339–49. Edited by R. M. Haines. London: H.M. Stationery Office, 1966.

Registrum Simonis de Sudbiria. Diocesis Londoniensis A.D. 1362–1375. Edited by R. C. Fowler. 2 vols. Canterbury and York Society 34. Oxford 1927–38.

Registrum Reginald Brian, Bishop of Worcester, 1353–1361. Unpublished register in the county record office in St. Helen's, Worcester.

Registrum William Whittlesey, Bishop of Worcester, 1364–1368. Unpublished register in the county record office in St. Helen's, Worcester.

Registrum William Whittlesey, Archbishop of Canterbury, 1368–1374. Unpublished register in Lambeth Palace Library, London.

Registrum William Lynn (or Lenn), Bishop of Worcester, 1369–1373. Unpublished register in the county record office in St. Helen's, Worcester.

The Register of Henry Wakefield, Bishop of Worcester, 1375–95. Edited by Warwick Paul Marett. Leeds: *WHS*, 1972.

Register Brian 2 (late fourteenth century). A precedent book or formulary, probably compiled during the episcopate of Henry Wakefield. County record office, St. Helen's, Worcester (unpublished). For an account of this volume see "Secondary Sources" below under Haines (1975).

The Register of Richard Clifford, Bishop of Worcester, 1401–1407: A Calendar. Edited by W.E.L. Smith. Toronto: Pontifical Institute of Medieval Studies, 1976.

Registrum Sede Vacante, Diocese of Worcester, 1301–1435. Edited by John W. Willis-Bund. Worcester Historical Society, 1893–97.

Stainer, C. L. *Compoti Collegii Aule Reginae.* 10 vols. Oxford, 1906–8. Handwritten copy in Library of Queen's College, Oxford.

Victoria County History. VCH.

Gloucestershire. Vol. 2, 1907.

Oxfordshire. Vols. 3 and 4, 1954 and 1979.

Other Primary Sources

Augustine. *The City of God.* Translated Henry Bettenson. Harmondsworth, Middlesex, Eng.: Penguin Books Ltd., 1972.

Bale, John. *Scriptorum Illustrium Maioris Brytannie . . .* Catalogus. *Catalogue of Illustrious British Writers.* 2 vols. Basel, 1557.

Biblia Sacra. (Vulgate.) Paris, 1947.

Bigland, Ralph. *Historical, Monumental and Genealogical Collections, Relative to the County of Gloucester.* London: John Nichols, 1791.

Boase, C. W., ed. *Registrum Collegii Exoniensis.* Oxford Historical Society vol. 27. Oxford, 1894.

Boase, G. C., and W. P. Courtney, eds. *Bibliotheca Cornubiensis.* 3 vols. London: Longmans, Green, Reader, and Dyer, 1874–82, 2:795–98, 3:1352.

Boase, G. C. *Collectanea Cornubiensis.* Truro, 1890. Col. 1090.

Brown, Edward, ed. *Fasciculus Rerum Expetendarum et Fugiendarum.* 2 vols. London, 1690. See 2:466–86 (FitzRalph's *Defensio Curatorum*).

Catalogus Librorum Manuscriptorum Bibliothecae Wigorniensis. Made in 1622–23 by Patrick Young. Edited by Ivor Atkins and Neil R. Ker. Cambridge, 1944.

Chaucer, Geoffrey. *The Riverside Chaucer.* General editor, Larry D. Benson. 3d ed. Boston: Houghton Mifflin Co., 1987.

Dibden, Thomas F., ed. Revision of Joseph Ames, *Typographical Antiquities . . .* 4 vols. London: W. Miller, 1810–19.

Forshall, J., and F. Madden, eds. *The Holy Bible Made from the Latin Vulgate by John Wycliffe and his Followers.* 4 vols. Oxford, 1850.

Froissart, Jean. *Chroniques de J. Froissart.* Edited by Luce et al. 15 vols. Paris: Société de l'Histoire de France, 1869–1975.

———. *The Chronicles of Froissart.* Translated by Sir John Bourchier, Lord Berners (1523–25). London: D. Nutt, 1901–3.

Goldast, Melchior, ed. *Monarchia S. Romani Imperii.* 3 vols. Hanover, 1612–14. See vol. 2, 1392–1410 (FitzRalph's *Defensio Curatorum*).

Gray, Irvine E., ed. *Guide to the Parish Records of the City of Bristol and the County of Gloucester.* London: Records Section of the Bristol and Gloucestershire Archaeological Society, 1963 (BGAS Records Section, v. 5), p. 257.

Gregory the Great. *Morals on the Book of Job*. Translated by J. Bliss. 3 vols. in 4. London: J. H. Parker, 1844–50. Library of the Fathers, vols. 18, 21, 23, 31.

Hearne, Thomas, ed. *Historia vitae et regni Richardi II, a monaco quondam de Evesham consignata*. Oxford, 1729. (See also Stow below.)

Hennecke, Edgar Ludwig T. *Neutestamentliche Apokryphen*. Vol. 1. Edited by W. Schneemelcher. Tübingen: J.C.B. Mohr, 1959.

————. *New Testament Apocrypha*. English translation edited by R. McL. Wilson Vol. 1. "Gospels and Related Writings." London: Lutterworth Press, 1963.

Holinshed. *Chronicles*. Edited by Henry Ellis. 6 vols. London, 1807–8.

James, M. R., trans. *The Apocryphal New Testament*. Oxford: Clarendon Press, 1924. Rev. ed., 1953.

Lake's Parochial History of the County of Cornwall. Edited by J. Polsue. 4 vols. Truro, 1867–72. Reprinted 1974 with a new introduction by Charles Thomas.

Leland, John. *Commentarii de Scriptoribus Britannicis*. Edited by Anthony Hall. 2 vols. Oxford, 1709.

————. *The Itinerary of John Leland*. Edited by L. Toulmin Smith. 5 vols. London, 1906–10. Revised with a foreword by Thomas Kendrick. Carbondale: Southern Illinois University Press, 1964.

————. See also "Secondary Sources" below, under Dorsch.

Le Long, J. *Bibliotheca Sacra*. Paris, 1723, pp. 424ff.

Lindstrom, Bengt, ed. *A Late Middle English Version of the Gospel of Nicodemus*. Uppsala: Almqvist and Wiksell, 1974. Studia Anglistica Upsaliensia, 18.

Mandeville. *The Bodley Version of Mandeville's Travels*. Edited by M. C. Seymour. London: EETS, Oxford University Press, 1953.

Norris, Edwin, ed. *The Ancient Cornish Drama*. 2 vols. Oxford, 1859; reprinted New York: B. Blom, 1968.

Oudin, Casimir (Casimirus Oudinus). *Commentarius de Scriptoribus Ecclesiae Antiquis . . .* 3 vols. Leipzig, 1722, 3:1043–46.

Pits, John (Joannes Pitseus). *Relationem Historicarum de Rebus Anglicis*. Paris, 1619.

Romanus, Aegidius (Giles of Rome, Archbishop of Bourges). *De Ecclesiastica Potestate*. Woodbridge, Suffolk; Dover, N.H.: Boydell Press, 1986.

Seymour, Michael C., et al. *Bartholomaeus Anglicus and His Encyclopedia*. London: Variorum, 1992.

Sisam, Kenneth, ed. *Fourteenth Century Verse & Prose*. Oxford: Clarendon Press, 1921. Contains brief selections of Trevisa's translation of Higden's *Polychronicon*, pp. 146–48.

Skeat, W. W., ed. *Piers the Plowman and Richard the Redeless*. (Parallel Texts) 2 vols. Oxford, 1886.

Smyth, John. *The Lives of the Berkeleys* [ca. 1622]. 3 vols. Edited by Sir John MacLean. Gloucester, 1883–85.

Somnium Viridarii. In *Revue du Moyen Age Latin*, 22:1–230. Edited by F. Chatillon et al. Strasbourg: Palais de l'Université, 1966.

Stow, George B., ed. *Historia Vitae et Regni Ricardi II Angliae Regis*. Philadelphia: University of Pennsylvania Press, 1977. (See also Hearne above.)

Thomas, Charles. See *Lake's Parochial History of the County of Cornwall* above.

Ussher, James. *Historia Dogmatica . . . de Scripturis et Sacris Vernaculis*. Edited by Henry Wharton. London, 1690. Appendix by Wharton beginning p. 305. "Auctorium Historiae Dogmaticae Jacobi Usserii Armachani de Scripturis et Sacris Vernaculis." London, 1689. On Trevisa, see pp. 426f, 430, 438f.

Waldron, Ronald. "Trevisa's Original Prefaces on Translation: A Critical Edition." In *Medieval English Studies Presented to George Kane*, pp. 285–99. Edited by Edward Donald Kennedy et al. Woodbridge, Suffolk; Wolfeboro, N.H.: D. S. Brewer, 1988.

Wanley, Humphrey. *A Catalogue of the Harleian Manuscripts in the British Museum*. 4 vols. London, 1808–12, 2:320.

Waterland, Daniel. *History of the Athanasian Creed*. London, 1724. 2d ed., 1728, p. 79f.

Wood, Anthony (Antonius à Wood). *Historia et Antiquitates Universitates Oxoniensis*. Oxford, 1674, lib. 2, p. 95.

SECONDARY SOURCES

Aston, T. H., general editor, *History of the University of Oxford*. Vol. 1, *The Early Oxford Schools*, editor J. I. Catto (London: Oxford University Press, 1984). Vol. 2, *Late Medieval Oxford*, editors J. I. Catto and R. Evans (London: Oxford University Press, 1992).

Bitterling, Klaus B. "Notes on the Text of the Peterborough Lapidary." *N&Q* 222 (1977a): 303–6.

———. "Zwei bisher unbeachtete Fragmente der Mittelenglischen Ubersetzungen von Bartholomaeus Anglicus, *De Proprietatibus Rerum*." *NM* 78 (1977b): 47–56.

Boyle, Leonard E. *A Survey of the Vatican Archives and of Its Medieval Holdings*. Toronto: Pontifical Institute of Medieval Studies, 1972.

Briggs, Charles F. "Manuscripts of Giles of Rome's *De Regimine Principum* in England, 1300–1500: A Handlist." *Scriptorium* 47 (1993): 60–73.

Carew, Richard. *Survey of Cornwall*. London, 1602, 1769, 1811. Reprinted, 1969.

Catto, J. I. "John Wyclif and the Cult of the Eucharist." In *The Bible in the Medieval World: Essays in Memory of Beryl Smalley*, edited by Katherine Walsh and Diana Wood, pp. 269–86. Oxford: Basil Blackwell, 1985.

Cawley, A. C. "Punctuation in the Early Versions of Trevisa." *London Mediaeval Studies* 1:1 (1937): 116–33.

———. "The Relationships of the Trevisa Manuscripts and Caxton's *Polychronicon*." *London Mediaeval Studies* 1:3 (1939/1948): 463–82.

Clarke, Maude Violet. *Fourteenth Century Studies by M. V. Clarke.* Edited by
L. S. Sutherland and M. McKisack. Oxford: Clarendon Press, 1937.

Cooke, James H. "On the Ancient Inscriptions in the Chapel at Berkeley Castle,
with Some Account of John Trevisa." *Transactions of the Bristol and Gloucester
Archaeological Society* 1 (1876): 138–46.

———. "Trevisa's Translation of the Bible." *N&Q* 5th ser. X. Oct. 5 (1878):
261–62.

Courtenay, William J. *Adam Wodeham: An Introduction to His Life and Writings.*
Leiden: E. J. Brill, 1978.

———. *Schools and Scholars in Fourteenth-Century England.* Princeton: Princeton
University Press, 1987.

Covella, Francis Dolores, trans. *Piers Plowman: The A-Text, An Alliterative Verse
Translation.* Introduction and Notes by David C. Fowler. Binghamton, N.Y.:
Medieval and Renaissance Texts and Studies, 1992 (Pegasus Paperbooks).

Dahmus, J. H. *The Metropolitan Visitations of William Courtenay, Archbishop of
Canterbury, 1381–1396.* Urbana: University of Illinois Press, 1950.

———. *William Courtenay, Archbishop of Canterbury, 1381–1396.* University
Park: Pennsylvania State University Press, 1966.

Deanesly, Margaret. *The Lollard Bible and Other Medieval Biblical Versions.* Cambridge: University Press, 1920. References to Trevisa, pp. 299–302.

Dictionary of the Middle Ages. Edited by Joseph R. Strayer. 13 vols. New York:
Scribner, 1982–89.

Dorsch, T. S. "Two English Antiquaries: John Leland and John Stow." *Essays
and Studies,* New Series 12 (1959): 18–35.

Doyle, A. I. "More Light on John Shirley." *MAE* 30 (1961): 93–101.

———. "English Books in and out of Court from Edward III to Henry VII."
In *English Court Culture in the Later Middle Ages,* edited by V. J. Scattergood
and J. W. Sherborne. London: Duckworth, 1983.

Dwyer, Richard A. "Some Readers of John Trevisa." *N&Q* 212 (1967): 291–
92.

———. "Arthur's Stellification in Lydgate's *Fall of Princes.*" *PQ* 57 (1979):
155–71.

Edwards, A. S. G. "A Sixteenth Century Version of Trevisa's *Polychronicon.*"
ELN 11 (1973): 34–38.

———. Notes on the *Polychronicon.*" *N&Q* 223 (1978): 2–3.

———. "The Influence and Audience of the *Polychronicon*: Some Observations." *Proceedings of the Leeds Philosophical and Literary Society.* Literary and
Historical Section 17, pt. 6 (1980): 113–19.

———. "John Trevisa." In *Middle English Prose: A Critical Guide to Major Authors
and Genres,* edited by A. S. G. Edwards, pp. 133–46. New Brunswick, N.J.:
Rutgers University Press, 1984.

———. "Bartholomaeus Anglicus and Medieval English Literature." *Archiv für
das Studium der Neueren Sprachen und Literaturen* 222 (1985): 121–28.

————. "The Unity and Authenticity of Anelida and Arcite: The Evidence of the Manuscripts." *Studies in Bibliography* 41 (1988): 177–88.

Ellis, P. Berresford. *The Cornish Language and Its Literature.* London and Boston: Routledge and Kegan Paul, 1974.

Emden, A. B. *Biographical Register of the University of Oxford to A.D. 1500.* 3 vols. Oxford: Clarendon Press, 1957–59.

————. "Northerners and Southerners in the Organization of the University to 1509." In *Oxford Studies Presented to Daniel Callus*, pp. 1–30. Foreword by R. W. Southern. OHS ns XVI. Oxford: Clarendon Press, 1964.

Ernle, Rowland E. P., Lord. *English Farming Past and Present.* London, New York: Longmans, Green and Co., 1912. 6th edition, 1961.

Erickson, Carolly. "The Fourteenth Century Franciscans and Their Critics." *Franciscan Studies* 35 (1975): 107–35.

Erickson, Norma N. "A Dispute Between a Priest and a Knight." *Proceedings of the American Philosophical Society* 111 (1967): 288–309.

Fabricius, J. A. *Bibliotheca latina mediae et infimae aetatis.* 6 vols. Hamburg, 1734–36: IV 450.

Floyer, John K., ed. *Catalogue of MSS: Preserved in the Chapter Library of Worcester Cathedral.* Revised by Sidney G. Hamilton. Oxford, 1906.

Forte, Stephen L. "A Study of Some Oxford Schoolmen of the Middle of the Fourteenth Century with Special Reference to Worcester Cathedral MS. F.65." 2 vols. Oxford, 1947. Typescript.

Fowler, David C. "John Trevisa and the English Bible." *MP* 58 (1960): 81–98.

————. "About the Author." Chapter 7 of *Piers the Plowman: Literary Relations of the A and B Texts*, pp. 185–205. Seattle: University of Washington Press, 1961.

————. "The Date of the Cornish *Ordinalia*." *Medieval Studies* (Toronto), 23 (1961): 91–125 (1961a).

————. "New Light on John Trevisa." *Traditio* 18 (1962): 289–317.

————. "A Middle English Bible Commentary (Oxford: Trinity College MS 93)." *Manuscripta* 12 (1968): 67–78.

————. "Poetry and the Liberal Arts: The Oxford Background of *Piers the Plowman*." In *Arts Libéraux et Philosophie au Moyen Age* (Actes du Quatrième Congrès International de Philosophie Médiévale), pp. 715–19. Montreal: Institut d'études médiévales; Paris: Librairie Philosophique J. Urin, 1969.

————. "John Trevisa: Scholar and Translator." *Transactions of the Bristol and Gloucestershire Archaeological Society* 89 (1970): 99–108.

————. "More about John Trevisa." *MLQ* 32 (1971): 243–54.

————. *The Bible in Early English Literature.* Seattle: University of Washington Press, 1976.

————. "The Middle English Gospel of Nicodemus in Winchester MS 33." *Leeds Studies in English* 19 (1988): 67–83.

————. "*Piers Plowman*: In Search of an Author." *Essays in Medieval Studies: Proceedings of Illinois Medieval Association* 5 (1988): 1–16.

Frank, Robert Worth. *Piers Plowman and the Scheme of Salvation: An Interpretation of Dowell, Dobet and Dobest*. New Haven: Yale University Press, 1957.

Fristedt, Sven L. *The Wycliffe Bible*. 3 vols. Stockholm: Almqvist and Wiksell, 1953–73.

Fuller, Thomas. *The Church History of Britain*. London, 1655.

————. *The History of the Worthies of England*. London, 1662.

Galbraith, V. H. "An Autograph MS of Ranulph Higden's *Polychronicon*." *Huntington Library Quarterly* 23 (1959): 1–18.

Gethyn-Jones, J. E. "John Trevisa—An Associate of Nicholas Hereford." *Transactions of the Woolhope Naturalists' Field Club* 40 (1971), Part 2: 241–44.

————. *Trevisa of Berkeley: A Celtic Firebrand*. Dursley, Glos.: Alan Sutton, 1978.

Goodman, A. *The Loyal Conspiracy: the Lords Appellant under Richard II*. Coral Gables, Fla.: University of Miami Press, 1971.

Green, Richard Firth. *Poets and Princepleasers: Literature and the English Court in the Late Middle Ages*. Toronto: University of Toronto Press, 1980.

Greenwood, Alice D. "The Beginnings of English Prose. Trevisa. The Mandeville Translators." *Cambridge History of English Literature*, 2:80–100. Edited by A. W. Ward and A. R. Waller. New York: G. P. Putnam's Sons; Cambridge: Cambridge University Press, 1908.

Greetham, D. C. "Models for the Textual Transmission of Translation: The Case of John Trevisa." *Studies in Bibliography* 37 (1984): 131–55.

Griffiths, Jeremy, and Derek Pearsall, eds. *Book Production and Publishing in Britain, 1375-1475*. Cambridge: Cambridge University Press, 1989. See General Index, under Trevisa.

Gwynn, Aubrey. "The Sermon Diary of Richard FitzRalph, Archbishop of Armagh." *PRIA* 44c (1937): 1–57.

Haines, R. M. *The Administration of the Diocese of Worcester in the First Half of the Fourteenth Century*. London: Church Historical Society, SPCK, 1965.

————. "The Compilation of a Late Fourteenth-Century Precedent Book—Register Brian 2." *Studies in Church History* 11 (1975): 173–85.

Hall, G. D. G. "Three Courts of the Hundred of Penwith, 1333." In *Medieval Legal Records, in Memory of C. A. F. Meekings*, edited by R. F. Hunnisett and J. B. Post, pp. 169–96. London: H.M. Stationery Office, 1978.

Hammond, Eleanor Prescott, ed. *English Verse between Chaucer and Surrey*. Durham, N.C.: Duke University Press, 1927. Reprinted New York: Octagon Books, 1965.

Hanna, Ralph, III. "Sir Thomas Berkeley and His Patronage." *Speculum* 64 (1989): 878–916.

————. "MS. Bodley 851 and the Dissemination of Piers Plowman." *The Yearbook of Langland Studies* (forthcoming).

Hilton, R. H. *A Medieval Society: The West Midlands at the End of the Thirteenth Century.* New York: Humanities Press, 1966.

———. *Bond Men Made Free: Medieval Peasant Movements and the English Rising of 1381.* London: Temple Smith, 1973.

History of the University of Oxford. General editor, T. H. Aston. Vol. 1: *The Early Oxford Schools.* Edited by J. I. Catto. Vol. 2: *The Late Middle Ages.* Edited by J. I. Catto and R. Evans. Oxford: Clarendon Press, 1984, 1992.

Hodgkin, R. H. *Six Centuries of an Oxford College: A History of the Queen's College, 1340-1940.* Oxford: Blackwell, 1949.

Holmes, George. *The Good Parliament.* Oxford: Clarendon Press, 1975.

Housman, J. E. "Higden, Trevisa, Caxton and the Beginnings of Arthurian Criticism." *RES* 23 (1947): 209–17.

Hudson, Anne, ed. *Selections from English Wycliffite Writings.* Cambridge: Cambridge University Press, 1978.

———. "John Purvey: A Reconsideration of the Evidence for His Life and Writings." *Viator* 12 (1981): 355–80.

———. *The Premature Reformation.* Oxford: Clarendon Press, 1988.

Hulme, William Henry. *The Middle-English Harrowing of Hell and Gospel of Nicodemus.* EETS 100, 1907.

Izydorczyk, Zbigniew. *Manuscripts of the Evangelium Nicodemi: A Census.* Subsidia Mediaevalia, 21. Toronto: Pontifical Institute of Mediaeval Studies, 1993.

Jeayes, Isaac Herbert. *Descriptive Catalogue of the Charters and Muniments in the Possession of the Rt. Hon. Lord Fitzhardinge at Berkeley Castle.* Bristol, 1892.

Kedar, Benjamin Z. "Canon Law and Local Practice: The Case of Mendicant Preaching in Late Medieval England." *Bulletin of Medieval Canon Law* ns 2 (1972): 17–32.

Kelley, J. N. D. *Early Christian Creeds.* 3d ed. New York: D. McKay Co., 1972.

Kendall, Bryan H. *The Art of Cornish Wrestling.* The Cornish Wrestling Association, Cornwall, no date.

Kenney, Anthony. *Wyclif.* New York: Oxford University Press, 1985.

Ker, N. R. "A Middle English Summary of the Bible." *MAE* 29 (1960): 115–18.

———. *Medieval Libraries of Great Britain.* 2d ed. London: Offices of the Royal Historical Society, 1964.

———. *Medieval Manuscripts in British Libraries.* 4 vols. Oxford: Clarendon Press, 1969–92. (Vol. 4 by A. J. Piper.)

Kingsford, C. L. "Life of Trevisa." *Dictionary of National Biography*, edited by Sidney Lee, 19:1139–40. New York: Macmillan, 1909.

Knowles, Dom David. "The Censured Opinions of Uthred of Boldon." *Proceedings of the British Academy* 37 (1951): 305–42.

———. *The Religious Orders in England.* 3 vols. Rev. ed. Cambridge: Cambridge University Press, 1956–57. See vol. 1, "The End of the Middle Ages," pp. 48–

54, 58–60.

———, and R. Neville Hadcock. *Medieval Religious Houses, England and Wales.* New York: St. Martin's Press, 1972.

Lawler, Traugott. "On the Properties of John Trevisa's Major Translations." *Viator* 14 (1983): 267–88.

Lawrence, W. T. *Parliamentary Representation of Cornwall.* Truro, n.d., pp. 36, 125, 141, 154, 168, 182, 195.

Lerner, Robert E. "Medieval Prophecy and Religious Dissent." *Past and Present* 72 (1976): 3–24.

———. "Poverty, Preaching, and Eschatology in the Revelation Commentaries of 'Hugh of St. Cher.'" In *The Bible in the Medieval World: Essays in Memory of Beryl Smalley,* edited by Katherine Walsh and Diana Wood, pp. 157–89. Oxford: Basil Blackwell, 1985.

Lewis, H., and H. Pedersen. *A Concise Comparative Celtic Grammar,* pp. 46, 123. Gottingen: Vandenhoeck and Ruprecht, 1937.

Lindberg, Conrad. "The Manuscripts and Versions of the Wycliffite Bible: A Preliminary Survey." *Studia Neophilologica* 42 (1970): 333–47.

———. ed. *MS Bodley 959 Genesis-Baruch 3.20 in the Earlier Version of the Wycliffite Bible.* Stockholm Studies in English 6 (1959), 8 (1961), 10 (1963), 13 (1965), 20 (1969).

———. ed. *The Earlier Version of the Wycliffite Bible* (Baruch 3.20-end of Old Testament from Christ Church Oxford MS 145), Stockholm Studies in English 29 (1973).

———. "A Note on the Vocabulary of the ME Bible," *Studia Neophilologica* 57 (1985): 129–31.

Literature of Medieval History, 1930–1975. Edited by Gray Cowan Boyce. 5 vols. New York: Kraus International Publications, 1981. A supplement.

Long, R. J., ed. *Bartholomaeus Anglicus On the Properties of Soul and Body: De Proprietatibus Rerum Libri III et IV.* Toronto: Toronto Center for Mediaeval Studies, 1979.

MacCracken, Henry N. "Vegetius in English." In *Anniversary Papers . . . for G. L. Kittredge,* edited by Robinson, Sheldon, and Neilson, pp. 389–403. Boston: Ginn and Co., 1913.

Magrath, J. R. *The Queen's College.* 2 vols. Oxford: Clarendon Press, 1921.

Mallet, Sir Charles. *A History of the University of Oxford.* 3 vols. New York: Longmans and Green, 1924–27.

Marcett, M. E. *Uhtred de Boldon, Friar William Jordan and Piers Plowman.* New York, 1938.

Mathew, Gervase. *The Court of Richard II.* London: Murray, 1968.

McEvoy, James. *The Philosophy of Robert Grosseteste.* Oxford: University Press, 1982.

McFarlane, K. B. *John Wycliffe and the Beginnings of English Nonconformity.* London: English Universities Press, 1952.

McIntosh, Angus, et al. *A Linguistic Atlas of Late Mediaeval English.* 4 vols. Aberdeen: University Press, 1986.

Minnis, A. J. "'Authorial Intention' and 'Literal Sense' in the Exegetical Theories of Richard Fitzralph and John Wyclif: An Essay in the Medieval History of Biblical Hermaneutics." *PRIA* 75c (1975): 1–30.

Mitchner, R. W. "Wynkyn de Worde's Use of the Plimpton Manuscript of *De Proprietatibus Rerum.*" *Library* 5th ser. 6 (1951): 7–18.

Monnier, J. *La Descente aux Enfers: Etude de Pensée Religieuse d'Art et de Littérature.* Paris, 1905.

"MS. Collections at Castle Horneck, 1720–1772." (Borlase, William Copland) *Quarterly Review* 139 (1875): 367–95, esp. pp. 369, 393.

New Cambridge Bibliography of English Literature. Edited by George Watson. 5 vols. Cambridge: Cambridge University Press, 1969–77.

O'Ceallaigh, G. C. "Dating the Commentaries of Nicodemus." *Harvard Theological Review* 56 (1963): 21–58.

Oliver, George. *Lives of the Bishops of Exeter and a History of the Cathedral. . . .* Exeter, 1861.

Orme, Nicholas. *English Schools of the Middle Ages.* London: Methuen, 1973.

———. *Education in the West of England, 1066-1548.* Exeter: University of Exeter, 1976.

Overy, Rev. Charles, and Arthur C. Tynsdale. "The Parentage of William Tyndale, Alias Huchyns, Translator and Martyr." *Transactions of the Bristol and Gloucestershire Archaeological Society* 73 (1954): 209–15.

Pacht, Otto, and J. J. G. Alexander. *Illuminated Manuscripts in the Bodleian Library Oxford.* Vol. 3. Oxford: Clarendon Press, 1963.

Padel, O. J. *Cornish Place-Name Elements.* Cambridge, 1985. English Place-Name Society, vol. 56/57, pp. 237–38.

Pantin, W. A. *The English Church in the Fourteenth Century.* Cambridge: Cambridge University Press, 1955.

Parrish, Verna M. "Batman's Additions from Elyot and Boorde to His English Edition of Bartholomaeus Anglicus." In *Studies in Language, Literature and Culture of the Middle Ages and Later,* edited by E. B. Atwood and A. A. Hill, pp. 337–46. Austin: University of Texas Press, 1969.

Parry, J. J. "The Revival of Cornish: An Dasserghyans Kernewek." *PMLA* 61 (1946): 258–68.

Perry, A. J. "Notes on John Trevisa." *MLN* 33 (1918): 13–19.

———. "John Trevisa: A Fourteenth-Century Translator." In *Manitoba Essays,* pp. 277–89. Toronto: Macmillan, 1937.

Peter, Thurston C. *The History of Glasney Collegiate Church, Cornwall.* Camborne, Cornwall: Camborne Printing and Stationery Co. Ltd., 1903.

Pfeffer, Bernhard. *Die Sprache des "Polychronicons" John Trevisa's in der Hs. Cotton Tiberius D. VII.* Duren, 1912.

Pitseus, Joannes. *Relationem Historicarum de Rebus Anglicis.* Paris, 1619.

Poole, R. L., ed. *John Bale's Index of British and Other Writers*. Oxford: Clarendon Press, 1902.

Pokorny, Julius. *Indogermanisches etymologisches Worterbuch*. 2 vols. Bern: Francke, 1959.

Postan, M. M. *The Medieval Economy and Society: An Economic History of Britain, 1100–1500*. London: Weidenfeld and Nicolson, 1972.

Power, Kathleen H. "A Newly Identified Prose Version of the Trevisa Version of the *Gospel of Nichodemus*." *N&Q* 223 (1978): 5–7.

Powicke, F. M., and E. B. Fryde, eds. *Handbook of British Chronology*. London: Offices of the Royal Historical Society, 1961.

Rashdall, Hastings. *The Universities of Europe in the Middle Ages*. 3 vols. Edited by F. M. Powicke and A. B. Emden. Vol. 3: *English Universities—Student Life*. Oxford: Oxford University Press, 1936.

Rigg, A. G. "Medieval Latin Poetic Anthologies (II)." *Mediaeval Studies* 40 (1978): 387–407.

Robson, J. A. *Wycliff and the Oxford Schools*. Cambridge: Cambridge University Press, 1961.

Rogers, John J. "Notice of John de Trevisa, a Cornish Mediaeval Author.—A.D. 1342–1412." *Journal of the Royal Institution of Cornwall* 2: 11 (April 1870): 147–54. Also supplemental note same journal 4: 15 (1874): 262–65.

Russell, G. H. "The Salvation of the Heathen: The Exploration of a Theme in *Piers Plowman*." *Journal of the Warburg and Courtauld Institutes* 29 (1966): 101–16.

Sabin, Arthur. "The Foundation of the Abbey of St Augustine at Bristol." *Transactions of the Bristol and Gloucestershire Archaeological Society* 75 (1956): 35–42.

Salter, Elizabeth. "The Alliterative Revival." *MP* 64 (1966): 146–50; 64 (1967): 233–37.

———. *Fourteenth-Century English Poetry*. Oxford: Oxford University Press, 1983.

Samuels, M. L. "Langland's Dialect." *MAE* 54 (1985): 232–47.

Saul, Nigel. *Knights and Esquires: The Gloucestershire Gentry in the Fourteenth Century*. Oxford: Clarendon Press, 1981.

Scase, Wendy. *Piers Plowman and the New Anticlericalism*. Cambridge: Cambridge University Press, 1989.

Se Boyar, G. E. "Bartholomaeus Anglicus and His Encyclopedia." *JEGP* 19 (1920): 168–89.

Seymour, Michael C. "A Middle English Abstract of Bartholomaeus, *De Proprietatibus Rerum*." *Anglia* 87 (1969): 1–25.

———. "More about a Middle English Abstract of Bartholomaeus, *De Proprietatibus Rerum*." *Anglia* 91 (1973): 18–34.

———. "Some Medieval English Owners of *De Proprietatibus Rerum*." *Bodleian Library Record* 9 (1974): 156–65.

————. "A *literatim* Trevisa Abstract." *NM* 93 (1992): 185–91.

Short, T. *A General Chronological History of the Air, Weather, Seasons, Meteors, &c . . .* London, 1749. Copy in the Bodleian Library. See p. 180.

Shrader, C. R. "A Handlist of Extant Manuscripts Containing the *De Re Militari* of Flavius Vegetius Renatus." *Scriptorium* 33 (1979): 280–305.

Shrewsbury, J. F. D. *A History of Bubonic Plague in the British Isles.* London: Cambridge University Press, 1970.

Sluder, Brenda. "Differences between Chancery English and the English of John Trevisa." *ELN* 27 (1989): 13–18.

Smalley, Beryl. "John Wyclif's *Postilla super totam Bibliam.*" *Bodleian Library Record* 4 (1953): 186–204.

————. *English Friars and Antiquity in the Early Fourteenth Century.* Oxford: Basil Blackwell, 1960.

————. "Wyclif's *Postilla* on the Old Testament and His *Principium.*" *Oxford Studies Presented to Daniel Callus,* OHS ns. 16 (1964), pp. 253–96.

————. *The Study of the Bible in the Middle Ages.* 3d ed. Oxford: Basil Blackwell, 1983.

Smith, A. S. D. *Cornish Simplified: Short Lessons for Self Tuition, Pronunciation . . .* 2d ed. Printed by J. Townsend, 1955.

Smith, David M. *Guide to Bishops' Registers of England and Wales.* London: Offices of the Royal Historical Society, 1981.

Smith, William James. "The Rise of the Berkeleys: An Account of the Berkeleys of Berkeley Castle." *Transactions of the Bristol and Gloucestershire Archaeological Society* 70 (1951): 64–80; 71 (1952): 101–21.

Southern, R. W. "From Schools to University." In *The History of the University of Oxford,* edited by J. I. Catto, 1:1–36. Oxford: Clarendon Press, 1984.

Steadman, John M. "Chauntecleer and Medieval Natural History." *Isis* 50 (1959): 236–44.

The Stonore Letters and Papers. 2 vols. Camden Society 3d ser., vols. 29–30. London: Offices of the Society, 1919. See 1:12–13.

Strayer, Joseph R. *The Reign of Philip the Fair.* Princeton: Princeton University Press, 1980.

————, ed. *Dictionary of the Middle Ages.* 13 vols. New York: Scribner, 1982–89.

Takamiya, T. "A Hitherto Unedited Manuscript of Trevisa's *De Proprietatibus Rerum.*" In *Philologia Anglica: Essays . . . Yoshio Terasawa,* edited by K. Oshitari et al., pp. 308–19. Tokyo, 1988.

Tanner, Thomas. *Bibliotheca Britannico-Hibernica.* Edited by David Wilkins. London, 1748.

Taylor, John. *The Universal Chronicle of Ranulf Higden.* Oxford: Clarendon Press, 1966.

Thomas, Charles. "The Society's 1962 Excavations: The Henge at Castilly, Lanivet." *Cornish Archaeology* 3 (1964): 3–14, esp. p. 11.

Thomson, John A. F. *The Later Lollards, 1414–1520.* London: Oxford University Press, 1965.

Thrupp, Sylvia L. *The Merchant Class of Medieval London, 1300–1500.* Chicago: University of Chicago Press, 1948.

Tischendorf, Constantine, ed. *Evangelia Apocrypha . . .* Leipzig, 1853.

Towneley, James. *Illustrations of Biblical Literature.* 3 vols. London, 1821. See 2:49–55.

Turner, Ralph V. "*Descendit ad Inferos*: Medieval Views on Christ's Descent into Hell and the Salvation of the Ancient Just." *Journal of the History of Ideas* 27 (1966): 173–94.

Ullmann, Walter. *Law and Politics in the Middle Ages.* New York: Cornell University Press, 1975.

Wakelin, M. F. *Language and History in Cornwall.* Leicester, 1975.

Waldron, Ronald. "John Trevisa and the Use of English." *Proceedings of the British Academy* 74 (1988): 171–202.

———. "Trevisa's 'Celtic Complex' Revisited." *N&Q* 234 (1989): 303–7.

———. "The Manuscripts of Trevisa's Translation of the *Polychronicon*." *MLQ* 51 (1990): 281–317.

———. "Dialect Aspects of Manuscripts of Trevisa's Translation of the *Polychronicon*." In *Regionalism in Late Medieval Manuscripts and Texts*, edited by Felicity Riddy, pp. 67–88. Cambridge: D. S. Brewer, 1991.

———, and Henry Hargreaves. "The Aberdeen Manuscript of Trevisa's Translation of the *Polychronicon* (AUL MS 21): A Workshop Crisis and its Resolution." *Scriptorium* 46 (1992): 276–82.

Walsh, Katherine. *A Fourteenth-Century Scholar and Primate: Richard Fitz-Ralph in Oxford, Avignon and Armagh.* Oxford: Clarendon Press, 1981.

Watson, Andrew G., and Malcolm Parkes, eds. *Medieval Scribes, Manuscripts, and Libraries: Essays Presented to N. R. Ker.* London: Scholar Press, 1978.

Weisheipl, J. A. "Ockham and the Mertonians." In *The History of the University of Oxford*, edited by J. I. Catto. 1:607–58, Oxford: Clarendon Press, 1984.

Wharton, Henry. *Appendix ad Historiam Literariam . . . Gulielmi Cave.* London, 1689.

Whiting, Bartlett Jere. "Miller's Head Revisited." *MLN* 69 (1954): 309–10.

———. *Proverbs, Sentences, and Proverbial Phrases: From English Writings Mainly before 1500.* Cambridge, Mass.: Harvard University Press, 1968.

Wilkins, H. J. *Some Chapters in the Ecclesiastical History of Westbury-on-Trym.* Bristol, 1909.

———. *Was John Wycliffe a Negligent Pluralist? Also John de Trevisa, His Life and Work.* London: Longmans, Green and Co., 1915. Supplement, 1916.

———. *Westbury College from c. 1194 to 1544 A.D.* Bristol, 1917.

Wilks, Michael. "Misleading Manuscripts: Wycliff and the Non-Wycliffite Bible." *Studies in Church History* 11 (1975): 147–61.

Williams, Arnold. "Relations Between the Mendicant Friars and the Secular Clergy in England in the Later Fourteenth Century." *Annuale Mediaevale* 1 (1960): 22–95.

Workman, Herbert Brook. *John Wyclif: A Study of the English Medieval Church.* 2 vols. Oxford: Clarendon Press, 1926.

Wright, Joseph. *The English Dialect Dictionary.* 6 vols. London: Henry Frowde, 1898–1905.

DISSERTATIONS

Andrew, M. R. "A Critical Edition of the Seventh Book 'On Diseases and Their Cures' of John Trevisa's Middle English Translation of the *De Proprietatibus Rerum* of Bartholomaeus Anglicus." Ph.D. dissertation, York University, 1972.

Blechner, Michael Harry. "An Edition of Book IV of John Trevisa's Translation of Bartholomeus Anglicus' *De Proprietatibus Rerum*." Ph.D. dissertation, Princeton University. DAI 32/11 (1971): 6366.

Briggs, Charles F. "The English Manuscripts of Giles of Rome's *De Regimine Principum* and Their Audience, 1300–1500." Ph.D. dissertation, University of North Carolina, 1993.

Brockhurst, E. J. "The Life and Works of Stephen Batman." M.A. thesis, London University, Westfield College, 1947.

———. "Bartholomaeus Anglicus: *De Proprietatibus Rerum*." Ph.D. dissertation, London University, Westfield College, 1952.

Cawley, Arthur C. "A Study of the Language of the Various Texts of John Trevisa's Translation of Higden's *Polychronicon*." M.A. thesis, University of London, 1938.

Childs, Herbert Ellsworth. "A Study of the Unique Middle English Translation of the *De Regimine Principum* of Aegidius Romanus (MS Digby 223)." Ph.D. dissertation, University of Washington, 1932.

Clinton, S. M. M. "The Latin Manuscript Tradition in England of the *De Proprietatibus Rerum* of Bartholomaeus Anglicus: An Analysis Based on Book Ten." Ph.D. dissertation, Northwestern University. DAI 43/06-A (1982): 1965.

Conroy, Kenneth C. "A Glossary of John Trevisa's Translation of the *De Regimine Principum* of Aegidius Romanus." Ph.D. dissertation, University of Washington. DA 25/12 (1964): 7241.

Erickson, Norma N. "A Dispute Between a Priest and a Knight." Ph.D. dissertation, University of Washington. DA 27/09A (1966): 2970.

Farley, Peter Paul. "Book XIII 'De Aqua' of John of Trevisa's Translation of Bartholomaeus Anglicus' *De Proprietatibus Rerum*: A Critical Edition." Ph.D. dissertation, Fordham University. DAI 35/06-A (1974): 3676.

Fischer, N. A. "Animal Illustrations in English Religious Prose of the Fourteenth and Fifteenth Centuries." Ph.D. dissertation, Leeds University, 1967.

Gaumer, Mahlon Conover. "John Trevisa's Translation of the *De Proprietatibus Rerum* of Bartholomew Anglicus: An Edition of the Plimpton Manuscript." Ph.D. dissertation, University of Washington. DAI 32/06-A (1971): 3249.

Hamilton, Ruth Elaine. "Of Fire and of Air: Notes and Commentary on Books 10 and 11 of John Trevisa's Translation of Bartholomaeus Anglicus' *De Proprietatibus Rerum*." Ph.D. dissertation, Northwestern University. DAI 43/10A (1983): 3313.

Harder, Bernhard David. "The Medieval Lapidary of Bartholomaeus Anglicus: A Critical Edition of John Trevisa's Translation into Middle English of *De Proprietatibus Rerum*, Book XVI." Ph.D. dissertation, University of North Carolina, Chapel Hill. DAI 32/10-A (1971): 5738.

Harris, Phyllis Pier. "*Origo Mundi*, First Play of the Cornish Mystery Cycle, the *Ordinalia*: A New Edition." Ph.D. dissertation, University of Washington. DA 25/03 (1964): 1912–13.

Hutchinson, Ann M. "An Edition of Book VI of John Trevisa's English Translation of *De Proprietatibus Rerum* by Bartholomeus Anglicus." Ph.D. dissertation, University of Toronto. DAI 38/10-A (1974): 6107.

Kim, Hack Chin, ed. "*The Gospel of Nicodemus*, Translated by John Trevisa." Ph.D. dissertation, University of Washington. DA 25/03 (1963): 1893.

Kinkade, Berte Leroy. "The English Translations of Higden's Polychronicon." Ph.D. dissertation, University of Illinois, 1934.

Lidaka, Juris Girts. "Bartholomaeus Anglicus' *De Proprietatibus Rerum*, Book XIX, Chapters on Mathematics, Measures, and Music: A Critical Edition of the Latin Text in England." Ph.D. dissertation, Northern Illinois University. DAI 48/10-A (1987): 2623.

Reilly, Robert. "A Middle English Summary of the Bible: An Edition of Trinity College, Oxford MS 93. Ph.D. dissertation, University of Washington. DA 27/12-A (1966): 4229.

Seeger, Richard A. "The English *Polychronicon*: A Text of John Trevisa's Translation of Higden's *Polychronicon* Based on Huntington MS 28561." 3 vols. Ph.D. dissertation, University of Washington. DAI 36/06-A (1974): 3663.

Index

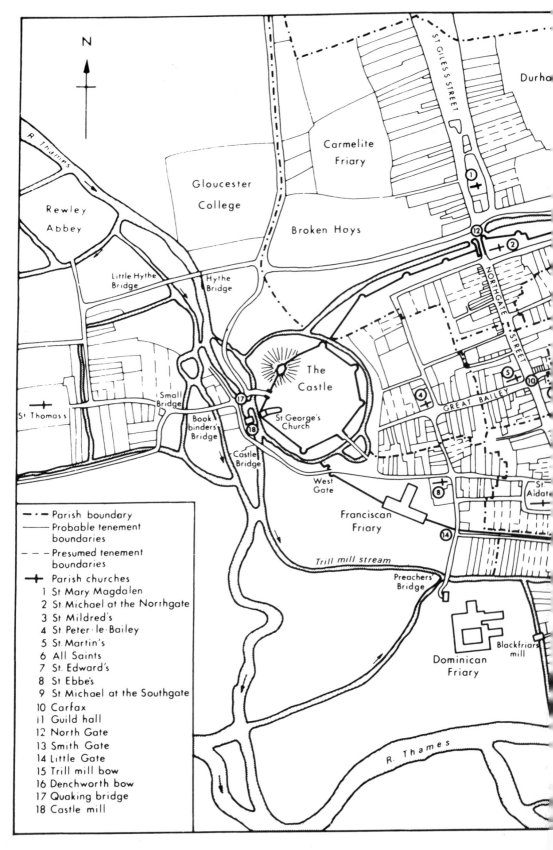

N

R. Thames

Rewley
Abbey

Gloucester
College

Carmelite
Friary

ST GILESS STREET

Durha

Broken Hoys

Little Hythe
Bridge

Hythe
Bridge

NORHGATE STREET

The
Castle

Small
Bridge

St. Thomas's

Book
binders'
Bridge

St George's
Church

GREAT BAILEY

St.
Aida

West
Gate

Castle
Bridge

Franciscan
Friary

Trill mill stream

Preachers'
Bridge

Blackfriars
mill

Dominican
Friary

R. Thames

— · — · Parish boundary
———— Probable tenement
boundaries
– – – Presumed tenement
boundaries
✛ Parish churches
1 St Mary Magdalen
2 St Michael at the Northgate
3 St Mildred's
4 St Peter-le-Bailey
5 St Martin's
6 All Saints
7 St Edward's
8 St Ebbe's
9 St Michael at the Southgate
10 Carfax
11 Guild hall
12 North Gate
13 Smith Gate
14 Little Gate
15 Trill mill bow
16 Denchworth bow
17 Quaking bridge
18 Castle mill